P9-AEY-993

HV8290 .K684 2006
Kovacich, Gerald L.
Security metrics
 management :
Northeast Lakeview Colleg
33784000127530

Northeast Lakeview College

33784 0001 2753 0

Security Metrics Management

SECURITY METRICS MANAGEMENT

How to Measure the
Costs and Benefits of Security

Dr. Gerald L. Kovacich
Edward P. Halibozek

ELSEVIER

AMSTERDAM • BOSTON • HEIDELBERG • LONDON
NEW YORK • OXFORD • PARIS • SAN DIEGO
SAN FRANCISCO • SINGAPORE • SYDNEY • TOKYO

Butterworth-Heinemann is an imprint of Elsevier

Butterworth–Heinemann is an imprint of Elsevier
30 Corporate Drive, Suite 400, Burlington, MA 01803, USA
Linacre House, Jordan Hill, Oxford OX2 8DP, UK

Copyright © 2006, Elsevier Inc. All rights reserved.

No part of this publication may be reproduced, stored in a retrieval system, or transmitted in any form or by any means, electronic, mechanical, photocopying, recording, or
otherwise, without the prior written permission of the publisher.

Permissions may be sought directly from Elsevier's Science & Technology Rights
Department in Oxford, UK: phone: (+44) 1865 843830, fax: (+44) 1865 853333,
E-mail: permissions@elsevier.com. You may also complete your request on-line
via the Elsevier homepage (http://elsevier.com), by selecting "Support & Contact"
then "Copyright and Permission" and then "Obtaining Permissions."

 Recognizing the importance of preserving what has been written, Elsevier prints
its books on acid-free paper whenever possible.

Library of Congress Cataloging-in-Publication Data
Kovacich, Gerald L.
  Security metrics management : how to measure the costs and benefits of security / by
Gerald Kovacich and Edward Halibozek.
     p. cm.
  Includes index.
  ISBN 0-7506-7899-2 (pbk. : alk. paper) 1. Private security services. 2. Security systems.
3. Corporations--Security measures. 4. Corporations--Security measures--Costs. I.
Halibozek, Edward P. II. Title.
  HV8290.K684 2006
  658.4'70681--dc22
                        2005025565

British Library Cataloguing-in-Publication Data
A catalogue record for this book is available from the British Library.

ISBN 13: 978-0-7506-7899-5
ISBN 10: 0-7506-7899-2

For information on all Butterworth–Heinemann publications
visit our Web site at www.books.elsevier.com

Printed in the United States of America
05 06 07 08 09 10   10 9 8 7 6 5 4 3 2 1

Working together to grow
libraries in developing countries

www.elsevier.com | www.bookaid.org | www.sabre.org

ELSEVIER   BOOK AID   Sabre Foundation
            International

Other Books by
Dr. Gerald L. Kovacich

- *Information Systems Security Officer's Guide: Establishing and Managing an Information Protection Program*, May 1998, ISBN 0-7506-9896-9, First Edition and July 2003, ISBN: 0-7506-7656-6, Second Edition; published by Butterworth-Heinemann (Czech translation of First Edition also available).
- *I-Way Robbery: Crime on the Internet*, May 1999, ISBN 0-7506-7029-0; co-authored with William C. Boni; published by Butterworth-Heinemann; Japanese version published T. Aoyagi Office Ltd, Japan: February 2001, ISBN 4-89346-698-4.
- *High-Technology Crime Investigator's Handbook: Working in the Global Information Environment*, September 1999, ISBN 0-7506-7086-X; co-authored with William C. Boni; published by Butterworth-Heinemann; Second Edition co-authored with Andy Jones to be published in early 2006.
- *Netspionage: The Global Threat to Information*, September 2000, ISBN 0-7506-7257-9; co-authored with William C. Boni; published by Butterworth-Heinemann.
- *Information Assurance: Surviving in the Information Environment*, September 2001, ISBN 1-85233-326-X; co-authored with Dr. Andrew J. C. Blyth; published by Springer-Verlag Ltd (London); Second Edition to be published in late 2005.
- *Global Information Warfare: How Businesses, Governments, and Others Achieve Global Objectives and Attain Competitive Advantages*, June 2002, ISBN 0-84931-114-4; co-authored with Andy Jones and Perry Luzwick; published by Auerbach Publishers/ CRC Press.

Other Books by Dr. Gerald L. Kovacich and Edward P. Halibozek

- *The Manager's Handbook for Corporate Security: Establishing and Managing a Successful Assets Protection Program*, April 2003, ISBN 0-7506-7487-3; published by Butterworth-Heinemann.
- Instructor's Manual for *The Manager's Handbook for Corporate Security: Establishing and Managing a Successful Assets Protection Program*, 2005, ISBN 13: 978-0-750-67938-1; ISBN 10: 0-750-67938-7, published by Butterworth-Heinemann.
- *Mergers & Acquisitions Security: Managing Security Issues Before, During and After a Merger or Acquisition*, April 2005, ISBN 0-7506-7805-4; published by Butterworth-Heinemann.

This book is dedicated to all the security professionals who try to justify their assets protection programs, their budgets, and their jobs!

A special dedication to a great criminologist, mentor and friend:
John P. Kenney, Ph.D., Professor Emeritus. Thanks, Jack! We miss you!

Contents

Preface

This book, *Security Metrics Management*, is designed to provide *simple* and *basic* guidance to security professionals and managers for establishing a baseline to begin the process of measuring the costs and benefits of their assets protection program—their security program—as well as its successes and failures—its effectiveness. We begin where all assets protection policies, procedures, processes, plans and projects should start—with the assets protection security drivers. In other words:

- Why is assets protection needed at all?
- What drives that need?
- If needed, why are the related security functions needed?
- Even if they too are needed, why are they being performed the way they are being performed?
- Is the assets protection program working?
- At what costs?
- How are their costs measured?
- Can it be done more effectively (better)?
- Can it be done more efficiently (cheaper)?
- How?

This book will provide some methods to enable the reader to answer these questions. The book also includes a discussion of how to use security metrics to brief management, justify resources and use trend analyses to develop a more efficient and effective assets protection program.

The security metrics management system that we discuss is not rocket science. It is a basic, rather simple and hopefully commonsense approach to help you *begin* your process of managing a cost-effective assets protection program, some part of that program, or providing management oversight of such an assets protection program.

Once you have established a security metrics management baseline, you can continue to improve upon it and make it work for your environment.

COVERAGE

The intent of this book is to provide:

- A holistic approach to developing, implementing, and maintaining a security metrics management program;
- for the corporate or government agency security professional (as well as corporate management);
- an approach that will be useful to both the new and experienced professionals; and

- for the reader and security practitioner, methods which can enable them to measure the costs and benefits, as well as the success and failures of their security functions and overall assets protection program.

The information provided is generic and broad in scope in that it covers all major security functions for a basic international corporation. The methods and processes we offer can be applied by any security professional in any country. It will help provide an international answer to the problems of measuring security costs, benefits, successes and failures across nations and societies.

To make this discussion more "real-world," we will use a fictional, international corporation, the International Widget Corporation (IWC), as the place where a security metrics management system is being implemented by the new Chief Security Officer (CSO).

Methods, processes and procedures will be provided to the reader that can be immediately implemented. An overview of the chapters and chapter abstracts are provided below:

Section I: Introduction to the Role of the Security Professionals and Security Metrics Management

This section provides the introduction into the security profession, its service and support to businesses and government agencies and an introduction to security metrics management.

Chapter 1: The Security Profession and its Role in Supporting Business and Government Agency Assets Protection Needs

This chapter will discuss the support role of security in supporting the needs of businesses and government agencies in today's global environment.

Chapter 2: Management and a Security Metrics Foundation

This chapter will look at security and security metrics management from the viewpoint of business and government agency management and executives (nonsecurity professionals). It will discuss what they should expect from their security staffs; what questions to ask relative to assets protection costs, benefits, successes and failures; and what they need to know to help them make better risk management decisions. It will also address how security professionals can help management come to the right asset protection decisions supported by a security metrics management system, as well as how such a system supports the security professional in meeting their security service and support objectives.

Chapter 3: Policies, Procedures, Processes, Plans, and Projects

This chapter will explain and provide examples of how to identify and describe corporate security duties, responsibilities, processes, plans, policies, procedures and projects on which security metrics management is based. It will lay the foundation for establishing a security metrics management system that can be applied by any security professional in any business and government agency in any country.

Chapter 4: Security Metrics Management Program—An Overview

This chapter will describe a method for establishing a successful security metrics management program (SMMP) to include a discussion of the processes, tools and measures that can be used, graphic depictions of the data collected to include types of charts, colors and styles. Some case studies will be provided.

Chapter 5: Case Study: Measuring Costs of Security
This chapter will use a fictitious international corporation, the International Widget Corporation (IWC), to discuss security metrics related to some basic security cost factors.

Chapter 6: Case Study: Six Sigma
This chapter will discuss one popular performance assessment methodology that can be applied to assets protection, to security functions, and to improving security processes. It is provided here so that the reader is made aware of another view of how to measure and improve performance by identifying and discussing this "popular" and successful methodology.

Section II: Administrative Security Metrics
This section describes the basic administrative security functions that should be performed as part of the duties and responsibilities related to an assets protection program and detailed analyses of those related security functions, as well as integrating security metrics management processes into each of the security functions. As with all security metrics processes identified in this book, some examples will be provided that can be easily copied and used by any security professional.

Chapter 7: Information Security
This chapter will discuss the function of information security and how to apply the process of metrics management to the function of information security in order to determine its costs, benefits, successes and failures.

Chapter 8: Personnel Security
This chapter introduces the function of personnel security and the process of personnel security metrics management identification and establishment to determine costs, benefits, successes and failures.

Chapter 9: Security Education and Awareness Training
This chapter will discuss the SEATP function and the process of security metrics management identification and establishment to determine costs, benefits, successes and failures.

Chapter 10: Security Compliance Audit
This chapter will address the administrative security organization's security compliance audit (SCA) function and the process of using security metrics to measure and manage its costs, benefits, successes and failures.

Chapter 11: Surveys and Risk Management
This chapter will address the use and measurements related to the conducting of security surveys and also the use of risk management metrics.

Chapter 12: Corporate Assets Protection Program
The corporate assets protection program (CAPP) is the primary reason security exists. The role of security is a protective role. Protection of people, information and physical assets is the purview of the security professional and the security organization.

For any corporation or government agency, the security organization and its CSO are chartered with the protection role.

Chapter 13: Contingency Planning
The fundamental elements of contingency planning and the process of contingency planning metrics management identification and establishment to determine costs, benefits, successes and failures will be addressed.

Section III: Physical Security Metrics
This section will address the various security functions that fall under the category of physical security and will address their specific drivers and metrics processes.

Chapter 14: Security Officer/Guard Force
This chapter will address the use of metrics relative to the guard forces, which is one of the most costly, labor-intensive aspects of an assets protection program.

Chapter 15: Technical Security Systems
Technical security systems, when used properly, can efficiently and effectively support assets protection processes. How to measure those systems and benefits will be discussed in this chapter.

Chapter 16: Locks and Keys
The lock and key function is generally a very human-intensive process for security and affected employees. Measuring the cost of lost productivity due to this function will be discussed, as well as how to find more cost-efficient processes to achieve objectives of this function.

Chapter 17: Fire Protection
Many security organizations are also responsible for the fire protection program. Fire protection programs usually divide into two areas: fire prevention and fire suppression. This chapter will address the fundamental elements of a fire prevention program and a fire suppression program and the process of fire protection security metrics management identification and establishment to determine costs, benefits, successes and failures.

Chapter 18: Executive Protection
This chapter will address the use of security metrics as a tool for managing an executive protection program. Although an executive protection program is a function requiring fewer resources than many other security functions, it is nevertheless a critical function. The focus of the executive protection program is the protection of the company CEO and other key senior executive leaders of the company. Executive protection is a high-profile function with little margin for error. Effectiveness of the program is critical. Metrics can help the CSO assess effectiveness.

Chapter 19: Event Security
Many companies, in particular publicly held companies, are involved in high-profile events, from annual shareholder events to trade shows. Protection of personnel, assets and information can become very complicated during these events, particularly when they occur in a foreign environment. This chapter will address its supporting security metrics management process.

Section IV: Security Operations Metrics

This section will deal with what we call the "operational" security functions as they relate to security metrics management.

Chapter 20: Investigations and Noncompliance Inquiries

This chapter will address the investigative and noncompliance inquiry security functions and the processes of security metrics management identification and establishment to determine costs, benefits, successes and failures.

Chapter 21: Government Security

This chapter addresses the fundamental aspects of a corporation's government security program, their related contracts and the process of government and contract security metrics management identification and establishment to determine costs, benefits, successes and failures.

Chapter 22: Information Systems Security

This chapter will address the information systems security function and the process of automated information and information systems security metrics management identification and establishment to determine costs, benefits, successes and failures.

Chapter 23: Mergers and Acquisitions Security

Mergers and acquisitions, as well as divestitures, are common strategic business processes that require security support. That support will vary depending upon the size, scope and complexity of the deal. As with the M&A process itself, the performance of security must be measured. How the cost, benefit and effectiveness of security in support of the M&A process is measured will be discussed in this chapter.

Chapter 24: Outsourcing

In this chapter the cost-benefits of outsourcing will be discussed, using security metrics management to support the outsourcing decisions, as well as monitoring the performance of service providers.

Section V: The Security Profession and Metrics Management in the Future

This section will address how security metrics management techniques can be used to support future security functional needs relating to costs, benefits, successes and failures.

Chapter 25: Security Metrics Management Technology of the Future and How to Prepare Now to Use It

Technology is rapidly changing all professions and the profession of security, of assets protection, is no different. This chapter will provide direction for the security professionals so that they can prepare now to integrate and apply new technology to more efficiently support future security metrics management systems.

WHO SHOULD READ THIS BOOK?

This book is for the new and experienced security professional, as well as those in government agencies, finance managers, and auditors who are involved with some aspects of understanding or managing security budgets and costs versus benefits.

It is believed that the information provided in this book can be easily adapted by any security professional in any nation since an asset is an asset, so to speak, and measuring assets protection performance uses fundamental measurement techniques, analyses, graphic depictions and project plans.

The use of security metrics management techniques is generic in nature and these techniques can also be used by executive management, auditors and finance specialists to identify and track assets protection costs and performance. We attempt to use somewhat of a global perspective in writing this book so that it appeals to and can be used by security professionals and others around the world.

In addition, the following professionals will find this book useful:

- Corporate executives who have responsibility for protecting corporate assets as part of their inherent responsibilities to the corporation, its board of directors, and to shareholders. This includes executives such as the CEO, CFO, COO, CIO, CSO, CHRO, and potentially many others. We will demonstrate how a security metrics management program can assist executive management in assessing the effectiveness and efficiency of their assets protection program.
- Corporate staff members who have specific responsibilities for specific assets: e.g., information technology staff, emergency services staff, and contingency/emergency planners.
- Professors, scholars and researchers interested in the protection of people, information and other assets within businesses or government agencies, as well as those that teach courses in business management, auditing, security and criminal justice at colleges and universities.

In this book, we provide real-world examples of the trials and tribulations—e.g., case studies—of a security professional based on our own experiences and those of others that we know, and show how security metrics management has helped support effective asset protection and management decisions.

When discussing the support agency—corporations, nonprofit agencies, government agencies and the like—we will for the most part use the term "corporation," "business," or "company" to represent all of these entities. We used this approach to make it easier instead of each time detailing an entire list of entities. A security metrics management program is applicable to all these entities where security costs, benefits, successes and failures should be assessed for effectiveness, efficiency and the contribution to the enterprise.

CLOSING COMMENTS

We believe that this book, in the described format and with the identified topics, provides an exceptional security measurement foundation for security professionals or business/government agency executives who have a variety of levels of security experience and knowledge—in any location in any modern nation-state.

Our emphasis is not only on a global, modern-day world of business and government agencies, but also on providing sufficient guidance and tools that will support the inexperienced security professional in actually building a useful security metrics management program.

Please note that the numbers, flowcharts, and drivers are only provided as examples. You will find this especially true with the data collections' numbers and their accompanying charts, which are fictional and are entered at random just to give you some samples. So, please concentrate on the methodology and the thought processes and do not try to concentrate on the accuracy of the numbers and whether the totals depict the cumulative numbers of whatever is being collected on a monthly or quarterly basis. Yes, we know that some of you out there will do that. So, one-plus-one may or may not show up as two. Again, (we stress) concentrate on the idea, process, formats, and methodology behind it all and not the actual numbers.

Some of the information provided on corporate security assets protection functions and related information is taken from our other published books. This was done so that we can provide a consistent and detailed background of information about corporate security functions that will help the reader understand our security metrics management program approach and philosophy.

Although not entirely redundant throughout each of the book's chapters, each chapter was written to be used as much as possible as an independent guide to one or more aspects of an assets protection program and its specific security functions. For example, if your focus is on guard forces and possibly other aspects of physical security and your security organization does not manage the information systems security function, you can go to the appropriate part of the book without reading about other security functions first. We try to offer the security functions in a manner that allows you to pick and choose which ones you want to know first vis-à-vis security metrics—after you have read Section I, which provides background information for all the security functions.

You will also find that we are always (hopefully) making the point that using security metrics management can assist you in identifying and reducing the costs of an assets protection program and the related security functions. After all, security is generally an overhead cost to a corporation and therefore not only adversely impacts a corporation's potential profits but also has that "hidden" cost of lost employee productivity. Helping the security professional (and others) maintain an efficient and effective assets protection program is our goal.

As you read through this book, you will find that the security metrics management program (SMMP) is basically viewed as a combination of:

- Data collection
- Data analysis
- Graphically depicting the data to understand and tell the story

Over the years, we have found that graphically depicting data in chart format is a useful and necessary part of any SMMP. That is because, as the old saying goes, "A picture is worth a thousand words." This is certainly true when it comes to an SMMP. One can look at pages upon pages of data incorporated into spreadsheets, and not be able to easily see the positive or negative trends. Furthermore, from a management standpoint, the graphic depiction of data makes the results of the data collection easier to analyze, communicate and generate corrective actions or make course corrections. Furthermore, executive management does not have time to view endless reams of data. Therefore, the charting of collected data is a good way to analyze data and brief management on anything from your assets protection program to why you need more budget, more resources and everything in-between.

This book[1] was developed primarily based on the knowledge and actual experience of the authors. Together the authors have a long and experienced record of managing large and complex security organizations supported by metrics management systems.

We thank you for reading it and would appreciate your comments, constructive criticism and suggestions for incorporation in a second edition at a later date. Please send all comments to us through our publisher.

Dr. Gerald L. Kovacich
Whidbey Island, Washington
U.S.A

Edward P. Halibozek
Los Angeles, California
U.S.A

---

[1] Some of the information in this book is taken from the authors' other book, *The Manager's Handbook for Corporate Security: Establishing and Managing a Successful Assets Protection Program:* April 2003, ISBN 0-7506-7487-3, published by Butterworth-Heinemann, because the need to introduce the security profession and its role in the world of business and government is the same whether discussing that role exclusively or as background information for a corporate SMMP.

Acknowledgments

This book was developed from our lectures at security conferences given over the years and from practical applications within the different businesses where we have worked or for whom we have consulted.

Although we have also provided limited discussions on security metrics management in a few of our other books, the feedback we received from our readers and the attendees at our security metrics management-related lectures included requests for more details about developing and implementing a security metrics management program. We thank them for their support and for suggesting that we write a book providing more of a "how to," detailed approach to this topic. This book is written to fulfill those requests.

We of course must always, in every book, thank our wives—Hsiao-yun Kovacich and Phillis Halibozek—for their patience, support and understanding. Without that, each of us would not have been able to walk into our individual offices on a daily and often nightly basis, close the door for hours and not be disturbed except for an occasional knock on the door with coffee, tea and sometimes a snack to keep us energized and writing!

We send special thanks also to:

- William C. Boni, Vice President and CISO Motorola Corporation, one of the "best and brightest" in the profession today, and especially for his Six Sigma information;
- Don Evans, who continues to be the "InfoSec Conferences' "workhorse" and security professional, even before computers used punch cards;
- Dr. Lou Guthrie, President, Guthrie Research Group Incorporated, for his benchmarking spreadsheet provided as an appendix; and
- Dr. Andy Jones, Team Group Leader, British Telecommunications, United Kingdom, a leader in the European security arena, computer forensics and security expert; and of course
- Motomu Akashi, security professional extraordinaire, mentor, great friend and now retired—thanks, Tom!

To the staff and project team of Butterworth-Heinemann—Mark Listewnik, Chris Nolin, Jennifer Rhuda-Soucy, hey, what can we say? You all continue to be the best of the best!

To those other professionals in the book publishing world of Butterworth-Heinemann, who helped make the manuscript into a real book, thanks for another great effort: Kelly Weaver, Heather Furrow and Kelly Johnson.

We are grateful to all of them, not only for their support on this project, but also supporting our other projects over the years.

We also thank you and our many other readers for your comments, suggestions and support over the years.

Foreword

When people first began to think about security—in other words, assets protection—the problem largely dealt with the physical theft of assets. It was usually just a matter of physical security and using guard forces to protect the assets and locks and keys to control access and egress.

The people who were involved in security came mainly from one of two groups: law enforcement or the military. Both groups believed that they understood how to apply protective measures and the associated issues. They believed the issues of security related to the physical environment, to procedures, and of course to personnel security, but only in regards to their physical protection. Privacy matters were not a concern. Nor were issues such as suitability and trustworthiness of employees. The early security practitioners did not have a solid appreciation of the gradual influence that technology development would have on the practice of security.

As time passed and the level of knowledge, experience and business acumen needed to effectively protect assets changed, there developed an increasing level of knowledge and a more comprehensive understanding of a holistic approach to security and the use of technology to assist in the protection of assets. This development allowed for improved security, but was a long way from the utopia of highly effective and efficient application of security measures. There were still improvements and changes needed.

The first of these was that security was not thought of as a business process. After all, why should it be when the main participants were retired or ex-government employees or retired or ex-military personnel who knew little of business principles and needs? After all, why should they? There didn't appear to be a need to view security as an integral part of business. It was more of a detached afterthought. The second was there was no good way of measuring any of the factors that were involved vis-à-vis costs versus defined benefits.

As the businesses' and governments' assets became more sophisticated and valuable, so did the manner in which they were protected. Furthermore, as the economy became complex, so did competition between individual businesses and even government agencies. In this new environment, security began playing a more important and sophisticated role as information in the form of trade secrets and proprietary processes grew in value, and as global competition became more aggressive.

In global competition, lower costs of production generally provides for a competitive edge. Since security is usually an overhead cost, it was, and is, often valued in terms of what must be done and not in terms of how security may add value to the enterprise. During difficult times this places security in the forefront for cost reduction. Within industry and government, security costs were a likely target for executives seeking cost reduction. In essence, higher levels of risks would be accepted in order to reduce security costs.

This is the prerogative of management but should be accomplished with a complete and accurate understanding of the cost versus benefit equation of the value of security.

In addition, with the spread of computing into the business community, it became increasingly necessary to deal with the security of these technologies that businesses had come to rely on in their business processes and to consider them along with any other aspect of the business. The same basically held true for government agencies.

In order to achieve the necessary amount of cost-effective security, the security expert who has come to understand the technology (or the "techie" who has gained an understanding of security) now has to understand the business. In addition, it is now necessary for the management of the business to understand and have some faith in the security processes.

Today, business is very much the driving force in the use of information technology and computers and it has struggled to integrate the way in which the security of the technologies can be dealt with in terms that are understood by the management. Security professionals have, in the past, managed with expressions of disaster if "security" is not taken seriously, but they have not, in the past, been able to provide detailed costs and benefits that the implementation of identified security measures would create.

In order for the business to be able to deal with security as it does with any other process, there is a need to be able to express security in the same type of business terms and to be able to apply metrics to it that are meaningful to management, such as costs and benefits.

Up to this point in time, this has not been achieved with any regularity or consistency. This book attempts to move the integration of security into the business one step closer, it has been written by two people with knowledge of and experience in both business and government security, as well as in measuring the effectiveness and efficiency of security. It has been written with not only the security professional in mind but also the nonsecurity individuals who oversee security and have assets protection responsibility for the company or government agency, such as executive management. It is aimed at assisting both the security professional and the management of organisations in dealing with the practical issues of the topic.

This book looks at the main aspects of assets protection (security) measurement and the types of metrics that can be applied to a range of security processes. It goes beyond the usual range that you might expect and extends to cover areas such as executive protection, contingency planning and investigations. At all stages, the book addresses the value of metrics in helping the individual understand how effective and efficient security processes are. In essence it covers the cost versus benefit proposition on the application of security measures as part of an assets protection program.

The book was written for the benefit of all those involved in the business of security, from the practitioner to the board member, and done so in terms relevant to each of these audiences (i.e., measurement and the languages of business).

Dr. Andrew Jones, MBE, MSc, MBCS
Team Group Leader
British Telecommunications
United Kingdom

Introduction

It is important to understand what is meant by "security metrics management." So, before we get into the details of the matter, let's define and discuss some terms.

WHAT IS A METRIC?

To begin to understand how to use metrics to support management of a corporate assets protection program (CAPP), it is important to understand what is meant by "metrics." For our purposes, a metric is defined as *a standard of measurement using quantitative, statistical, and/or mathematical analyses.*

WHAT IS A SECURITY METRIC?

A security metric is the application of quantitative, statistical, and/or mathematical analyses to measuring security functional costs, benefits, successes, failures, trends and workload—in other words, tracking the status of each security function in those terms.

There are two basic ways of tracking costs and benefits. One is by using metrics relative to the day-to-day, routine operations of each security function. Examples would be analyses of the costs of a security briefing program and conducting noncompliance inquiries (internal investigations into loss of assets). In more financial terms, these are the recurring costs.

Metrics can be and are used as individual data points. They are often best used in the depiction of trends. For example: is the cost of security at company X going up or down?

The other way of tracking costs and benefits is through the formal project plans. Remember that security functions are "level-of-effort" (LOE), never-ending, daily work, while projects have a beginning and ending date with a specific objective and associated discrete costs.

So, in order to efficiently and effectively develop a security metrics management program, it is important to establish that philosophy and way of doing business. Everything that a corporate security manager and security staff do can be identified as fitting into one of these two categories: routine operations (LOE) or projects.

In other words, project plans provide project schedules and are a tool to track time and expenses in relationship to the accomplishment of a task. Both time and costs (money) are metrics in and of themselves and are included in a project plan. A project plan establishes criteria and metrics (time, costs, milestones accomplished) that are used to measure performance to plan.

WHAT IS SECURITY METRICS MANAGEMENT?

Security metrics management is the managing of a CAPP and related security functions through the use of metrics. Security metrics management is the application of an individual metric or a set of metrics as a means of assessing the performance of a security process, security processes or an entire security program. Through the use of metrics, the security cost versus benefit analysis becomes more quantitative and easier to understand and communicate in common business terms. Metrics help the security professional and others better understand the efficiency and effectiveness (value) of an assets protection program.

METRICS, MEASUREMENT AND MANAGEMENT

There are several other generally accepted forms of measurement. These include:

- The Capability Maturity Model for Software (also known as the CMM and SW-CMM) which "has been a model used by many organizations to identify best practices useful in helping them increase the maturity of their processes... In 2000, the SW-CMM was upgraded to CMMI® (Capability Maturity Model Integration)." (See http://www.sei.cmu.edu/cmm/)
- There is the Six Sigma which, according to Motorola's Bill Boni (See Chapter 6), "has proven itself a very capable tool with wide applicability in a number of disciplines including engineering, operations and systems management. Motorola originated Six Sigma in the mid-1980s as a response to severe quality challenges to the company's products. The original goal was to reach a state where there was a reduction in defects and variability in processes."
- There are also others which relate to metrics measurement and management, such as the continuous productivity (or process) improvement (CPI) and total quality management (TQM) philosophies and related models.

Some metrics are unique to their environment—e.g., software—while others can be ported to various environments. What we are offering here for the security professional is not some scientific, complicated or "formal" methodology that requires training classes, nor years of experience to understand and efficiently and effectively use.

What we will be discussing throughout this book is a very *basic* and *commonsense* approach to *begin* to get a handle on the problem of identifying costs, benefits, success and failures of assets protection programs and their related security functions.

Parts of that, as a Chief Security Officer, you already do—budgeting, for example. What we offer is an outline—an approach—that takes the methodology of metrics measurement and the philosophy of metrics management and combines them into a security metrics management program. In other words, putting it all together and using it as a security management tool to manage a corporate assets protection program.

Now that you have an understanding of what we mean by security metrics management, we can move on to an introduction to business and government agency security followed by detailed discussions of developing and implementing a security metrics management program as an integral part of an assets protection program and its related security functions, culminating into a look into the future of business security supported by metrics.

Section I

Introduction to the Role of the Security Professionals and Security Metrics Management

Starbucks Tracks Everything That Moves…Starbucks Metrics insight: rigorous tracking of processes leads to improvements and business value…[1]

This section provides an introduction into the security profession, its service and support to businesses and government agencies, and an introduction to security metrics management.

- Chapter 1: The Security Profession and Its Role in Supporting Business and Government Agency Assets Protection Needs
- Chapter 2: Business and Government Agency Management and a Security Metrics Foundation
- Chapter 3: Policies, Procedures, Processes, Plans, and Projects
- Chapter 4: How to Develop and Use a Security Metrics Management Program—An Overview
- Chapter 5: Case Study: Measuring Costs of Security
- Chapter 6: Case Study: Six Sigma

Section I begins with an introduction to the security profession and the role of the security professional in supporting businesses and government agencies primarily through their assets protection needs. The support role of security to the needs of businesses and government agencies in today's global environment will be reviewed.

Next, we will look at assets protection as it relates to security metrics management from the viewpoint of the business and government agency management (nonsecurity professionals). It will include a discussion of:

- What they should expect from their security staffs;
- What questions to ask relative to assets protection costs, benefits, successes and failures; what they need to know to help them make better risk management decisions;
- How security professionals can help management come to the right asset protection decisions supported by a security metrics management system; as well as
- How it supports the security professional in meeting their security service and support objectives.

---

[1] Quoted from CSOONLINE.COM, "Where the Metrics are" article, February 2005 issue.

We will explain and provide examples of how to identify and describe corporate security duties, responsibilities, processes, plans, policies, procedures and projects on which security metrics management is based. It will lay the foundation for establishing a security metrics management system that can be applied by any security professional in any business or government agency in any country.

Finally, we will describe a method for establishing a successful security metrics management program (SMMP). This discussion will include a description of the processes and tools that can be used, types of graphic depictions (charts), colors, style to use, along with case studies.

Chapter 1

The Security Profession and Its Role in Supporting Business and Government Agency Assets Protection Needs

This chapter will introduce and discuss the role of security in support of the needs of corporations and government agencies in today's global environment. It is provided to set the stage for a basic foundation for security, and assets protection managed through a security metrics management program.

INTRODUCTION

The world of the security professional has changed, as have so many professions, due to the technological changes and advances that have led to the phenomena of instant and mass global communications. Today's corporations can no longer afford to think locally or even nationally. Now, they must not only think globally but also compete in the global marketplace. Sure, some can survive in their small world of local or nation-based business (within a specific niche)—for now—but even they will be positively and negatively impacted by what is referred to as the "global economy."

Security professionals have been slow to recognize or admit that this change has impacted their profession. One just has to look at the ever-expanding threat agents and their sophisticated techniques for attacking corporate assets to see that the environment in which they work has changed and will continue to change, probably faster than ever before. However, that is only one of the many issues facing the security professional.

The role of security is often viewed in a much-maligned way—even by some security professionals. Employees (and that includes management) often consider security professionals as an extension of law enforcement. They imagine the security staff operating in an enforcement role, watching them and "making" them behave in a certain way—a way not necessarily conducive to good business practices, inconvenient and not in-line with their preferences. After all, today's employees are like most people. They are not receptive to constraints, particularly when they don't understand the reasons for them or the value the constraints bring to the business.

All too often, security professionals believe it is the "job" of employees to understand them and to be automatically supportive of them and security's role to protect business assets. The security specialists may grow impatient when they don't get the support they believe they need, require or deserve. After all, don't corporate employees understand how important the security job is? The answer is, "No, they probably don't and really don't think about it very often, if at all!"

When such an attitude is present, it is up to the security professionals to win over the employees with the help and support of management. This may not be what the security professional wants to do or hear, but in order to be a successful security professional and manage a successful assets protection program for the business, that is what must be done.

Yes, justifying one's job is not as enjoyable as performing it, but one way to look at it is to consider each new supporter as one more victory in the game of gaining assets protection program support. A security metrics management program (SMMP) can help the security professional explain security decisions, policies and practices in a way that employees and management can understand and appreciate—using the business language of costs and benefits instead of security lingo.

On the brighter side, the security profession has come a long way as a profession and is no longer using (in most cases anyway) what was often termed "the guard force mentality." The perception was, and is sometimes still true, that the security staff was made up of retired law enforcement or military personnel looking for a retirement job. Most of these individuals had little concept of the business world and of dealing with executive management whose priority is profits and not "following the rules" or "patriotism" at all costs.

Even today, retired law enforcement, intelligence or security professionals are often given the opportunity to lead security organizations in business over those business security professionals who "grew up" within the business. In many cases, executive management does not understand or appreciate the talents and the job done by the security professionals within their own companies. Furthermore, the security professionals have done a rather poor job of educating corporate management as to what it takes to be a 21st century security professional—and being an ex-spy or investigator is not the same as establishing and managing a corporate assets protection program. Again, using an SMMP can help the security professional, regardless of the prior background of the individual who is responsible for assets protection.

Another problem with some security specialists is that they may even consider that the business assets are "theirs" and they are responsible for their protection, like parents worry about their children. They may fail to realize that it is not their property. It is the property of the owner(s) who have delegated protection of those assets to the corporate management team.

Management and other business employees are slow to realize the change to a more educated, intelligent and technical security profession. However, this change has been gradually taking place over the last several decades. The security profession has become more complex and requires far more skilled security professionals, not only in security-related functions, but also in various other disciplines of the business world.

So, who are these security professionals in the 21st century and what is their role in the world of business? To understand that, let's look at the reasons for the increased need for security professionals in today's business world.

THE NEED FOR SECURITY PROFESSIONALS IN BUSINESS

Is there a need for business security professionals today? The answer may be obvious if you are in the security profession. However, you may be surprised to know that there are many in the corporations of the world that might not agree with you. You may wonder how anyone in a corporate management or leadership position could think that way. Although you may be able to rationalize employees feeling that way, since many of the assets protection requirements can cause them to operate in a way that they do not agree with.

You should remember that most people prefer to operate without, or with minimal, constraints. That includes management. People are basically the same throughout the world, and this is basic human nature. Ask yourself if you like being constrained. The answer is: of course not. A business security professional must keep that in mind. After all, you must try to get people to understand the need for and value of complying with security requirements or "constraints" which are needed to protect business assets. An SMMP helps you make the case for those security requirements. If you can't make the case with or without an SMMP, then perhaps you are the one who is wrong in that situation. That is possible you know, and something you as a security professional should always think about when making assets protection decisions—is it possible that this decision is the wrong one?

> *After the attacks of "9/11," security changes included giving airline passengers plastic knives instead of metal ones, but allowed metal forks. How much damage can one do with a metal butter knife versus a sharp metal fork? Passengers consider such security requirements illogical and give security professionals a bad name.*

However, the security professional should not take attitudes of other employees personally. After all, security specialists not only provide guidance and direction as they establish operating constraints, but security is also an overhead cost. Therefore, as you often will be reminded throughout this book, if not done effectively and efficiently, security can be a "parasite on the profits." Management, as well as the corporate owners, feel the same way about any other function within the business that is a "profit parasite." They want those functions to be as effective and efficient, and the least intrusive as possible on their core business activities.

All that said, then why have corporate security? If it is a publicly held company, a lack of security may at a minimum violate some government laws or regulations. In other words, the responsibilities of executive management include protection of assets and much of this is accomplished under the direction and control of security. Another reason assets protection is needed is the lack of trustworthiness of a small number of employees. Most employees are very conscientious and are honest enough to do the right thing regardless of any security staff or business policies. However, as is often the case, resources are allocated for security to protect the business and the honest employees. The goal is to protect them from the few who, for some reason, have it in their nature to take what does not belong to them or to do harm. Actually, if you are a security professional, you should thank those miscreants from around the world for being dishonest, even for only a moment. Why? Because you owe your job and the growth of the security profession to the miscreants of the world; without them, security professionals would not be needed.

So, yes, security is necessary. Without it, as without a law enforcement presence in societies, there would be uncontrolled losses of business assets and maybe even human lives. With that being said, as the leader of the security department and therefore the one responsible for the protection of corporate assets, you must still justify your decisions that impact productivity and other costs. As you can guess by now, we believe that the SMMP can help justify assets protection decisions.

One thing that is seldom talked about but helps rationalize security personnel and assets protection that is integrated into our daily lives and that is it is often a form of psychological security. (It makes us feel protected, although we may not be protected as well as we think. Some of it may be an illusion.) Think about it. How often do you hear about items getting through the airport checks, the fact that cargo is not checked, and other such security processes, and yet old ladies and children are included in random physical searches at airports and other locations. Let's face it; unless we want to live in a total police state—maybe even then—no one can protect people, information or facilities with 100% certainty that no one can get through the "security net" and steal, damage, or destroy some valuable asset. It is all a matter of deciding on what are acceptable levels of risks based on costs and benefits. As can be seen by the 9/11 attack, some management risk-related decisions can have a terrible impact on corporations and people.

Remember also that security costs money. Protection of people, physical assets and information costs an organization in terms of convenience, productivity and dollars. Executive management and security professionals make risk assessments based upon threats and vulnerabilities every day. If there is no specific threat, fewer resources are allocated for protection, regardless of the vulnerability. If the threat is high and controls in place leave the system vulnerable, then more resources may be allocated for protection.

In the case of airport and airline security controls, since the threat to the system pre-9/11 was presumed to be low, management at that time could get away with few or minimal security controls and less capable, poorly trained security personnel. They could afford to accept the risks associated with minimal security controls. In hindsight, now that the threat is better understood, it was a hard and costly lesson to learn.

The acts of terror committed in New York and Northern Virginia are hopefully a rare but highly visible example of inadequate security. However, there are many other less-visible examples that also demonstrate a need for security just as clearly, if not as catastrophically.

> *In 1985, a company called* Recon Optical, *operating out of Barrington, Illinois, in the United States, experienced severe economic damage as a direct result of espionage. Representatives from another country (a nation-state allied with the United States, and not some rogue adversarial nation-state) were able to obtain sensitive technical data from Recon Optical, allegedly giving that foreign nation-state and its businesses a competitive advantage. The damage to Recon Optical's future business was severe and it took them years to recover. Apparently, Recon Optical did not have sufficient information protection controls in place, leaving them vulnerable to economic espionage. In this case, both threats and vulnerabilities were high, creating a major risk. Controls protecting against this risk were apparently inadequate, resulting in extensive loss.*

Corporations have an obligation to their shareholders to protect their interest and competitiveness of the company. This includes protecting people, information, facilities and other physical assets. Shareholders want the company they invest in to be profitable, as do all owners of businesses. Anything that threatens the competitiveness or profitability of a company requires risk mitigation. Loss of information and physical assets, harm done to employees and/or customers, or damage to company products and business reputations can severely affect the profitability of a company.

In 1982, Johnson and Johnson experienced severe damage to the reputation of one of their major product lines. An unknown person or persons tampered with the pain reliever product, Tylenol. Product capsules were laced with cyanide, causing the sudden and inexplicable deaths of seven people. This incident and several other copycat tampering episodes that occurred over the next 10 years, led to major changes in tamper-proof packaging. The result was a relatively simple but highly effective security feature that has just about eliminated product tampering. However, this also increased costs to the company. This new packaging is still used today.[1]

Companies have a legal right to protect their own property. Shareholders and stakeholders expect executive management to exercise that right and protect the viability and profitability of the enterprise. Furthermore, many state and federal laws and regulations require that employers provide safe and secure work environments for employees and customers. Even insurance providers now mandate protective measures as a part of the underwriting process. Employees expect to work in an environment that is reasonably safe—safe from a variety of hazards, and safe from the potential threat of workplace violence.

The vice president for internal controls and public affairs at Eddie Bauer, a retail chain of stores, expressed a responsibility and obligation to employees and customers for their safety.[2] *Bill Gates of Microsoft now considers "security the number one priority." (We know what you are probably thinking—"Yeah right! Sure they are!"). Look at it this way: at least by saying it, the topic of security (and safety) is raised to a new awareness level and, at least in the public relations arena, security is elevated to a more serious and more important level.*

What does all of this mean to businesses in the context of "why business security?" The events of 9/11 may be looked upon as one of a kind—at least that is the hope. The closest comparison takes us back to Pearl Harbor in December 1941. Can we be certain they will never happen again? The Ricon Optical and Johnson and Johnson situations may or may not be extreme, but not rare examples of economic damage so significant that recovery was difficult and took a very long time. On a daily basis, businesses face the loss of product, information, physical assets and reputation.

Even the large international business, Microsoft, has now apparently decided enough is enough. At Microsoft, security seemed to take a back seat in software development. The attitude seemed to be that if a security hole was found, let the customer or hacker find it, and then Microsoft would offer a security patch later. Microsoft is obviously one of the biggest targets in the world. Bill Gates was once rumored not to be too keen on security; after all, few "computer techies" like security. However, maybe that is changing. Maybe the public pressures, the latest successful attacks, and the increased vulnerabilities of inadequately protected systems are taking their toll on the public image of Microsoft. After all, sometimes the best way to get security support in a business is for

---

[1]   See http://www.personal.psu.edu/users/w/x/wxk116/tylenol/
[2]   See http://www.onpatrol.com/cs.privsec.html

the business to have a poor public image because of losses and public derision, often through the Internet and news media.

Getting back to the question, "Is there a need for business security?" The answer is a resounding yes! Furthermore, businesses should employ security professionals to fill that need and not rely on nonsecurity staff members to be responsible for that job as an "additional duty." However, we again stress that the need may be perceived, but how assets protection should be applied is often the argument, even among security professionals.

CORPORATE SECURITY TODAY

The security organization today is shaped by many influences. The specific needs, concerns and vulnerabilities of a corporation, the capabilities of its security team, and the perception of management as to the value of security all contribute to the security organization's structure and role. Even business downsizing trends influence the role of security. Since downsizing affects all aspects of business, security too has to learn to operate in a leaner environment with greater demands and higher expectations, while at the same time working in an environment of increased threats and risks. The challenges to security professionals are ever-increasing. The use of an SMMP can assist the security professional in dealing with issues of squeezing more effectiveness and efficiencies out of the security processes—but more on that later.

In large businesses, security organizations are generally structured as independent departments staffed with security professionals. The overall security profile is one of compliance and loss prevention. Often, safety, fire prevention, and ethics functions are linked to security. Smaller companies may even link more disciplines and tasks to security, but this is a product of manpower limitations and general needs as opposed to a direct association, or close relationship with the compliance and loss-prevention missions.

In small businesses, security is often an additional duty assignment to the human resources or law department. Small security departments, with few resources, generally rely on security professionals with broad and general experience as opposed to the highly specialized security professionals often used in larger companies.

Many businesses today, of various sizes, are outsourcing their security needs to companies that specialize in such matters. These include security functions such as the obvious—security guards—to the less obvious—for example, investigations, or information systems security. Many businesses are doing so because they require security but find that outsourcing it saves them money. The SMMP can provide supporting data to help make the outsourcing decision.

As usual, business management must look at security costs. It is expected that this trend will continue and more businesses will be aggressively trying to minimize security costs while at the same time security companies will be competing for these outsourced security contracts.

THE ROLE OF THE CORPORATE SECURITY PROFESSIONAL

The role of the corporate security professional is a protective role: the protection of people, information and physical assets that belong to, or are part of, any business. It is more than just a checklist of duties to be performed and responsibilities to be met. It is a commitment to the management and employees of a business to provide a safe and secure work environment.

A safe and secure work environment reduces the chances of disruptions to the business. Disruptions can be in many forms—for example, breaches of security and loss of information or physical assets—and can degrade the quality of the work environment and negatively impact the profitability of the business. The Chief Security Officer (CSO) has the lead in this protective role. Other security specialists provide their skills and efforts in support.

Because security professionals are involved with all departments within a business, they should have some of the best overall knowledge as to the state of the business as it relates to employee morale, business projects, and problems within various departments. They also know basically what is going on throughout the business. In fact, the security staff, if they are out and about in the business as they should be, probably has a better understanding of the state of the business than anyone else in the business (in terms of security, employee morale, vulnerabilities and risks), including the CEO.

CEOs hear what executives and managers tell them. Sometimes, some corporate managers may resent the intrusion of security requirements into their departments. They may even say that "this unnecessary security" is costing the department time and money. This may be especially true if the executive managers are discussing with the CEO why their department is over budget.

The security staff sees and hears what those doing the hands-on jobs are saying about their work. Therefore, the security staff can and should provide an overall idea of the state of security within the corporation and all its associated costs. In doing so, and to refute or defend allegations, the costs of security and its impact on employees' productivity, an SMMP can provide the data to support assets protection decisions.

THE REQUIRED SKILLS OF THE SECURITY PROFESSIONAL

Protecting business information, physical assets and people is not a simple job. Years ago, it would suffice to place a guard at the door to ensure no one, or anything, went in or out without proper authorization. That worked in an environment where everything was contained. The skills required for that tasking were minimal. Much more is expected from today's security professional, as today's business environment differs from yesterday's business environment. There are many important qualities a security professional must have to be effective. The following are some of the most essential:

- Must be technology and computer savvy.
- Needs good communication skills—written and verbal.
- Must possess a good understanding of how business works.
- Must understand the global business environment.
- Possesses college or university general education supplemented by a degree in business as an ideal major, or communications, human relations or psychology (the importance of understanding human behavior cannot be overstated). Furthermore, formal training in information systems has gone beyond being useful to being a necessity.
- Has strong analytical skills.
- Has good command of the language (ideally more than one, for example, Spanish, Chinese, Japanese) both verbal and written.
- Possesses an ability to work with and lead project teams.
- Has an interest in experiencing different roles and responsibilities.
- Has some international experience, preferably business.
- Has experience with, or an understanding of, other cultures and languages.

WHAT KIND OF PEOPLE ARE NEEDED?

Good security professionals must be recruited, trained, and retained. The business must be able to provide an interesting and attractive environment consistent with the needs and demands of most professional people in order to make them want to work there. To retain them, they must be provided with challenging work supplemented by competitive compensation. The CSO should provide the security staff with continued and relevant training and opportunities for professional and personal growth.

> *Part of an SMMP can include a costs-benefits analysis as to what training, at what location, at what costs, are to be provided the security staff that will best serve the needs of the department in its assets protection program.*

For security professionals, trustworthiness is of particular importance. Security professionals are charged with "minding the store." Because they are in a position of trust, the potential damage they can do is extensive. The security professional is responsible for the protection of company information, people and physical assets. They contribute to the company's continuity and therefore its overall performance and success. They must be trustworthy, competent and capable of providing protection. They must understand the fundamental precepts of security. As a CSO, how can you know that the security personnel you are hiring have the necessary qualifications?

Generally speaking, an SMMP cannot help in this regard but it can be used as part of another SMMP, separate from an assets protection-supported SMMP. This separate SMMP would be an integral CSO-supporting tool to measure the performance of the security staff. The more the SMMP can be used means that the performance measurement will be more objective instead of based on subjective performance, which always leaves room for debate between the CSO and the security professional being evaluated.

To perform, succeed, and survive, security professionals must also be learners. In a world of constant change, the ability and willingness to learn is essential. Successful companies learn and change to maintain competitiveness in the marketplace. The security professionals who protect them must do the same, or else their efficiency and effectiveness will degrade and the value they bring to the corporation will be less than what is necessary. Furthermore, without a willingness to learn, they could not be considered true professionals, only security employees who have "jobs" and not security "careers."

How do you know if someone has a willingness to learn? One way to determine this is to look at their history. Are they interested in learning? Have they engaged in learning activities? There is no single means to make this determination. The CSO should discuss learning with all prospective security employees, and maintain an interest in their learning, supporting their learning goals after they are hired.

An SMMP can be used to track security staff's learning against objectives supported by costs-benefits analyses.

WHY THE CORPORATE SECURITY PROFESSIONAL?

Global markets, uniqueness of product, diversity of the workforce, customers, and a rapidly changing technological environment make business security tasks more complex. Understanding how a business works is necessary but not sufficient for providing an appropriate level of protection. It takes more than just an understanding of the business to develop and implement a successful security, or as it is often called, assets protection program. It also takes an understanding of fundamental security principles. This is why security professionals should manage the task of providing assets protection for a corporation. Do you want an auto mechanic to do brain surgery on your daughter? No, of course not. So, executive management should not take the security role lightly either, for it can literally cost lives and jobs.

WHERE IS SECURITY'S PLACE IN THE CORPORATION?

There are many opinions as to where the responsibility for security best fits into a business structure. Some suggest that, inasmuch as security is a compliance function, it should be part of a larger compliance organization, such as audit, or part of the legal department. Others suggest security's role is closely aligned with people and therefore ought to be part of the human resources organization. Some in management suggest security is integral to the continuity of the enterprise and ought to be part of a business continuity organization. Effective arguments can be made for security belonging to any of these functions and several others.

> *Remember it is* corporate assets *and not* security assets! *Executive management makes the risk decisions!*

Regardless of where in the business structure security is placed, the CSO must have direct access to executive management. More specifically, the CSO needs access to the business's most senior executives, such as the CEO, COO, CFO, and CIO.

Ultimately, the overall security profile for any business is the responsibility of its CEO. An inability to adequately protect people, physical assets and information can have a negative impact on the corporation's profitability. Profitability is clearly a concern for any CEO and others in executive management. This is not to say that a CEO ought to be involved in the day-to-day management of security or the business' assets protection. That is the role of the CSO and all security professionals.

The CEO must be aware of what is being done to protect the business' assets and provide an "open door" to the CSO. One reason is that if something happens, the CEO can no longer get away by saying, "I didn't know; that is not my job; that is security's job." In today's global business environment, with more and more laws and regulations being implemented to protect the public, and the corporate owners, the CEO must know. The use of an SMMP and its related briefings to management can assist the CEO in "knowing."

Although the importance of the security functions has a direct correlation with the number and value of the corporate assets, many CEOs don't see security as an important, mission-critical, function. Also, it appears that, for some reason, some CSOs shy away from contact with executive management instead of trying to become more involved through formal and informal communications channels with them. Some look upon discussions with the corporate CEO as "out of their league." A CSO that is so inclined is in the wrong job. The CSO must make it a goal to actively and continually find good reasons to communicate with the CEO and executive management, for without their support, security will not succeed in its mission.

Using an SMMP can help the CSO use meaningful metrics to periodically provide executive management with a summary of security program successes. Using SMMP techniques, the CSO can build a briefing and provide executive management with an overview of security showing:

- the state of the corporate assets protection
- why assets are protected the way they are being protected
- how compliance with laws and regulations is being accomplished
- costs broken down by various elements, such as individual security functions, compliance with individual laws and regulations

SUMMARY

The role of security, primarily an assets protection role (people, information, facilities and other assets), has been evolving over the decades. It is no longer a "retirement" position for law enforcement or military personnel. The security professional of the 21st century must understand business, the political and global environment in which the business operates, and what laws and regulations affect the business and the security environments.

Today's security professionals must not only be business oriented but also provide a working business environment that is safe and secure based on the requirements of today's laws and regulations; as well as the risks that executive management are willing to take.

The security professional, to be effective, must gain the support and respect of the business's employees. The position of a security professional—the CSO—in a business is one of service and support by providing the best protection of business assets in an effective and efficient manner. The use of an SMMP helps focus the security staff and executive management on that goal, as we will show in the coming chapters.

Chapter 2

Management and Security Metrics Management Foundation

This chapter will look at security and building a foundation for a security metrics management program (SMMP) from the viewpoint of business and government agency management (nonsecurity professionals). It will discuss:

- What management should expect from their Chief Security Officer (CSO) and security staff;
- What questions to ask relative to assets protection costs, benefits, successes and failures;
- What they need to know to help them make better asset protection risk management decisions;
- How the CSO can help management come to the right asset protection decisions supported by an SMMP. That is to say, how to use measurement data of security processes in the decision-making process; and
- How management can support the security professional in meeting their security service and support objectives, and thus the needs of the business.

INTRODUCTION

In the vast majority of security-related books, the view is that of the security professional dealing with such topics as managing a security department, establishing an assets protection program, emergency planning and preparedness, physical security, and other more traditional security subjects. However, as a security professional, one must see the role of security and assets protection through the eyes of the receivers—of corporate management and shareholders—in order to better understand how best to communicate with management and gain management support. This chapter may help the security professional better understand executive management's assets protection risk decisions.

SECURITY FROM AN EXECUTIVE MANAGEMENT PERSPECTIVE

Management often considers security professionals to be a necessary expense in order to help the business comply with a wide variety of government regulations that range from those specific to security, such as Department of Defense and Homeland Security regulations, to recently enacted Sarbanes Oxley regulations and those established by the United States Security Exchange Commission. These regulations require that executive management protect the business assets for the business owners—the stockholders. Management often views security, in terms of cost, as a "parasite on the profits" of the business. (These may be harsh words but they make the point.) Money not spent on security can be spent in others areas of the business that make a more obvious contribution to the bottom line.

As we previously stated, executive management, like the other people in business, are not generally receptive to working with "more constraints." However, they do tolerate some "interference" by security professionals with regards to protection of the business assets, since most realize that, in our currently dangerous world, security professionals are needed as opposed to being a luxury function. The CSO and staff operate within the corporate environment out of necessity; it's not as though corporate management has any real choice these days.

What Business Management Should Expect from Their Security Staff

What management generally expects from their CSO and staff is that they provide only an appropriate (which often translates to minimal) amount of assets protection at the lowest possible cost while maintaining compliance with the applicable government laws and regulations and company policies.

However, this is usually not the preference of the security professional. They usually want to provide the best assets protection program for the corporation as is possible with minimal (and sometimes no) risk to the corporate assets. This can contribute to an adverse relationship between the CSO and senior management. If this is the case, management will constantly question security decisions and, in the back of their minds, may be thinking that the function of the security professional is not really necessary to the degree and cost provided by the CSO.

> *Security professionals who understand the corporate and global environment have a better chance of personal and professional success than those who do not.*

Business management wants and needs to be able to trust the CSO, and all security professionals, to make the right assets protection decisions based on the perspective and philosophy of management. That is, they want security professionals to think of assets protection from a business point of view and that view is all about costs, profits and managing risks. Using an SMMP can help the CSO manage the costs of a corporate assets protection program (CAPP) and show corporate management that the function is being handled using business sense.

Therefore, the CSO and all of the security professionals on staff must think of assets protection from the perspective of a business person and business owner. Business management expects the security staff to provide them with quality low-cost solutions and an estimate of risks involved when management is to make assets protection decisions, as well as available alternatives. These alternatives must always include the opportunity to do nothing. For example, if no decision is made, what are the (management) options; in other words, what will happen? What would that cost? As the CSO, remember to address these issues when developing your SMMP.

What Questions Should Corporate Management Ask Relative to Security Matters?

In general, corporate management must know assets protection costs, benefits, successes and failures, and what they (management) need to know to help them (management) make better security risk management decisions. Specifically, they should ask their security staff (and are likely to ask) the following questions:

- What is driving the need for assets protection as planned?
- If laws or regulations require assets protection as envisioned, which ones specifically? (NOTE: The corporate legal staff should also be involved in these discussions or, better yet, the CSO should coordinate the legal issues with the legal staff in advance. In this way, the CSO can say that the legal staff has been consulted and they have rendered their advice (concurrence, disagreement, recommendations). Of course, if they disagreed with the CSO, the CSO must have a very good reason should a contrary path be selected; however, in the vast majority of cases, the legal opinion must be adhered to in the context of following the law, and seriously considered in the context of liability and risk versus benefit.
- Are your (CSO) recommendations based on an interpretation of the laws or regulations so that we can provide the minimum needed for compliance?
- What will it cost the corporation in terms of expenditure of resources (money) and other less tangible considerations?
- Are the costs based on providing minimal and reasonable protection to the assets?
- Is the plan based only on a lowest-cost approach?
- What are the risks involved in providing a lowest-cost, minimal assets protection program?
- On what specifically do you base your recommendations—for example, experience of other corporations, benchmarked against other corporations' assets protection programs, or what?

What Corporate Management Should Know to Help Them Make Better Risk Management Decisions

It is important for corporate management to understand the basics of an assets protection program and the protection philosophy behind such a program. Times have changed and, in more and more countries, executive management is being held personally accountable to the stockholders and stakeholders for ensuring that the business assets are properly safeguarded.

Corporate management, and by that we mean primarily executive management, including CEO, CFO, COO, CIO, and in general, officers of the company, should require at least an annual briefing on the state of the corporation's assets protection program, as well as its impact on productivity of the employees and its other costs.

It would also behoove the CSO to recommend such a briefing in order to help provide "awareness training" to executive management. The better they understand the assets protection program and philosophy, the more apt they are to support it—assuming the CSO's approach makes good business sense.

Some security professionals are sensitive about having their experience, skills and decision-making questioned when it comes to matters of security. After all, they are the experts, are they not? This is generally not the case in terms of business decisions. In fact, the CSO should welcome such exchanges as it will help the executive management better understand why assets are protected the way they are. Also, even though management may not be "experts" in assets protection, they may approach it more from a "common business sense" point of view.

The CSO should not look upon this exchange as adversarial, but rather as everyone making their contribution to ensure the best decisions are made. After all, if nothing else, a profitable business will help ensure the CSO's position in the business.

> *Leave your ego at the entrance to your workplace. You can always find it again after work, if you must.*

An SMMP can be used to support briefings for corporate management and, if done correctly, the CSO will welcome the exchange of ideas and information about the CAPP and its impact on the corporation.

> *By using a well-prepared SMMP, the CSO can have the confidence to explain and support the CSO's assets protection decisions, which are proven and supported by the SMMP to be the best course of action for the corporation.*

How Can Security Professionals Help Business Management Make the Right Risk Management Decision?

The CSO may want the corporate management to "just trust me" and not question the CSO's decisions and judgment. This may work once in a while, sometimes, or even often, depending on the corporate management's attitude. However, it is important to remember that the less interest management has in the CAPP, the less support they will probably give it—and you. Furthermore, if something does go wrong—well, the phrase "ignorance is bliss" comes to mind, as management will be "ignorant" of CAPP requirements and will not have bought-in to them, which is never an advantage for the CSO. Thus, they will say it is your fault and not theirs, as they didn't know—even though they should have. Luckily, as numbers of corporate executives have recently found out, that doesn't work with trial juries hearing testimony of massive corporate frauds.

To help executive management make the best protection-related decisions, it is very important that the CSO ensure that management understands:

- Basic assets protection concepts;
- How those concepts are applied in the business;
- Philosophy behind each assets protection application/process;
- Costs of the assets protection program and individual security functions and processes;
- Why security applications and processes are implemented as they are;
- What is done to ensure that a reasonable amount of risk is incorporated into the assets protection program, thus keeping costs lower;
- What is done to ensure that each assets protection application and process is implemented as efficiently as possible;
- What is done to ensure that each assets protection application and process is implemented using principles of risk management (that includes a cost-benefits analysis);
- What is being done to continuously look for ways to provide for a more effective assets protection program? That is, balancing costs with risks for the protection of company assets.

How Can Corporate Management Support the CSO in Meeting Security's Service and Support Goals?

It may be obvious by now, but corporate management must support the CAPP. After all, assets protection is management's responsibility. The CSO and security professionals employed in the corporation are the designers, implementers and managers of a CAPP. They are the "in-house security consultants" for management. It is the executive management's CAPP, because it is a corporate and not exclusively a security program.

Executive management, in fact all levels of management, must understand their role and responsibilities for the protection of corporate assets, as should all employees. Once they understand that role and agree to that role, they must support the CAPP, which includes supporting the CSO and security staff. Management must also be vocal about their support with their employees.

> *You should lead the assets protection program, but be sure that executive management understands that it is their program too.*

Corporate management must play an active role in the assets protection program and not a passive role. This is not to say that they micromanage the business' assets protection program, but they should macromanage it to some extent—obviously prioritized with their other duties and responsibilities.

In doing so, management should ask for periodic briefings and reports concerning the business' "state of security" on at least an annual basis, if not semiannually or quarterly. Therefore, the CSO should propose and offer an awareness program for executive management, to be accomplished through periodic briefings and also periodic reports as to the state of the corporate assets protection and its related costs. For example, an annual briefing with quarterly reports would provide a good balance in time and effort by all participants. The CSO should try to have the annual briefings coincide with the executive management's budgetary decision period. In that way, the CSO can help management understand the need for the assets protection budget and the consequences of a decreased budget.

> *As you read through these initial chapters, you can begin to see how an SMMP can help in meeting both the goals of corporate management and those of the CSO and security staff with regard to the CAPP.*

SUMMARY

In providing an effective and efficient assets protection program for a corporation, a team effort is required, with that team made up of employees who will comply with the policies and procedures of a CAPP, management who support the program, and a CSO and security staff who will lead the program.

In order for such a program to be successful, each employee, each level of management, and security professionals on staff must understand each others' point of view when it comes to security and the CAPP.

It is up to each to do their part. This triad—employees, management, and security staff—is like a three-legged stool. If one leg is removed or weak, the stool will topple. Such is the case with a CAPP. To be successful, each part of the assets protection triad must work together and each must do their part.

The SMMP developed and led by the CSO and security staff can provide visibility into how the CAPP is being managed, as well as its related costs, benefits, successes and failures.

Chapter 3

Policies, Procedures, Processes, Plans and Projects

In the previous two chapters, we generally discussed what the Chief Security Officer (CSO) and corporate management, specifically executive management, should know and do relative to a successful corporate assets protection program (CAPP).

This chapter will explain and provide examples of how to identify and describe business security policies, procedures, processes, plans, and projects, as well as how they are used to fulfill the CSO's duties and responsibilities. Furthermore, in this chapter, we will continue to lay the understanding and foundation for establishing a security metrics management program (SMMP) that can be applied by any security professional in any business or government agency in any country.

INTRODUCTION

If the security professionals employed by corporations are to lead a successful CAPP, they must be able to determine if the CAPP is meeting all the expectations of the corporation's executive management.

In order to provide some assurance that the CAPP is working as planned, an SMMP can be used. However, before an SMMP can be developed, it should begin on a solid foundation—but what is that foundation? (See Figure 3-1.)

The answer is CAPP-related:

- Drivers
- Policies
- Procedures
- Processes
- Plans
- Projects

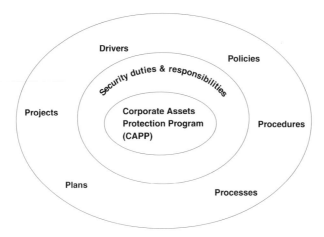

Figure 3-1   A simplified version of the relationship between security duties and responsibilities, security drivers, policies, procedures, processes and plans.

TRIAD OF ASSETS PROTECTION AND SECURITY FUNCTIONAL DRIVERS

It is important for you to have a basic understanding of what drives a CAPP, as well as the security functions that support a CAPP, as it provides the foundation on which an SMMP is developed to oversee and monitor the CAPP and related security functions. (See Figure 3-2.)

Laws, Regulations, Company Policy
and Procedures, Ethics, Privacy, &
Good Business Practices

Figure 3-2   The triad of security drivers relative to the CAPP and assets.

PART ONE OF THE SECURITY DRIVERS' TRIAD: RISK MANAGEMENT DRIVERS

A corporation's or government agencies' CAPP must, or at least should, be based on the identified needs, which have their origin in identifying the threats, vulnerabilities and risks to the assets, usually through a process called risk management, which includes risk assessments, risk analyses, and best security practices.

Risk management is defined as the management decision-making process related to identifying and minimizing various risks to the business or organization. It looks at a combination of threats to assets, the vulnerabilities of those assets to the related threats, and the chances that any particular threat can or will take advantage of a vulnerability. Risks can be identified using a statistical method; for example, the chances are 12:1 that an attack will occur within a year and that attack on an asset will be successful. It can also be done through the use of qualitative methods using such indicators as "High," "Medium," or "Low." Either method will work in an SMMP. Whichever one you use, however, should be consistent throughout the risk management program that supports an SMMP.

Costs-benefits analyses are added to the risk management program to assist in determining how to lower the risks to a manageable level at the lowest possible costs. Regardless of what you might hear from some PhD in statistics or risk management "experts," this still most often boils down to a best, educated guess.

For example, if you had conducted a risk assessment to determine the impact to your corporation of the potential destruction of offices in, say, Sri Lanka, Phuket and Aceh due to a massive earthquake causing massive tsunami effects, you would probably have said that the chances were "low" or even improbable. Your analyses would have been correct! Why? Because the chances of that catastrophic event occurring was low, and yet it happened. That tells you that there are *always* risks to assets. You can never have a completely safe asset that is so protected that the chances of any adverse effects to that asset are zero.

Risk management is a process used to help design and implement security policies, procedures, and processes that are applicable and effective for protecting corporate assets. Risk management assessments also influence the design and development of plans and projects. For example, if an unacceptable level of risk is identified relative to some asset or assets, a plan or project may be initiated to lower the risk to the identified asset(s).

Furthermore, risk assessments are tools to be used when providing support to executive managers who often make risk-related decisions. Managing risks requires management to take into consideration many factors that contribute to the vulnerability, threat and probability of occurrence equation. Part of that equation includes the availability of resources (budget, money) to be used to protect that asset.

PART TWO OF THE DRIVERS' TRIAD: CORPORATE DECISIONS' DRIVERS

The second driver in our driver triad is management direction. Management direction is just that—direction given by management, or those that are in your organizational chain of command, such as your boss, the boss's boss, and so forth.

This is considered an asset protection driver because these managers will determine how much risk they are willing to accept on behalf of the corporation. Hopefully, if you have done your job well and presented the risk options to management, they will decide on the best course of action. That course of action will drive how well and at what costs the corporate assets will be protected.

> *Remember that it is* not *the job of security personnel to accept the risks associated with business assets protection. That is the job of executive management who are responsible to the business owners, whether they be stockholders of a publicly traded company or private owners.*

Often, security professionals think that assets protection decisions regarding risks are theirs to make. No, they are not. Security professionals are the in-house security consultants and advisers. That is their role. They develop a CAPP, present it to management with its related costs and risks included, and management decides to accept it, reject it entirely and send you either packing or back to the planning stage, or accept it in part, rejecting some parts while accepting more risks.

Yes, you may make risk management decisions every day on behalf of management and as delegated by executive management. However, somewhere in that decision-making chain of events, you should be able to trace each decision back to management responsibility—and management accountability. They are the ones who are accountable to the corporate owners.

> *Management can delegate risk management decision authority to you, but they cannot delegate away their responsibility for the overall protection of corporate or government agency assets. Based on management decisions, you—the CSO—implement and manage the CAPP accordingly.*

Remember to use the risk management process to support sound business decisions with regard to assets protection by incorporating the results of risk management findings into the executive management decision-making process, backed up by a good SMMP.

This, coupled with the other security drivers of laws and regulations (to include contractual requirements that are legally binding) and management direction, provide the basis for building the CAPP. These are called security drivers, as they "drive" the need for security or assets protection. Think about it: one should not arbitrarily build a CAPP that includes any requirements that cannot be traced back to some required obligation or security driver and/or good business practice—even if "you have always done it this way"!

Following the identification of the drivers, one can then look at their related policies, procedures, processes and projects—generally in that order. Once these matters are addressed, they will provide the necessary information on which to build an SMMP.

PART THREE OF THE DRIVERS' TRIAD: LAWS, REGULATIONS, BEST BUSINESS PRACTICES, ETHICS AND PRIVACY DRIVERS

Laws and Regulations

Each business, regardless of location in the world, and each government agency, regardless of the country that it supports, must comply with government laws and regulations. Obviously, failure to do so would not only cause chaos in the country or maybe even globally, but also would be a cause for some civil or criminal action being taken by a government or other injured party.

If corporations always complied with the applicable laws and regulations, it would provide for a fair competitive environment. However, as we have seen over the years, this has not always been the case—and is still not the case today, as fraud and corruption reports are seen in the news almost daily. Although most employees, managers and executives work hard and "do the right thing," there are those few that don't and that causes problems or even disasters for everyone else. One possible use of an SMMP is to look for indications of fraud or other wrongdoing. This is what is usually called a "slippery slope," as we have seen in the past. Those committing fraud and other criminal acts may be those in positions of authority and trust, who you would be seeking support from on your program to detect fraud.

Even in a corporation where executives and employees are extremely honest and ethical, there may be a reluctance to actively seek out problems. High levels of trust or a false sense of security may lead to low emphasis placed on fraud detection efforts. Moreover, concern for unwanted and negative attention, particularly that of shareholders, customers and the media, may cause decision-makers to look for problems less than aggressively.

Part of a CAPP has to do with monitoring compliance with applicable laws and regulations. You might wonder what this has to do with a CAPP. The answer is that if the laws and regulations under which a business is to operate were violated, that could—actually, would—lead to a diminishing stakeholder trust. If that occurs, the stock of a publicly held company would go down. Also, customers may not want to do business with that corporation and thus revenue would decrease. This might also lead to layoffs, indictments, civil and/or criminal penalties and fines.

So, any SMMP should include metrics for ensuring compliance, but not only with the government's laws and regulations, but also the CAPP's policies and procedures, since the policies and procedures are in place to provide processes for meeting the business's governmental laws and regulations. (See Figure 3-3.)

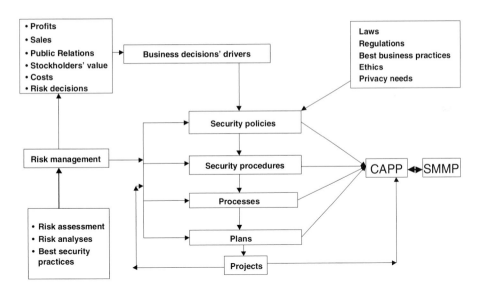

Figure 3-3 The additional relationship of laws, regulations, and so forth to the security policies, procedures, etc.

Other Potential Drivers

Best Practices

In addition to laws and regulations, other drivers related to security duties and responsibilities, CAPP, and security policies is "best business practices" and "best security practices." Just because a corporation or a CSO designs and implements a business practice does not mean that it is good or effective. A good way to help ensure the business practice implemented is a quality practice/process is to benchmark with others. That is to say, compare your process or practice with what other companies are doing. Others may perform the same or similar practice or process but more effectively. Learn from them and don't "reinvent the wheel." Benchmarking is a good process to incorporate into an SMMP.

Ethical Conduct

Ethical conduct is another related driver. To violate a security directive would of course be unethical. Ethics is a major concern for the public when dealing with public figures and business executives, particularly those leading publicly held companies. Ethics violations or breaches are not necessarily violations of laws or regulations, although they can be. Ethics violations are activities or behaviors that step outside of acceptable behavior. Acting ethically means "doing the right thing." For example, if you see someone cheating on their travel expenses, this is probably a violation of company policy, perhaps a fraudulent act against the government (depending on the circumstances), and without doubt not a good practice. It is an example of unethical behavior. Just knowing this places you, the observer, in an ethical dilemma. You haven't broken any law, but reporting the violation would be the right thing to do. Not reporting it is unethical in itself.

Privacy Demands

The need for privacy is addressed in the laws and regulations of many countries. Corporations and government agencies most often have specific policies defining their approach to privacy and why privacy is important to the corporation. Historically, privacy issues have been treated differently from corporation to corporation, with many simply not taking the issue of privacy seriously. This is changing due to public concerns and rampant violations of individual's privacy rights. From identity theft to the protection of company private information, privacy has become a highly important and politically charged issue. Failing to have adequate privacy policies and protective measures in place can impact organization performance and even the most important "bottom line."

SUMMARY OF DRIVERS

As we have just discussed, the assets protection drivers—the security drivers—are where one begins to build a CAPP. Once the CAPP is established, the SMMP can be developed, implemented and maintained. This is very important because neither part of a CAPP nor any security function should be implemented unless it can be shown to be a necessary requirement based on drivers. To do otherwise would be wasting resources such as money and productivity. (See Figure 3-4.)

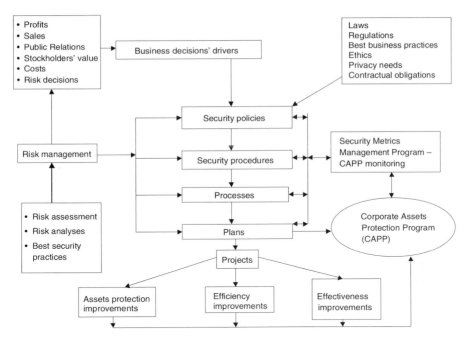

Figure 3-4   Another example of a summary chart of assets protection and security functional drivers as they relate to a CAPP and SMMP.

CAPP-RELATED POLICIES

In the security flow, the security drivers are used to establish security policies. Security policies are those directives that set the rules for the protection of corporate or government agency assets. These directives tell those who have access to the assets what assets need to be protected, and sometimes how they should be protected.

> *Policies are defined in the dictionary as "…a principle, plan or course of action, as pursued by a government, organization, individual, etc.…."*[1]

CAPP-RELATED PROCEDURES

Security procedures are further set forth in department or work-unit work instructions. Work instructions take procedures a step further and address the details of how to protect the corporation's assets. Security procedures may be set forth in any type of environment from that of the security department, engineering, information technology, manufacturing, etc. They may be broad in scope, covering the entire business, or may be narrow in scope—for instance, covering how to securely manufacture a product where a proprietary process is being used.

> *Procedures are defined in the dictionary[2] as "…the act, method or manner of proceeding in some process or course of action; esp., the sequence of steps to be followed…a particular course of action or way of doing something…"*

---

[1]   Webster's New World Dictionary
[2]   Ibid.

Keep in mind that policies are very high level and broad in scope. Procedures are linked to policies but go into greater detail in defining operating parameters.

CAPP-RELATED PROCESSES

What is a process? As used here when discussing an SMMP, it is a series of steps or actions taken to produce products or services. (See Figure 3-5.) To measure it first requires an understanding of the process itself:

- What are the requirements that drive the process?
- What are the assets protection policies that drive the process?
- What are the assets protection procedures that drive the process?
- In other words, why do it at all?
- What is the final product or service delivered?
- Who are the customers?
- Are their needs and expectations being met?
- How does the process itself work?
- Are there dependent subprocesses?
- Who are the process owners?

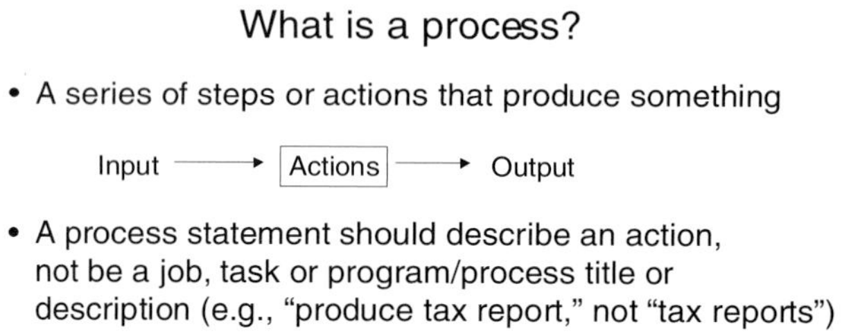

What is a process?

- A series of steps or actions that produce something

Input ──────▶ Actions ──────▶ Output

- A process statement should describe an action, not be a job, task or program/process title or description (e.g., "produce tax report," not "tax reports")

Figure 3-5   Summary of the process concept.

These are the basic questions to which you will need to know the answers in order to successfully assess security and assets protection processes' effectiveness using the SMMP.

> *The dictionary defines a process as "...a series of actions taken towards a particular aim..."*[3]

It is important that processes be identified and also supported by flowcharts or flow diagrams indicating all the steps in the assets protection process. This will be useful for security audits and comparing the established (approved) processes with the actual work being performed—in other words, determining if the assets are being safeguarded using the approved methods. These then can be measured and analyzed as an integral part of the SMMP.

The security processes, along with the security drivers, policies, procedures and processes form an integral baseline or foundation for a CAPP and SMMP. The security processes' flowcharts are also exactly what are needed in order to analyze the processes

---

[3]   Encarta World English Dictionary; St Martin's Press, Microsoft Encarta, 1999.

as part of any "total quality management/continuous process improvement (TQM/CPI) functions, as well as an SMMP. "Total quality management" is a disciplined approach to the art of management.[4]

> *Flowcharts depict the sequence of steps or actions as they are designed to occur and also how they actually occur.*

As security processes relate to the SMMP, the flowcharts will be used to develop individual security functional metrics and also analyze the steps being taken. The analyses will identify where some steps in a security process are or are not:

- Required by policy, regulations or laws
- Needed to be accomplished in order to successfully accomplish the task at hand
- Taking too much time to accomplish
- Being done in the most effective manner (Could be done better?)
- Being done in the most efficient manner (Could be done cheaper?)

PROCESS MANAGEMENT

To determine the effectiveness of any single assets protection or security process (how security functions are performed), it is necessary to measure that process. What is measured will depend upon how the process works. For example, a transactional process may require measuring the cycle time of each transaction.

In some cases, the amount of what is being delivered is most important. In other cases, the frequency of delivery matters most. In any event, determining what gets measured is a product of what the process is intended to do. In other words, the process is designed to do something. Does that something get done? If so, how efficient, effective, frequent, or costly is the process of getting it done?

As mentioned earlier, an important tool used to assist in developing an understanding of how a process works is the process flow diagram. In this diagram, each step in any process is identified and examined in regards to how that step fits into the whole process. Furthermore, the value of each step itself is assessed. In other words, is it necessary to perform that step and does it bring value to the customer? By placing each step of the process in a flow diagram form, an assessment can be made of each step individually. Unnecessary or non-value-added steps should be eliminated or redesigned into value-added steps. Furthermore, the costs of each step and its impact on employees can also be measured at those points.

Once a process is diagramed and refined, measuring the actual performance of the process against the desired outcome is essential. This will tell just how effective the process is. For example, if the CSO needs to be able to produce a company employee identification badge at a cost of $5.00 per badge and delivered within 24 hours of the request then what gets measured is the cost to make the badge and the amount of time it takes to deliver that badge. Comparison of the actual cost and production time to the desired cost and production time will tell the CSO if they are effective and efficient, or not. The next step in the analysis would be to find ways to do it cheaper and faster.

---

[4]   http://www.johnstark.com/fwtqm.html

PERFORMANCE MANAGEMENT

The CSO should understand that determining the success of the security organization and assets protection program can be, and usually is, measured in many ways. Some processes like producing badges may be measured by the cost to make the badge and the amount of time it takes to produce a single badge, as well as adding any time spent by the employee in the process of obtaining a badge. The employee's time is nonproductive time when viewed in the context of what the employee was being paid to do for the corporation. Obviously, the employee was not hired or paid to apply for and receive a corporate access control badge.

Other areas of security, such as compliance with laws and regulations, are usually measured through the government or regulatory agency inspection process. Here a government organization with oversight responsibilities will conduct an inspection at a site or facility to assess the level of compliance. Any areas found noncompliant will require corrective action and may lead to the issuance of a citation—for example, fire safety. Using the SMMP, such costs should be measured. In some instances, government inspection costs can be billed back to the government agency that may have contracted for products or services to the corporation being inspected.

Compliance with corporate policy and procedures is usually measured through the internal audit process. Additionally, every security program should include a self-inspection process and possibly a security audit program. Self-inspections should be conducted periodically by the security organization and used as a tool to help understand the organization's level of performance and help prepare for external agency reviews. Inspections can also be conducted by the individual corporation departments. Furthermore, such tools can be offered to department managers for their own self-inspections.

CAPP-RELATED PLANS

When we talk about the CAPP, depending on the environment, the CAPP may also incorporate "subplans." The CAPP is the "umbrella" plan which incorporates the other related plans. These include the contingency plan, emergency plan, automated information backup plan, event security plan, disaster recovery plan, and any other plan that has to do with protecting assets. (See Figure 3-6.)

> *A plan is defined as "...to devise a scheme for doing, making, or arranging..."*

A plan, a course of action, can be used to build a CAPP, for example. Plans go into very specific detail about a specific event, activity or objective.

Often plans provide the "big picture," such as a business marketing or sales plan. But just as often, they can be very detailed, addressing every aspect of actions necessary to achieve an objective. In order to successfully develop and implement a plan, it can be handled through a project or a series of projects—for example, one for each milestone.

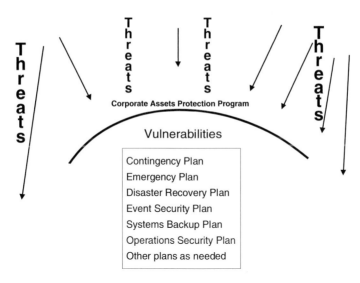

Figure 3-6   The CAPP umbrella.

CAPP-RELATED PROJECTS

There are two basic types of work performed by the CSO and staff which would comprise the SMMP. They are:

- Level of Effort (LOE) (refers to the routine amount of security work performed on a regular basis in support of accomplishing the security mission and fulfillment of CAPP objectives and on-going tasks—the day-to-day security functions)
- Projects

Projects are established where some tasks related to the CAPP and/or security functions must be completed but they are not on-going tasks. It is imperative that the CSO be intimately familiar with and experienced in project management, as well as time management.

Remember that the criteria for whether or not some task should be a project are as follows:

- A stated objective (generally in one clear, concise and complete sentence);
- A beginning date;
- An ending date;
- Specific tasks to be performed to successfully meet that objective;
- A project leader;
- Specific personnel to complete each task and the time period when each task will be completed.

Also often included are the costs of the project to subsequently compare against the planned costs and benefits. If there are cost overruns, then management must look at the way the project was estimated, take away some lessons learned, and correct the process used in estimating project costs. An automated or manual project management chart or form should be used to track the project. (See Figure 3-7.)

> *Projects have many uses but the three best uses from an asset protection and security viewpoint are as follows: Assets protection improvements; Security efficiency improvements; Security effectiveness improvements*

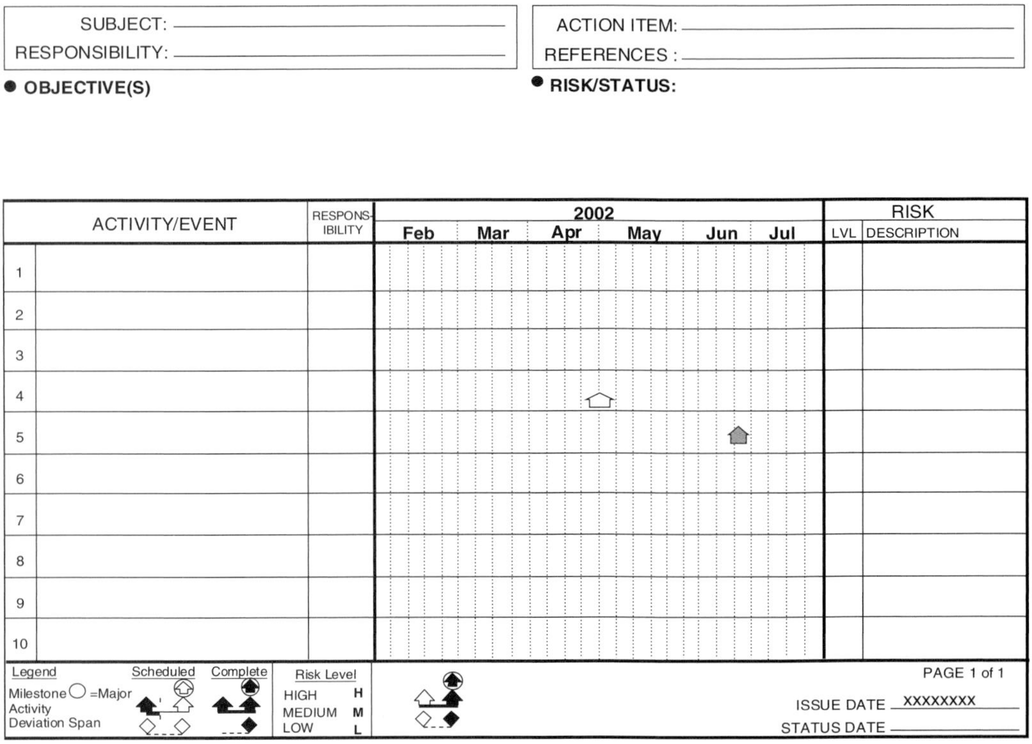

SUBJECT: ————————————

RESPONSIBILITY: ————————————

ACTION ITEM: ————————————

REFERENCES : ————————————

● **OBJECTIVE(S)**

● **RISK/STATUS:**

Figure 3-7   Example of a project management chart that can be on-line for easier modifications, and can be used to track CAPP and security functional projects. There are other commercially available versions of project management plans. Use what you determine to best meet your organizational needs.

Project Management Case Study—CSO and IT

Let's assume that the CIO sent a memo to the CSO based on a conversation that the CIO had with the director of information technology (IT). It seems that they had a meeting and during the meeting the discussion turned to IT projects related to their projects of upgrading systems—for example, hardware, software, and their general maintenance. The CAPP policy called for such upgrades and maintenance efforts to ensure that the assets protection environment relative to information be maintained in compliance with the requirements set forth in the CAPP.

The director stated that the IT staff did not know if that was always the case when they made changes to systems. Consequently, the director suggested that members of the CSO's organization be part of the IT project teams with responsibility for determining if the changes kept the business information environment secure. The CIO agreed and sent the CSO a letter to that effect. When the CSO received the memo, the CSO discussed the matter with the senior systems security engineer. It was decided that a project plan be developed in order to establish a process and function to comply with the CIO's and director of IT's request.

It was also determined that the project should include a member of the IT department to ensure that the project results met their need with minimal adverse impact on getting their upgrade and maintenance done in a timely fashion.

As a CSO, you should be able to identify several issues that must be resolved apart from initiating this project:

- The director of IT and the CSO should be working closely together and, by doing so, they could have dealt with this matter without the involvement of executive management
- The CIO, by sending a memo to the CSO instead of just calling the CSO on the phone or meeting personally with the CSO, indicates that the communication and working relationship between the CIO and CSO must be improved
- The CSO must take action to immediately begin improving the communication and relationship with the director and CIO.

Those aside, using Figure 3-7 as an example, let's develop a project and fill-in-the-blanks for major portions of the chart:

- *SUBJECT*: The project name: Security Test & Evaluation Function Development, for example.
- *RESPONSIBILITY*: The name of the project leader: John Doe, Security Senior Systems Security Engineer.
- *ACTION ITEM*: What is to be accomplished: IT requires CSO support to ensure information and systems protection are integrated into IT systems' integration, maintenance and update processes.
- *REFERENCES*: What caused this project to be initiated: See memo to CSO from CIO, dated November 2, 2005.
- *OBJECTIVE(S)*: State the objective of the project: Develop a security test and evaluation function to support IT systems' integration, upgrading and maintenance of systems and similar IT projects.
- *RISK/STATUS*: State the risk of not meeting the objective(s) of this project: Due to limited staffing and multiple customer projects being supported, this project may experience delays as higher priority LOE and projects take precedence.
- *ACTIVITY/EVENT*: State the tasks to be performed: e.g., meet with IT project leads.
- *RESPONSIBILITY*: Identify the person responsible for each task: The security department's Senior Systems Security Engineer, John Doe.
- *CALENDAR*: The calendar could be a year long, monthly, quarterly or a six-month calendar with vertical lines identifying individual weeks. Using the six-month calendar, the Project Lead and assigned project team members would decide what tasks had to be accomplished to meet the objective and using the "arrows" and "diamonds" identified in the legend, mark the beginning and ending dates of each task. The arrows are filled-in when the task is started and when the task is completed, while using the diamonds to show deviations from the original dates.
- *RISK—LVL*: In this space, each task is associated with the potential risk that it may be delayed or cost more than allocated in the budget for the task. Using "High," "Medium" or "Low" or "H," "M" or "L," the Project Lead in concert with the person responsible for the task, assigns a level of risk.
- *RISK—DESCRIPTION*: A short description of the risk is stated in this block. If it requires a detailed explanation, that explanation is attached to the project plan. In this block the Project Lead, who is also responsible for ensuring that the project plan is updated weekly, states "See Appendix."
- *ISSUE DATE*: The date the project began and the chart initiated goes in this block.

- *STATUS DATE*: The most current project chart date is placed here. This is important because anyone looking at the project chart will know how current it is and can compare it with the ISSUE DATE to determine how long the project has been in existence.

Other types of charts can also be developed to show project costs in terms of labor, materials and the like. A good, automated project plan software program is well worth the costs for managing projects.

The CSO uses the project charts to brief management relative to the on-going work and the status of the CAPP. The CSO receives weekly updates on Friday mornings in meetings with all the CSO's project leaders, in which each project lead is given five minutes to explain the status of the projects. Basically, all the CSO requires is that the project lead states the status of the project. For example, "The Project is still on schedule" or "Task #2 will be delayed because the person assigned the task is out sick for a week; however, it is expected that the project completion date will not be delayed because of it."

The CSO holds an expanded staff meeting the last Friday of each month. All assigned security personnel attend these meetings, which last two to three hours. At these meetings, one hour is taken for all project leads and security functional leads to brief the status of their LOE and projects to the entire staff. The CSO does this so that everyone in the organization knows what is going on—a vital communications tool. Also during this time, other matters are briefed and discussed, for example, the latest risk management techniques, or conferences and training available. (And the CSO should bring the donuts!)

Project Management Case Study—SMMP

If you are going to develop an SMMP, it is obviously a perfect project to be managed through a formal project plan. After all, there is a clear objective to be accomplished, it has a beginning date, an ending date, and a specific task to be accomplished by members of your (you are the CSO) security staff, with you as the project lead. After all, this is a major project with long-term benefits and consequences. It is not something to be delegated to others, although the majority of individual tasks can be delegated to staff.

The example below is by all means not complete in detail. Much of the information to be added in detail would depend on how well-documented your assets protection program and security functions are relative to drivers, policies, procedures, flowcharted processes, and so forth.

Using the format above, the following is a sample, in narrative terms, as to how an SMMP can be developed using a project plan methodology:

- *SUBJECT*: Security metrics management program (SMMP) development.
- *RESPONSIBILITY*: Chief Security Officer.
- *ACTION ITEM*: An SMMP will be developed, implemented and managed in order to identify costs, benefits, successes and failures of the company's assets protection program and related security functions.
- *REFERENCES*: This project was initiated based on a decision by the CEO to identify all business-related costs and to reduce those costs as much as possible in order to be globally competitive.
- *OBJECTIVE(S)*: Develop an SMMP to identify and lower assets protection and related security costs consistent with acceptable levels of risks.

- *RISK/STATUS*: The risk of not meeting the project's objective is considered "MEDI-UM" based on its high priority and lack of adverse impact on assets protection priorities, but due to its complexity, and duration, it cannot be considered "LOW".
- *ACTIVITY/EVENT*: The tasks to be performed are as follows:
  - Identify all assets protection drivers.
  - Identify assets protection drivers subdivided by each security function as follows:
    - Administrative Security.
    - Physical Security.
    - Outsourced Security.
    - Personnel Security.
    - Security Education & Awareness Training.
    - Fire Protection.
    - Contingency Planning.
    - Investigations.
    - Government Security.
    - Information Security.
    - Executive Protection.
    - Event Security.
  - Identify or develop security functions related to each driver.
  - Identify or develop assets protection policies.
  - Identify or develop assets protection policies subdivided by each security function.
  - Identify or develop the security functions' flowcharts used to support each major policy and procedure.
  - Identify data collection points for each flowchart and security function based on tracking costs in time, personnel, productivity and material.
  - Identify or develop the charts' formats, colors and design schemes as boilerplates.
  - Develop a detailed list of each of the security functions' charts beginning with an overall security functional chart.
  - Develop individual high-level security functions' charts, one for each function showing level of effort (LOE), impact, costs and benefits.
  - Develop lower-level charts for each security subfunction.
  - Chart each major aspect of the CAPP to drivers and security functions.
  - Develop an overall chart for each security function.
  - Develop budget charts in terms of dollars, people and other resources for each security function.
  - Develop total budget chart.
- *RESPONSIBILITY*: The person responsible for each security function-identified task is the current lead for each security function.
- *CALENDAR*: This project will begin on (date) and completed by (date). NOTE: Each individual task will of course be identified with a beginning and ending date; however, those dates cannot exceed the overall project due date.
- *RISK—LVL*: The project lead for each security function and its associated milestone(s) will set the risk factors. However, any risk factor other than "Low" must be explained to, and discussed with, the CSO prior to setting the final risk level. The CSO needs this information in order to set the overall risk factor, schedule of project completion, and understand the reasons for the time needed. NOTE: The subproject lead may try to extend the development time so as not to come in late (sometimes known as the "Fudge Factor").

- *RISK—DESCRIPTION*: The risk of delay of this project is considered "Medium" due to its complexity and the needs to identify all security requirements and document the procedures and processes of those function for which that task has not been previously accomplished. Further delays could be experienced due to the LOE of the security staff and nonplanned activities directed by management.
- *ISSUE DATE*: (date.)
- *STATUS DATE*: (Status date should be weekly for the first month and then monthly thereafter, assuming the project is on schedule without impediments seen coming in the future.)

SECURITY DUTIES AND RESPONSIBILITIES

The responsibilities, duties and functions of the CSO and security staff are directly related to the security drivers. Security drivers, along with executive management's business decisions, establish the baseline for the CSO and security department.

Once they are established, it is up to the security professionals, led by the CSO, to develop security policies, procedures, processes and plans. They will use risk management techniques to help ensure that the business assets are protected consistent with the business needs. (See Figure 3-8.)

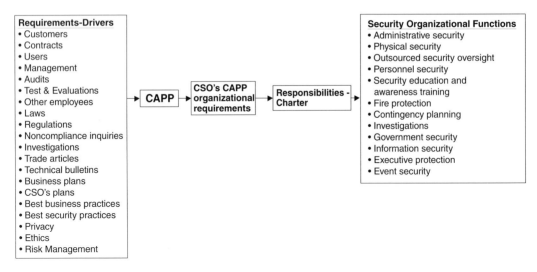

Figure 3-8   The relationship of drivers to security functions.

CORPORATE ASSETS PROTECTION PROGRAM (CAPP)

The CAPP is THE most important plan that the CSO and staff are responsible for establishing, implementing and maintaining. If a corporation does not have a cohesive, efficient and effective assets protection program as specified and implemented through the CAPP, one wonders how a corporation can possibly ensure that it is doing its utmost to protect corporate assets consistent with the needs of the business.

Due to its importance, it must be supported by an SMMP in order to provide continuous management oversight as to its status, costs, and benefits. It is the most important job of the CSO.

SUMMARY

A CAPP and security duties, responsibilities and functions should be based on the security drivers which are:

- Management direction
- Laws and regulations
- Ethics
- Best practices
- Risk management

Assets protection drivers are the foundation for a CAPP. The drivers then are used to build assets protection:

- Policies
- Procedures
- Processes
- Plans
- Projects

Together they help drive the security policies, procedures, processes, plans and projects. They are also needed to facilitate a strong foundation for the building of a security metrics management program (SMMP).

Chapter 4

Security Metrics Management Program—An Overview

This chapter will provide an overview describing a method for establishing a successful security metrics management program (SMMP). The SMMP is a tool for security management to use to assist in the evaluation of security processes for effectiveness and efficiency. For each process measured, the metrics used must be those that effectively measure what needs to be measured and help drive performance toward results.

INTRODUCTION

Some of the most common complaints of Chief Security Officers (CSOs) are that management doesn't support them and, as the famous U.S. comedian, Rodney Dangerfield, was known for saying, "I get no respect." The other major complaint is that the costs and benefits of a corporate assets protection program (CAPP) are difficult to measure. More specifically, the effectiveness and efficiency of the program is difficult to measure.

As for these complaints, the security professionals do get support because they are being paid—and these days more often than not, quite handsomely (although they might not think so)—and they have a budget that could have been part of corporate profits. Furthermore, respect is earned. If the security professionals wanted to be popular, they are definitely in the wrong profession.

One often hears executive management ask:

- "What is all this security costing me?"
- "What am I getting for the money I spend?"
- "Is it working?"
- "How do you know it's working?"
- "Can it be done at less cost?"
- And of course, when some adverse event occurs: "Why isn't it working?" "What went wrong?"

The more difficult question to answer is "What are the measurable benefits of a CAPP and of the security functions?" An SMMP can support the CSO in getting answers to these questions.

FIRST STEPS IN THE DEVELOPMENT OF AN SMMP

The first step in the development of an SMMP to help answer your own and management's questions concerning security costs and benefits is to identify its uses. As we have discussed in the previous chapters, an SMMP can support security professionals in many ways. Some of the ways it can help are as follows:

- Identify the costs of an assets protection program.
- Analyze the security functional processes to identify individual functional costs.
- Identify areas where efficiency gains can be made.
- Identify the effectiveness of security functions.
- Track the costs and benefits of changes to security processes.
- Measure the successes of a CAPP.
- Demonstrate to management changes/improvements in the efficiency and effectiveness of security processes.
- Provide management with a performance assessment of the CAPP.

> *When you go slowly, you go faster—lay the foundation before building the SMMP or it will crumble on a weak foundation.*

Remember, it is imperative that, before developing an SMMP or in the first stages of its development, a series of actions should occur:

- Identify the security drivers—the reasons for having a CAPP or security functions which include, but are not limited, to legislation, regulations, contracts, organizational policies and values.
- Identify the statement of work (SOW)—what must be accomplished.
- Identify the processes used to accomplish the statement of work—how does the work get done? Include the daily tasks performed by security professionals (and sometimes others) to implement the CAPP or related security functions.
- Conduct a process analysis using tools such as process flow diagrams—these diagrams depict and document how each process works.

After the processes are documented in detail, the next step is to determine what is important about each process: What its purpose is or what it produces and then determine how it can be measured. For example: if the objective is to conduct a certain number of security awareness briefings each month, then what gets measured is the actual number of briefings conducted each month. If the goal is 50 per month but only 40 are accomplished, the goal was not met. The metric (number of briefings) compared to the goal will allow a determination to be made on the effectiveness of the process. There may be many other factors influencing the number of briefings, but in its simplest sense, the goal was not met.

It also supports identifying the efficiencies of the processes: for example, 50 briefings were determined to be the optimum for maximum efficiency in the performance of that security function.

Each security function, CAPP policy, assets protection procedure, or process must have a purpose and that purpose should be directly tied to the security drivers. For example, what does the security function or process produce? What results are expected? For each process a measure must be established. That metric must reflect the purpose of the process. It must reflect what is being accomplished by that process. In total, the steps to accomplish this effort are the following:

- Identify each assets protection function/process.[1]
- Determine what drives that function/process: e.g., labor (number of people or hours used), policies, procedures, systems, etc.: In essence, why does the function exist or why is the process used at all?
- Develop detailed security processes flow diagrams. They depict how the process works.
- Determine what gets measured.
- Establish a data collection process. The collection process may be as simple as filling out a log of transactions for later summarization and analyses. The use of a spreadsheet that can automatically incorporate assets protection actions/statistics into graphs is another method.
- Determine how the information should be depicted. For example, some data, to be useful, should be depicted in the context of trends. Other data should be depicted in terms of volume, cycle times, numbers of occurrence, or percentages. The tool used to meaningfully depict the metric will depend upon the metric itself and the message being communicated.

If you are not entirely clear on this approach, don't worry, as we have provided some built-in redundancies to assist you in understanding all of this as we provide details and examples throughout this book. Right now, our goal is to explain to you the overall philosophy and systematic approach to establishing and managing an SMMP.

The decision to establish a process to collect data relative to a particular assets protection function or process should be decided by answering the following questions:

- What specific data will be collected?
- How will the data be collected?
- When will the data be collected?
- Who will collect the data?
- Where (at what point in the function's process) will the data be collected?
- What will the data depict?
- How will it be communicated?
- In what form will it be displayed?

By answering these questions for each proposed metrics chart, the CSO can better analyze the process as to whether or not a metrics collection process should be established for a particular security-related function. This thought-out process will be useful in helping explain it to the security staff or management, if necessary. It will also help the CSO decide whether or not the security staff should continue maintaining that particular metric collection process after a specific period of time.

The goal is to measure every process. Some processes more readily lend themselves to measurement than do others. All work should be measured eventually; however, perhaps only a critical few process metrics will be needed to determine the effectiveness and efficiency (cost versus benefit assessment) of the security function's process itself. Much depends on the environment in which you work—that is, your security duties and responsibilities.

> *Building a good SMMP requires planning, project management and continuous maintenance in order to constantly improve it over time.*

---

[1] It is assumed each function costs time (e.g., labor hours), money, and equipment to perform.

Let's look at it from a CSO's actions. The CSO began with:

- an analysis of assets protection requirements (drivers);
- which led to identification of a CSO charter of duties and responsibilities;
- which led to the identification of assets protection functions and processes;
- which were graphically depicted in process flow diagrams.

Now that most of the work is done, the remaining task is to develop process-specific measures or metrics. As mentioned earlier, metrics should capture the essence of what the process is designed to accomplish. The metric should be meaningful in that it contributes to a better understanding by the CSO or process owner just how that process works and performs. Since needs and requirements change, all metrics should be reviewed, evaluated and reconsidered for continuation on some periodic basis—annually, for instance— or when a requirement changes or the function must be changed. Keep in mind, as part of a quality management program, there must be the goal of "continuous process improvements."

Remember that, although the collection of data to develop robust and meaningful metrics for security processes will help the CSO better manage the assets protection duties and responsibilities, there is a cost incurred in the collection of data and the maintenance of measurement processes in terms of resources. These resources include:

- *People* who collect, input, process, print and maintain the metrics for you;
- *Time* to collect, analyze and disseminate the data; as well as
- *Cost* of materiel: e.g., information systems hardware and software needed and used to support the effort.

SECURITY METRICS MANAGEMENT IS NOT ROCKET SCIENCE

One thing you must remember: the use of metrics is one tool to support many of the CSO's decisions and actions; however, it is not perfect. Therefore, the CSO must make some assumptions relative to the data to be collected. The CSO must remember that security metrics measurement and management is not rocket science, only a tool to help the CSO take better-informed actions and make better-informed decisions, as well as keep management abreast of the status of the CAPP.

It can also help you and executive management make better risk management decisions. However, as the CSO you should never get carried away with the hunt for "perfect data" or the "perfect metric," or become so involved in metrics data collection that "paralysis by analysis" takes place.[2]

Keep in mind that tools used for metric collection and analysis such as spreadsheets, databases and computer graphics programs can become very complicated with links to other spreadsheets and elaborate 3-D graphic depictions. That may work for some, but the CSO should use the KISS (Keep It Simple Stupid) principle when collecting and maintaining metrics—at least to start. This is especially true if you, the CSO or security specialist, is just getting started and has no or little experience with metrics.

---

[2] The authors have each used 47 or more data collection points and metrics charts at various times to assist in managing several large security functional organizations.

> *When choosing between automation and manual data collection, use what works the fastest to get started. Improvements can be made over time.*

One may find that the project leads that are developing the "automated statistical collection" application are expending more hours developing the application that never seems to work just quite right, than it takes to manually collect and calculate the statistical information. When in doubt, go manual. You can always work on the automated collection processes over a longer period of time. Remember, such projects are perfect for managing through the project management systems. This will keep the applications developers "on their toes" and not allow them to treat the project in an informal and lackadaisical manner.

> *Standardize all metrics charts to show a holistic, systematic and organized SMMP.*

It is also important from a managerial and "story-telling" viewpoint that all graphic depictions, charts, statistics, and spreadsheets be done in a standard format. This is necessary so that they can be ready at all times for reviews, analyses and briefings to upper management or external customers. This standard is indicative of a professional organization and one that is operating as a focused team.

Those CSOs who are new to the CSO position, or to management in general, may think that this is somewhat ridiculous. After all, what difference does the format make as long as the information is as accurate as possible and provides the necessary details? This may be correct, but in the business environment, standards, consistency, and indications of teaming, are always a concern of management. Your charts are indicative of those things.

It is hard enough for the CSO to obtain and maintain management support, so this should not be made more difficult than it has to be. Another negative impact concerning nonconformance of format is that the charts will be the topic of discussions by the attendees and not the information on them. Once the "nonconformance to briefing charts' standards" is discussed, management will have already formed a negative bias. From that point on, it will be more difficult to:

- get the point across,
- gain the decision desired, and
- meet the established objective of the briefing.

It is better to just follow the corporate standards that are set than to argue their validity. It is better to save the energy for arguing for those things that are more important.

> *When choosing colors for your charts, make them simple, clear and readable.*

Of course the number, type, collection methods, etc., that the CSO will use will depend on the environment and the CSO's ability to cost-effectively collect and maintain the metrics. Find out and use the business-approved briefing chart formats, style, colors, etc. Such things as colors to be used are always important. For example, "green" often means good or satisfactory (denoting something positive) while "red" is used to identify unsatisfactory (negative), while "yellow" is used for caution.

Don't communicate a positive message using a negative color. Although the color yellow may be used to show caution, this color should be avoided unless it can show up very clearly on a chart. That is because such colors as yellow and lighter shades often do not clearly stand out on a chart. Undoubtedly someone in the audience will point that out to you, and this detracts from the point you are trying to make with the chart.

Lines on metrics charts must be "thick" as thin lines are unreadable.

It is also important, when using line charts, to make the lines thick enough so that they are clear to the members of the audience in the back of the room. In fact, all charts should be developed based on the person in the worst position (usually the back of the room) being able to clearly see the information on the charts.

If using text on charts, be sure they can be read by the members of the audience furthest from the briefing screen.

When using text on the charts, be sure that the text is also clearly visible. Do not use smaller fonts so that you can get all the required information on one chart. It is better to rework the chart and make two or more by subdividing the information and points you want to make.

One other point about charts: photocopying charts in color may be cost-prohibitive and you always want to have copies of your presentation to give to each member of your audience (however, this is dictated by the size of the audience, purpose of the briefing, etc.). The copies of the charts as a handout to the audience may all be done in black and white. If that is the case, it is imperative that the information on each chart be as differentiated in black and white as it was by using colors. This may require you to design your charts with various contrasting color shades so that they can also be differentiated in black and white. For line charts, it is usually best to use a solid and then various dotted lines so that they also can be differentiated in black-and-white reproductions.

If metrics charts are presented in color but hardcopies made in black and white, be sure that the information shown is just as clear and understandable.

As noted earlier, it also wouldn't hurt to determine what executive management prefers in chart formats, colors, and so forth. This may seem ridiculous, but believe it. As trivial as it may seem for an executive of an international, multibillion dollar company to be concerned about chart formats and colors, it does happen.

Another way of stating this is to know your audience. Understand what your audience's expectations and preferences are as you build the presentation. Having a receptive and friendly audience at the onset of a briefing sets a positive and professional tone. Remember, each audience is not the same; they all have different expectations and preferences and it is incumbent on the briefer to learn this.

You may be wondering why we are spending so much time on this topic. The answer, if you haven't discovered it so far, is that data collection usually must be converted into charts. As the old saying goes, "A picture is worth a thousand words." Besides, by using the charts to manage a security department and CAPP, you can easily show the trends, status, costs and so forth of your efforts. Furthermore, it is a great tool for briefing executive management, your staff, visitors, and the like.

> *Make charts using the styles, colors and formats that executive management prefers, to be sure you set the tone for them to concentrate on your charts' messages and not the charts themselves.*

To add emphasis: your secretary or administrative assistant is often in the best position to get the information on chart preferences and formats, as they often share the same tasks, albeit at a different bureaucratic level. Therefore, they may be in a better position to successfully work together on these issues while the CSO deals with other matters. NOTE: As a CSO, always be good to all the secretaries and administrative assistants in the business, as they are your best allies and hold the power associated with their bosses. They can be a valuable asset for you.

QUESTIONS CONCERNING DATA COLLECTION

Let's look at a method for determining security functional data (some may call it "statistics", but we will use the term "data") by asking and answering some basic questions concerning security functions as noted below. These are questions the CSO or project lead for an SMMP should be asking at the outset of an SMMP development, and periodically through the life of the SMMP to ensure it remains a reliable and useful tool.

• **Why should these data be collected?**
One should be able to clearly state in one or two sentences why specific data is being collected.

• **What specific data will be collected?**
The specific data that will be collected will be determined based on the security function and the specific need to track costs at specific points in the process. It is also collected to determine other information that would be of interest to management and the CSO—and if it is of interest to management, it obviously better be of interest to the CSO.

• **How will these data be collected?**
The data can be collected in a number of ways. They can be collected manually or through an automated data collection program. Generally speaking, it is usually more cost-effective to collect the data automatically; however, the development of an automated system may be too costly compared to a manual system. One must be cautious in that regard as the collection process should be done cost-effectively and efficiently. Again, remember KISS.

• **When will these data be collected?**
When data are to be collected will be dependent on the need for the data. If a monthly report, annual report, quarterly report or recurring briefing is to be accomplished, that may be the driver. However, as CSO managing a security department and CAPP, it would be logical to collect the data at the end of the month or the first week of each month, showing the previous month's data.

• **Who will collect these data?**
The data should be collected, input and maintained by the project leaders responsible for each security function. That way, they are part of the SMMP process and are also owners of their particular function. Furthermore, they should be responsible for leading the effort to identify more effective and efficient means of performing their security function(s).

- **Where (at what point in the security function's process) will these data be collected?**

The collection of data will be based on the need for the metrics and at the point where the data can be collected to fulfill that need. For some processes, it may be at the end of an individual security functional task, such as making a badge. Using that as an example, one would probably want to know how long it takes to process one badge for one new employee. After all, in today's environment, an employee identification badge is a critical tool and the employee "can't go to work" without a badge. Therefore, getting that person a badge the first day of employment may be mandatory.

One must remember that the longer it takes the new employee to process through the security badge office, the more it will cost the business in lost productivity for that new employee. The same would hold true when an employee must get a badge change or badge replacement.

SMMP CHART DESIGNS

We have alluded to the design of charts based on the data collected as part of the SMMP. However, this is such a crucial issue that we want to offer some "reinforcing guidance" on the topic.

The issue that will often come up when designing charts is what type of charts to use: bar, line, pie, etc. The choice should be to use the format that meets the chart's objective in the most concise and clear way, consistent with executive management briefing chart standards.

A CSO sometimes comes across numbers that are out of balance with each other—for example, 135 satisfactory security inspections ratings, 13 marginal. If the chart chosen were a line chart or a bar chart, the smaller number would be so dwarfed as to be almost unreadable. In this case, the pie chart may be the solution. The other solution could be to label each point in the chart with its number. For example, the bar or line designating 13 marginal ratings would have the number 13 over that point in the chart. This might give the perception that the marginal ratings were somewhat meaningless even though you, as a CSO, are aware that is not the case and that, in fact, it indicates increased vulnerabilities to successful attack on those assets. The pie chart, on the other hand, still shows that the number is small, but it at least appears larger on the graph. This allows the audience to look at that number as being more significant a matter than would be shown on the line or bar chart.

USING TECHNOLOGY TO DELIVER METRICS DATA

Some available technologies are quite obvious to the CSO and have been in use for some time. Others may even reside within the company and are just waiting to be tapped. Many information technology tools and capabilities already exist which, if properly deployed, would help provide professional-looking metrics charts at least cost.

There are many reasons to deploy technology in the effort to develop, implement and maintain an SMMP. Technology (computer-related hardware and software) can be used to improve the efficiency of how security services and products are delivered and this cost-benefits philosophy can be shown through security metrics charts. For example, you could make the case of costs-benefits through the charts to purchase new or upgraded computers and software, showing a return on investment graphically portrayed through metrics charts.

> *The use of technology to assist in performing security functions or supporting an SMMP may help but is not the "Holy Grail" answer.*

In today's tight resource environment, efficiency and timeliness are not the only motivation to seek alternative means of service and product delivery. The lack of budget to explore other options or add staff may drive you to seek help from technology. Furthermore, if you can't get additional budget for additional resources that you have determined to be necessary to improve, then the use of technology to free already committed resources would help you provide assets protection as needed through security staff reallocation. In other words, this should allow you to re-deploy those freed resources to other areas where they may be needed. An SMMP can provide the visibility needed to make the correct management decisions when looking at integrating more technology into security functions and the CAPP.

QUALITY AND OVERSIGHT

Remember that security is usually a cost center and not a revenue-producing entity; therefore, it is in competition with other organizations for budget. How that budget is obtained varies and is often dependent upon the demonstrated added value of the assets protection or security program to the corporation. As an example: if through an inspection it is determined that a security program is out of compliance and this noncompliant condition could adversely impact sales or a contractual obligation, management will divert resources to correct this problem. Yes, they will allocate money toward correcting the noncompliant condition, but you must prove your case. An SMMP helps you do just that.

The only concern you may have as the CSO is that someone other than you may be the person who receives the additional resources to fix the problem. This is of course assuming that the noncompliant condition was a result of something you did or did not do. It is not necessary to be completely dependent upon budgetary discretion of management. The solutions may rest within your own creativity as a CSO and willingness to explore other options. Furthermore, it is better to identify and correct security department and assets protection deficiencies before they are discovered by management. The SMMP can help you do just that. We suggest you take the initiative to do this on your own and not wait for a budget or compliance crisis.

It is a mixed blessing that security programs are often subject to very close oversight. It is good to have an external (outside of the security organization) perspective and assessment. But, dealing with these activities and organizations is time-consuming and can be difficult. Internal audit programs, government inspections or customer security reviews are some of the various methods employed to determine the effectiveness of a security program. Dealing with audits and inspections takes much time and effort. However, they provide a CSO with periodic feedback on the condition of the security program. An SMMP can be developed and used as a quality and oversight support program. The other downside is that, more often than not, the focus is on compliance and not on efficiency. Efficiency needs to be measured and the good news is that the CSO can do this through an SMMP.

> *SMMP can help in a supporting role as a tool to operating effectively and efficiently but, like any other tool, it is only as good as its user.*

Perhaps the most important methods for measuring the efficiency and effectiveness of any security program is to have solid metrics in place (badge example stated earlier), measuring all key processes for delivering products and services, and to conduct self-assessments (or self-inspections). Conducting self-inspections helps a security organization understand where they stand in relationship to all compliance obligations (i.e., policy, procedures, regulations and contractual obligations).

Conducting self-inspections allows a CSO to tailor the inspection or assessment process to focus on issues of efficiency and effectiveness. During a self-inspection or self-assessment, special emphasis can be placed on assessing efficiency or effectiveness of processes and the delivery of products and services. This in turn can be documented by the SMMP.

SECURITY METRICS AND PROCESSES

Because processes are such an integral part of an SMMP, let's look at them in more detail. Remember that basically a process is a series of steps or actions that produces something. In our case, the steps taken help protect assets.

When developing processes, a process statement should be developed that describes the actions to be taken and not the job or task. For example, "Produce a physical access violation report" and not "Physical Access Violation Report." In other words, there is action, using a verb instead of a noun.

Upon completion of that task, you must then decide how to produce the right metric or metrics. In order to do so, you must ask yourself:

- First: Are you measuring the product or the process which produces it?
    - An example would be looking at an employee climate-sensing product and process relating to their support for an asset protection program.
    - If you're tracking the climate itself (employees more or less are supporting the CAPP), you're measuring the product.
    - If you're tracking how well you obtain that climate data (e.g., How long does it take to get it? How accurate is the data?), you're measuring the process.
- Next, select the proper product or process metric, so as to measure its performance to target or customer specification; for example:
    - Product
        - Metric: % of reports delivered on time
        - Measurement: 98 of 100 reports were delivered on time
        - Result: 98% of reports were delivered on time
    - Process:
        - Measure a key characteristic of the product or the process itself (often cost, quality, cycle time or customer satisfaction)
        - Look for trends over time
        - Make sure it's a key characteristic the process has input to or control over. For example:
            - Measuring the number of alarms a guard force responds to that are false alarms—they don't cause or control the alarm

    –   Measuring how quickly they respond or the percentage that are actual alarms that they respond to in less than five minutes—they do control that

COST-AVOIDANCE METRICS

As a CSO, you may want to use the SMMP approach to be able to quantify the savings of some of your decisions. For example, when analyzing your budget and expenditures, you note that travel costs for your staff is a major budget item. This is logical since staff, as well as you, must travel to the various corporate offices to conduct assets protection inspections or assessments.

Again, using the project management approach, you lead a project team of yourself, staff members and a representative from the Contract Office and Travel Office. Your goal is to find ways to cut travel costs while still meeting all CAPP objectives and fulfill your charter responsibilities. In other words, you are trying to avoid costs.

USING METRICS CHARTS FOR MANAGEMENT BRIEFINGS

The data collected must be shown in some meaningful way. The use of security metrics management charts is just such a way. When using these metrics charts for management briefings, remember the purpose of the briefing. A succinct message is being communicated to management. This is most effectively accomplished with graphic depictions of data in a meaningful way.

How that data is depicted will depend upon the message being communicated and the type of metric being used. For example, if a cost of security trend over a five-year period is being depicted, the use of a bar chart suits the metric well. Or would a line chart be better? You decide based on your environment and briefing standards.

When the best form of depicting the metric is not clear, the CSO should experiment with various types of graphic depictions, as the use of line, bar, scatter and pie charts can be very useful in delivering a point. It is recommended that the charts be kept simple and easy to understand. Remember, the old saying, "A picture is worth a thousand words." The charts should need very little verbal explanation. The message must be kept clear and concise. Do not get bogged down in details which detract from the objective of the chart's message.

> *Remember that is it difficult to argue with facts and an SMMP provides facts that can support your assets protection positions.*

One way to determine if the message the charts are trying to portray is clear is to have someone unfamiliar with the subject look at them and determine if the data is easy to understand. A CSO may choose to have security staff members look at the charts and describe what the chart tells them. If it is what the chart is supposed to portray, then no changes are needed. If not, the CSO should then ask the viewer what the chart does seem to represent and what leads them to that conclusion.

The CSO must then go back to the chart and rework it until the message is clear and it is exactly what the CSO wants the chart to show. Each chart should have only one specific objective and the CSO should be able to state that objective in one sentence; for example, "This chart's objective is to show that assets protection support to the business is being maintained without additional budget although the workload has increased 13%." In such a chart, emphasis is on showing that the workload has increased, budget has not increased, but assets are being adequately protected. That view should be perceived with little or no additional commentary.

SEQUENCE OF ASSETS PROTECTION CHARTS FOR MANAGEMENT BRIEFINGS

The following paragraphs identify some basic examples of assets protection metrics that can be collected to assist a CSO in managing a CAPP and informing management on the success or failures, costs and benefits of a CAPP and the security organization. By the way, when establishing a briefing to management in which the metrics charts will be used, it is recommended that a sequence of charts be developed. Think of it as telling a story. It has a beginning, middle and an end. In this case, the story of security or a security function or issue is being told. It may even include the "moral" of the story—not in the true sense but in the context of something learned from the effort. The sequence may look something like the following:

- Assets protection drivers
- Specific drivers showing relationship with each specific security function
- Flowchart of each security function
- Flowcharts of each security subfunction using a work-breakdown type of approach
- The metrics charts for each part of a flowchart where time (productivity) and costs can, and should, be measured

When developing an SMMP, it is important to first outline the SMMP starting with an overall outline, which then includes details down to each flowchart of each security function. This process can be done by viewing it through the security functional view of the security department or through the view of the CAPP, the difference being that the security functional view only deals with security activities whereas the CAPP view deals with assets protection from an overall business perspective—what business employees must also do. Another way of looking at this is to start with the micro (a single security process or function) and move to the macro (the entire CAPP or maybe the entire security department or both). You may instead want to start with the overall CAPP view and gradually move to a more micro view.

The approach you use will be dependent on your philosophy as a CSO or your executive management needs, or how management wants to see such things. One way to find out how management generally likes to have the briefings done is to talk to those that prepare executive management briefings and also the executive management administrative staff. As we mentioned earlier, the secretary and other staff members have a clearer view of what their bosses would like to see than you would.

Remember that if executive management has some quirks about briefing charts, you should find out about it first so that your briefing is well-received instead of generating complaints about the types of charts or colors used. This has happened more than once, and in the end, the objective of the briefing was lost!

If you recall, in Chapter 3, we discussed a sample project plan format and also how to develop a project plan incorporating that format. It is again stated here to give you the opportunity to re-familiarize yourself with this type of project plan approach. In this case it will be used to develop an SMMP. When viewed at a high level, the individual tasks may look something like the following:

1. SMMP objective: Establish a program to track costs, benefits, successes and failures of a CAPP and related security functions.
2. Identify assets protection drivers—develop chart of all drivers.
3. Identify security processes related to each driver—develop charts connecting drivers to security processes.
4. Identify assets protection policies—develop charts to relate each major policy to the drivers and security functions.
5. Identify the security processes flowcharts used to support each major policy and procedure.
6. Develop individual high-level security process charts, one for each process showing level of effort (LOE), impact, costs and benefits.
7. Develop lower level charts for each security subprocess as in #6, above.
8. Chart each major aspect of the CAPP to drivers and security processes.
9. Develop total budgetary chart and subcharts based on budget breakdown.

It is recommended that, to begin this process, the outline should concentrate on an SMMP from the view of the CSO looking inward at the security department's security processes and functions. This reason for this is that it addresses most of what is needed when viewing the CAPP but also would be a higher priority view from the CSO's point of view. Why? Because the CSO will be spending most of the time managing the department in a macro sense, driving down into the micro when problem-solving or change is necessary. (See Figures 4-1 and 4-2.)

Figure 4-1   A simplified example of a chart depicting the link between security drivers and security functions that could be used as part of a briefing.

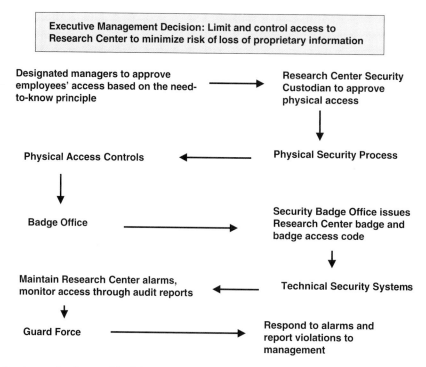

Figure 4-2   A sample of a specific driver to specific security functions.

Of course, as the CSO, you would want to get more specific and track to a more detailed level of granularity than may be required for executive management briefings. In fact, the security staff responsible to lead a specific function should be tasked with developing the charts relative to their function, based on standard formats or boilerplates. That way, the staff knows exactly why they are doing what they are doing.

The next step would be for them to track their workflow and analyze it. At the same time, they would also look at current costs and cost-savings, with the goal of identifying more efficient ways to successfully accomplish their jobs.

> *The benefit of such an approach is to get the security staff involved so that they feel ownership with their security function and therefore will be in a position to help identify steps to improve the processes, as they are closest to the function and processes.*

CASE STUDY: METRICS DATA COLLECTION EXAMPLE—BADGE-MAKING PROCESS

Using the flowchart for the security badge processing as an example, data must be collected at two points in the process: when the employee first enters the badge-making office and when the employee leaves the badge-making office (is issued a new badge). For example: collect the employee's:

- *Name*: The name is needed to connect the person to the badge for accountability. In addition, if the employee continuously damages or loses the badge, this would be something to bring up to the employee's manager.
- *Organization*: This can be used to develop a metric showing the number of new, replaced, and lost badges by each organization. This information can be converted

to lost productivity information in the form of hours lost and dollars lost. A chart can be developed comparing all organizations. The information can be used by organizational management to emphasize the organization's position relative to other organizations, emphasize the waste of resources, and encourage employees do a better job of controlling their badges.

- *Time of arrival in the badge-processing office*: This information is used to track the amount of time an employee spends in getting a badge and how much time the security person takes in making a badge. Both of these individuals' tasks could be averaged out for cost considerations.
- *Purpose of visit, e.g., new badge, replacement badge, change in badge due to change in access to various areas of the business*: This helps determine the reason the person is getting a new badge. Except for the employees getting their first badge, and those getting a replacement for changing their accesses within the corporation, all other reasons for obtaining a badge (lost it) are unacceptable and a goal should be established and tracked through the SMMP to eliminate or at least continually decrease the number of such incidents.
- *Time the employee signed for the new badge*: This time when used with the arrival time discloses how long the person was in the office. In addition, an average time to and from the employee's workplace to and from the badge office should also be considered when analyzing lost productivity and associated other costs.

> *Data collection costs time and therefore money—use both wisely.*

SMMP AND EXECUTIVE MANAGEMENT

Remember that the data collected costs time and of course "time is money." Therefore, it is again emphasized that the data collected must be only that data that is needed and not "nice-to-have" data, which is a waste of time and therefore money. Also, no data should be collected for "just in case we need it later." However, this is a CSO or management decision which may be based on management's track record of asking "unexpected" questions for which the CSO has been more than once caught off guard.

> *Assets protection must be viewed as a product and sold to management and all employees.*

Remember that a CSO is also an assets protection "salesperson" and must effectively advertise and market assets protection to management and the business' employees. So, the SMMP can assist in:

- Justifying the need for more budget and other resources;
- Indicating that the CAPP is operating more efficiently; and
- Helping to justify why budget and other resources should not be decreased.

When deciding to develop metrics charts to track workload, efficiency, costs, or other measures of a function, always start at the high level and then develop charts in lower levels (more details) that support the overall chart. This is done for several purposes:

- The CSO may have limited time to brief a specific audience and if it is an executive management briefing, the time will be shorter since busy executives have much responsibility and little available time. They often focus on the "bottom line" or the essence of an issue

- The "top-down" approach will probably work best. If you have time to brief in more detail, the charts will be available.
- If executive management has a question relative to some level of detail, then the other charts can be used to support the CSO statements and/or position in reply to the majority of the audience's questions.
- As part of the CSO's use of the SMMP, the top-down approach also provides flexibility for the CSO when using a systems approach to the data analyses—looking for costs, negative and positive trends in various levels of details, for example.

CASE STUDY: USE OF METRICS IN TIMES OF DOWNSIZING SECURITY STAFF

The CSO can also use the SMMP data when budget cuts are required. The data and supporting charts can be shown to management and modified to show what would happen if the security staff were cut by one person, two people, etc. One example may be that the average employee's initial access to corporate facilities in terms of creating the employee's area access badge turnaround time would increase. Management may or may not want to live with those consequences. In this case, that cost can be quantified in terms of taking the average hourly wage of the employee, identifying lost productivity time with access coming within one business day, and access due to laying-off a badge processor, thus delaying the employee's access by two business days.

For example, an employee earns $15 an hour. The employee showed up at the desk of a badge processor at the start of the business day, 8 a.m. That employee was authorized system access in 24 hours (by 8 a.m. the next day); a loss of at least 8 hours of productivity at $15 an hour would be the normal cost of the assets protection function of access control, or $120 per employee (using an eight-hour day). However, if the badge was not authorized until the day after, the costs per employee in lost productivity would be $240. NOTE: Yes, we are aware of the use of temporary badges; however, this is just an example to make a point of how to use an SMMP during corporate downsizing.

The chart can show the CSO where staff cuts can be made and still meet the expected goals. The CSO can also use this information when deciding to reallocate resources (transfer a person) to another function where the goals are not being met and where the fastest way to meet the goal is to add headcount. A word of caution here—adding or decreasing headcount is usually considered a fast, simple solution. However, it is not always the answer.

> *Adding more bodies to a problem is not always the best approach to solving a problem. Using an SMMP can guide the CSO in the right direction.*

Many project leaders and CSOs have found over the years that projects and level of effort problems are not always solved by adding "more bodies." One should first look at the process and systemic problems. It is usually a more cost-effective and more long-term approach to solving these types of problems. For example, using the example of the newly hired employee getting first-time access, suppose a way was found to cut that time down to one hour of processing time. The cost saving would be from the normal $120 to $15, or a saving of $105 per new employee. Such charts can be used for management briefings and will show specifically how the CSO and staff are lowering assets protection costs, at least for that particular assets protection function. It makes for a great "public relations" tool!

MORE ON SMMP AND DOWNSIZING

Because corporations continue to look for ways to save more and be more competitive in the global marketplace, they often look first to reductions in the employment force—downsizing. CSOs are constantly involved in looking for ways to save budget. However, there must be a balance between saving budget and adequately protecting corporate assets.

All CSOs at one time or another in their careers face the need to downsize: layoff, fire, or terminate security staff. However, if you are operating at peak efficiency and have not built any excess staff into meeting your security duties and responsibilities, you can possibly make a case for not terminating staff, or terminating fewer personnel.

Many managers, and CSOs are no exception, tend to forget that they are hired to do a job, and that job is *not* to build an "empire" or bureaucracy. The key to success is getting the job done efficiently and effectively—good and cheap.

If on the other hand, you have a small number of staff and a smaller budget, you have a better chance of protecting what you have because it is the minimum needed to get the job done. That approach, coupled with SMMP techniques and periodic briefings to executive management, will help you continue to get the job done as you deem appropriate, even though other organizations are losing staff. (NOTE: We have used our SMMP in the past and, due to periodic briefings to our bosses and executive management, who understood what we were doing to operate "lean and mean," we were able to save security jobs during lay-off periods—it does work!)

Let's look at the following figures showing various ways of presenting information based on metrics management's data collection efforts:

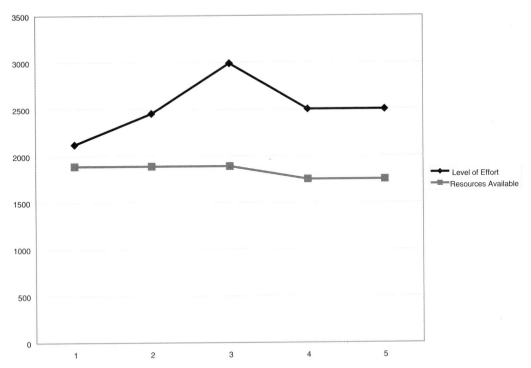

Figure 4-3 A five-year period tracking the level of effort in hours of work of the security staff per year (left-side of chart) per individual, compared to the hours of work that was budgeted per year per security staff member.

This LOE (as previously stated, this is defined as the normal everyday work of the security staff performing their security functional processes) versus project support charts that shows that the security organization has been supporting the projects of other departments and the workload is not "nice-to-have" projects. These are projects that require the support of the CSO and security staff. It also shows that the CSO and staff are an integral part of major projects and are functioning as part of their service and support duties in a corporate team effort.

Taking this chart as an example, similar charts can then be developed using the same template but showing the workload per function versus budgeted hours for each function.

A chart that is important for briefing management is one that shows the LOE versus the hours available for the security staff. The difference between LOE and time available can be shown to be part of a briefing on work backlog or used to show the difference is overtime being work. A subchart can show the details as to the amount of backlog and its impact on the cost of doing business. It can also show the overtime costs being paid and maybe a comparison of that cost with the cost of hiring one or more additional staff. Seeing this comparison would help in making decisions as to which is cheaper—paying overtime or hiring more staff.

These charts must also be accompanied by others showing productivity, and drivers of workload, as shown by some of the charts previously discussed. This is necessary because management will ask why you must do the things you do and why must you do them in the way you are doing them. This quest for productivity and efficiency gains will be a constant chore for the CSO. It is a challenge but one that can be supported by an SMMP.

Layoffs are a fact of life in business and metrics charts can help the CSO justify headcount and work, as shown by some of the charts above. Other charts may also help, such as that shown in Figure 4-4. The chart can show measurement in terms of headcount or hours that are equivalent to headcount.

Generally, when management decides to cut costs, they lay off employees, since this is the fastest method to cut costs. They often apply these reductions across the organization, directing each organization to cut a certain percentage of staff, such as 20%. However, although the fastest way, this is not the best way, as loss of skilled and trained employees can have a negative impact on productivity and performance. As we all know, executive management sometimes has a short-term view and approach to managing their parts of the business. You must consider such things when developing and using metrics charts to support your information.

> *Using SMMP, one can make a valid case for not laying off security staff in the numbers and/or in the time period requested—but be sure you are right and not just building your "empire" or just trying to save a person's job that really is not required.*

Security metrics management can help the CSO "plead the case" to not cut 20% of staff. One word of caution: as the CSO, this should be done objectively and based on providing effective and efficient service and support to the corporation. It should never, ever be based on keeping a large staff and bureaucracy for the sake of status, power, ego or other nonbusiness reasons.

Along with the chart shown in Figure 4-4, the CSO would include information relative to the impact of both your directed layoff numbers and your recommended impact

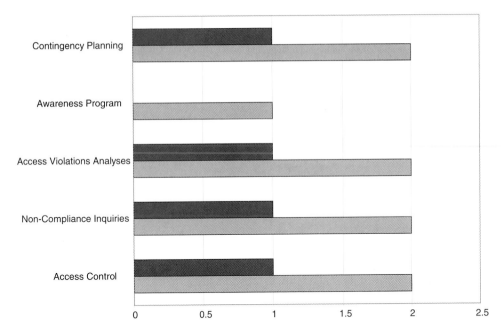

Figure 4-4 The comparison of CSO executive management-requested layoff versus a counter-proposal by the CSO where the function is noted on the left-hand side and the number of security personnel noted on the bottom of the chart.

and alternatives. This must be objectively done, based on a business rationale. This information would include the security functions described below as increasing the level of risks to corporate assets. As you read through this portion, think of what data would be collected to provide the information needed for you to make your point to management. Also, what charts would you develop to help support your rationale?

- *Contingency Planning:* Contingency, emergency, and disaster recovery testing and plans' updates will be delayed. The result will be anything from "no impact" to not being able to effectively and efficiently deal with an emergency.
- *Awareness Program:* Employees may not be aware of their responsibilities, thus leaving the assets open to potential attacks or an increase in the potential of the loss of sensitive information.
- *Access Violations Analyses:* There will be delays of between 48 and 72 hours in the analyses of access control records. Thus, an attack against assets may not be known for at least 48–72 hours. During that period, assets may be at higher risk. (However, if an attack were a denial of service attack or similar attack, it would be known when it was successful.) The opportunity to have possibly identified the initial attempts at these attacks over a period of time would be lost and with it the opportunities to mount defenses before the attacks were successful. The results may include theft, damage, or destruction of assets.
- *Noncompliance Inquiries:* The average time it would take to complete an inquiry would be increased by more than two weeks on average. Thus, no action to adjudicate the alleged infraction would be possible until the report was delivered to management. Furthermore, the alleged infraction may have called for the temporary revocation of access privileges of the employee or employees who are the subject of the inquiry. Thus, their ability to be a productive employee during that time would be negated.

- *Access Control*: It is assumed that the number of new employees hired would be drastically reduced and that could mitigate some of the level of effort expended by the access controllers. However, employees requiring changes in privilege would have those access changes delayed an additional 48–72 hours from the average now of 8–12 hours. This may adversely impact their productivity. Allowing departments to conduct their own employee's privilege changes was evaluated under a previous project and found not to be realistic. This change would just be the transferring of costs; doing so is less efficient, and would not save any additional corporate resources.

All of the above information would be shown in supporting charts to the main charts concerning workload and layoffs.

Although the information provided is a small example of how the SMMP techniques can be used when the need for budget cuts occurs, it provides some insight into how it helps mitigate the risks of budget and staff downsizing when such downsizing will hurt the CAPP. Thus, one can see that the use of SMMP techniques can help the CSO make the case to executive management. Furthermore, if the CSO, supported by the SMMP approach, has been periodically briefing management of the CAPP and CSO's projects and level of effort, the CSO will have gained the confidence of management as a reliable manager who gets the job done as efficiently and effectively as possible.

Other types of charts can also be developed to show project costs in terms of labor, materials and the like. A good, automated project plan software program is well worth the costs for managing projects. (See Chapter 3, Projects, for information on using a project chart format.)

CASE STUDY: CHARTING ASSETS PROTECTION INFRACTIONS AS PART OF AN SMMP AND BRIEFING MANAGEMENT ON THE RESULTS

The use of an SMMP chart may show security or assets protection infractions by individual departments. That means each department head will internally compare his or her department against the others, thereby causing a covert competition to begin. No department head wants their department to look bad and, in fact, because of their competitive nature, the department heads will push to have a "zero" for each month. Each will want to know what exactly the individual noncompliance inquiries (NCIs) were for. The CSO must be prepared to answer them—using individual charts per department. Is this a lot of work? Yes. However, the benefits are that each department's head will be pushing to have zero noncompliance inquiries conducted, which means the department heads will be overt supporters of the CAPP and will push their staffs to follow the CAPP—if for no other reason as they don't want to look bad to the CEO, which may impact the amount of the bonus.

This also often leads to the CSO joining the staff meetings of the departments' executives and presenting the individual analyses of each department or sub-department. The CSO should also then be in a position to explain what can be done to minimize these infractions, as well as minimize the loss of productivity, and thus dollars expended by each infraction. Showing the cost in lost productivity in hours per each noncompliance inquiry can have a major impact on the department's management and staff. This can then also be shown as losses in terms of budget using an average employee's salary or hourly wage, which can often be obtained from the Finance or Human Relations staffs.

The CSO should also take to these briefing one or more of the assets protection security department staff who have some responsibility for the information presented. This provides an opportunity for the staff members to become involved in seeing how their work affects the security department. It also helps them become part of the entire process of working the assets protection issues, as well as gives them the opportunity to show confidence and support for assets protection staff. By no means should they be used as a scapegoat or allowed to be the target of abuse by managers defending or rationalizing that a noncompliance inquiry was groundless, should not have been conducted, or the like.

The CSO should at all times take the blame and give the credit to assets protection (security) staff members. Furthermore, the CSO must keep the focus of the meeting on the material being briefed and discuss the numbers, and should not allow "finger-pointing" and NCI data critique. This is not often easy to do as the department managers try to defend themselves. The meeting objective and ground rules for discussion should be established in advance by the CSO and the department executive.

CASE STUDY—USING METRICS TO DETERMINE SUCCESS

The overall security process rating can be determined by a roll-up of the performance-to-target/product metric for the key processes. The formula is as follows:

1. Establish the percentage of success of each key process:
   Score/100 = percentage to success (e.g., the goal for Security Awareness Training was 100%. During this particular rating period, we achieved this 95% of the time. 95/100 = 95%. On the other hand, if you have a numerical score as in Access Control, set an arbitrary rating scale; the goal is 0 occurrences of unauthorized access, but you might set a scale whereby 0 incidents = a score of 100, 1 = a score of 99, etc.)

2. Average the results of the key processes; this gives you the overall security rating. To convert this to the standard stoplight chart, use the following scale:
   - 100 – 90 = green;
   - 89 – 80 = yellow;
   - <80 = red;

   with one exception: any score of less than 100 on certain critical key processes (for example, not responding to the Research Center alarms in under five minutes) requires a rating of "yellow" no matter how high the overall numerical rating is. Two consecutive months of less than 100 in those critical key processes requires an automatic red, as does more than two incidents in a quarter or four within a year.

You may wish to change these breakpoints to reflect realistic performance or customer sensitivity to certain processes in your environment.

SUMMARY

Metrics management techniques will provide a process for the CSO to support assets protection and other security-related decisions. The CSO should understand that:

- Metrics management is an excellent method to track security processes and functions related to LOE, projects, effectiveness, efficiency, costs, proper deployment of resources, etc.
- It provides a methodology for measuring the success of a CAPP.
- The information can be analyzed and results of the analyses used to:
  - identify areas where efficiency improvements are necessary;
  - determine effectiveness of security functional goals;
  - provide input for performance reviews of the assets protection staff (a more objective approach than subjective performance reviews of today's CSO's); as well as
  - where security services and support to CSO requires improvement, to meets its goals, etc.

Building a successful security metrics management program requires the use of a formal process to validate each step. Once that is completed for each security function, it can be summarized as a sort of abstract of that security function. (See Figure 4-5.)

Security Functional Process Summary

1. *Process Name*: Investigations and NCIs

2. *Process Description*: Provide professional investigative and NCI support to all the corporate sites

3. *Supplier*: Customers and employees

4. *Input*: Complaints, allegations, requests for assistance, asset protection requirements

5. *Subprocesses*: Investigations, NCIs, Crime Prevention Surveys

6. *Customers*: Management

7. *Output*: Investigative reports, Security assessment reports, Briefings, Survey reports, Testimony

8. *Requirements and Directives that Govern the Process (Drivers)*: CAPP, policies, laws, regulations, management decisions

---

Figure 4-5   Example of a security function summary.

Chapter 5

Case Study: Measuring the Costs of Security

This chapter and subsequent chapters will use a fictitious international corporation, the International Widget Corporation (IWC), to discuss a security metrics management program (SMMP) related to some basic security cost factors.

INTRODUCTION

Throughout the remainder of this book, we will be referring to IWC in order to hopefully provide more of a realistic view of establishing and managing a security metrics management program (SMMP).

We have discussed, albeit only in an introductory way, security and assets protection drivers, their associated policies, procedures, processes, plans, and projects and, to some extent, types of measurements.

Another important matter when building a corporate assets protection program (CAPP) is to be able to know your assets protection environment. This is important not only from a CAPP perspective but also an SMMP perspective. Why? Well, you cannot accurately measure and analyze assets protection and security functional costs if you do not know what type of assets you are dealing with and their location. For example, what if some assets and assets protection aspects were not included? What if only physical assets were identified and protected and intellectual assets were not? The analysis of the CAAP may indicate a robust and effective protection program but only of physical assets and not of intellectual assets.

In this and subsequent chapters of the book, we will be using a newly assigned Chief Security Officer (CSO) who has recently been hired to:

- Update the IWC CAPP and ensure that the CAPP is being managed as effectively and efficiently as possible based on acceptance of a reasonable level of risk to those assets.
- "Get a handle" on the assets protection costs, as the prior CSO did not know what the CAPP and security functions were costing IWC, except to refer back to the sum of the security department budget.

IWC ASSETS PROTECTION SURVEY QUESTIONNAIRE

To begin this process of understanding IWC's assets protection environment, the new CSO needed to know exactly the "size" of the IWC assets protection environment. Using an "IWC Assets Protection Environment Questionnaire," the CSO's security staff at all locations throughout the world were directed to conduct a survey in an attempt by the CSO to learn as much about corporate assets as possible. In essence, the CSO needed to know just how big an "elephant" had to be dealt with.

The individual locations' survey results would be kept as individual survey reports but also rolled-up into an overall IWC assets protection environment report. That way, the CSO would know the size of the "elephant" and also be able to deal with each location separately, and compare the costs for all or certain functions at each location. Therefore, using security metrics tools, the CSO could see where one location's costs were higher than others or lower, and find out why. There may be good reason for such differences—for example, cheaper labor costs—but maybe not. One location may not be using an efficient process for some security function, where another location may be using a very efficient process.

The SMMP can also be used to compare like "sub-CAPPs" and security functions across all IWC locations. The one with the most effective and also the most efficient operations could then be identified. Then that method, assuming it is not unique to that particular working environment, can be adopted throughout IWC. This would be one way to standardize assets protection and/or security functions using the most efficient and effective processes. A side benefit is that employees transferring or visiting other IWC facilities would have a basic understanding of the assets protection policies, procedures, and so forth. Thus, they are less likely to inadvertently violate them and increase the risks to the assets.

When doing the comparisons, one must be sure to not only consider the various unique environments, but also convert all costs to one form of currency for easier comparison. In addition, it is likely that such things as labor costs in Asia would be lower than those in the United States. All such matters must be considered when doing comparisons. Ensure apples are compared to apples and oranges to oranges.

The following IWC Assets Protection Environment Questionnaire was used to gather the initial information as part of the overall survey:[1]

IWC Assets Protection Environment Questionnaire

This questionnaire is to be completed under the supervision of the local security manager. It is intended to be used to determine the size of IWC's assets protection environment and to identify the basic assets that require protection. This information is being gathered to support the IWC CAPP and to comply with a request from the IWC CEO and executive management to determine the costs of the IWC CAPP and to establish an objective to make it as efficient and effective as possible, consistent with acceptable levels of risk.

---

[1] This questionnaire is a modified version of that generously provided by Lou Guthrie of Guthrie Research Group and identified as the Appendix in this book.

Country Identification: _____

I. Questionnaire Database
This report includes assets protection information from the following site(s):

Site: _____ Population: _____

Location (City, State): _____

Type of work being performed _____

Site: _____ Population: _____

Location (City, State): _____

Type of work being performed _____

Site: _____ Population: _____

Location (City, State): _____

Type of work being performed _____

(Attach additional page if necessary)

II. Site Security Resources
Instructions for Section II A—Money:
This section is designed to capture all assets protection expenses incurred by the reporting office during 2005 and those projected for 2006. These expenses include:

- Wages & Salaries,
- Fringe—for company employees,
- Travel,
- Capital expenditures,
- Other Included Expenses (OIE)—supplies, graphics & printing costs, etc.

Amount allocated for Outsourced Services refers to those dollars spent on security services, i.e., guard services, alarm monitoring, etc., purchased from an outside vendor, e.g., outsourced.

A. Money
  1. 2005 Expenses—All locations within the reporting country
  - Amount of dollars spent on security $ _____
  - Amount spent on outsourced assets
    protection services by the security organization $ _____
  - Amount spent on capital expense items by the
    security organization $ _____
  - Total amount spent on assets protection $ _____

  2. 2005 Budget—All of the locations in this country
  - Amount allocated for security expenses $ _____
  - Amount allocated for outsourced
    security services $ _____
  - Amount allocated for capital expenditure $ _____
  - Total amount allocated for assets
    protection at all sites in 2005 $ _____

Instructions for Section II B1—International Widget Corporation Security Employees:

This section is designed to capture the number of corporate employees either working in the Sector security departments or performing security duties. These numbers must be expressed as headcount *and* the number of Equivalent People (EP) used to perform assets protection work.

Reporting Headcount—For those employees who are spending less than 100% of their time doing assets protection work, estimate the percentage of time that they are spending on assets protection, and add these percentages. When the total of these percentages becomes 100% add one employee to the total.

Reporting Equivalent People[2]—One EP = 2080 hours (an employee's working calendar year, excluding holidays and such). Add the total number of hours worked on security tasks and divide by 2080 to get the total EP.

B.   Sector Security Employees

    1.   International Widget Corporation Employees *Heads on Board & EP:*

        a)   Number of nonuniformed assets protection employees
            Heads_____ EP_____

        b)   Number of uniformed employees—Guard Force
            Heads_____ EP_____

        c)   Total number of IWC assets protection (Security) employees a) + b)
            Heads_____ EP_____

Instructions for Section II B 2—Contract Labor Employees:

This section is designed to capture the number of contract labor employees working in the Sector's security departments. This number should be expressed as Equivalent People. One EP = 2080 hours (an employee calendar year). Add the total number of hours worked by contract labor employees during the year and divide by 2080, which will give you the total EP.

    2.   Contract Labor Employees   EP:_____

        a)   Number of nonuniformed contract labor employees_____

        b)   Number of uniformed contract labor employees—
            Guard Force _____

        c)   Total number of contract labor security employees   a) + b)_____

III.   Country's Cost Drivers

  A.   Assets Protection Population

        a)   Total number of IWC employees_____

        b)   Total number of employees from other countries or in-country locations that you host and support_____

  B.   Facilities

    Total number of buildings or sites where assets protection measures are in place_____

  C.   Assets Protected Material Holdings
    Proprietary Material

      •   Describe the type and amount of proprietary material on site*

      _____

---

[2]   Be sure to take into account the variations in what makes up an EP at IWC's various locations. For example, the hours may vary due to the various holidays for which the employees are given time off. As one knows, different countries have different holidays: e.g., Chinese New Year in Asia, Fourth of July in the U.S.

*IWC Assets Protection Manual, Chapter 2. Control and Accountability 2-21 Policy. The document accountability system for proprietary, sensitive, and trade secret material, must be used at all times.

Sensitive Material

- Describe the type and amount of sensitive material on site*

---

*IWC CAPP Chapter 2. Sensitive Information. Paragraph 2-12a Accountability. Accountability of sensitive research material shall be determined and approved in writing by the CSO or designee at the time the sensitive material is produced. A separate accountability control system may be required for each sensitive research project.

Trade Secret Material

- Does the site possess trade secrets? If so, discuss type and identify.

High Value items

- Does the site possess high-value equipment and assets other than information? If so, discuss type and identify.

D. **Need-to-Know Proprietary-Sensitive-Trade Secret Approvals**
   - Total number of people who have access to IWC assets protected material
     _____
   - Total number of people who have need-to-know (NTK) for access to proprietary information_____
   - Total number of people who have NTK approval for sensitive information
   - Total number of people who have NTK approval for access to trade secret information_____

   International Security
   - Number of foreign nationals working in IWC facilities (your location):
     _____

E. **Unsatisfactory/Marginal Inspections (Complete this section only if you have had Unsatisfactory or Marginal-Rated Inspections at your site during the period covered by this report, e.g., self-inspections, customer inspections)**
   Provide details of the Unsatisfactory/Marginal Security Compliance Inspections, including name of the inspecting organization, a description of the findings, your plan of corrective action, and current status. (Use additional sheets if required)

   _____
   _____
   _____

IV. **Site Security Issues**
   A. **Pre-Employment Investigations (PEIs): Are PEIs being conducted on all new hire personnel and personnel with access to the site?**
      - Number of PEIs performed in 2005:_____
      - Cost per potential employee:_____
      - Total costs to date for 2005 employees: _____
   B. **Workplace Violence Prevention (WPV) Program: Is there a workplace violence prevention program in effect at the site?** _____
      - Number of WPV incidents occurring during the calendar year
        _____

- Costs of each occurrence: _____
- Total costs of all occurrences: _____

C. **Information Security**
- Number of your local area networks (LANs) that transmit, display, store or process IWC proprietary, sensitive and/or trade secret information

  _____

- Number of your wide area networks (WANs) that transmit, display, store or process IWC proprietary, sensitive and/or trade secret information

  _____

- Number of your standalone systems that transmit, display, store or process IWC proprietary, sensitive and/or trade secret information

  _____

- Have there been any intrusion attempts to any of the systems listed above?

  _____

- How many?_____
- Costs of inquiries into their cause:_____
- Costs of loss or damage:_____

D. **Security Alarm Monitoring**
- Who monitors your security alarms? _____

  _____

- Who installs your security alarms? _____

  _____

- Who services your security alarms? _____

  _____

V. **(Country) Security Manager Signature:** _____
Date:_____

Once this survey is completed, the CSO then determines with some reasonable certainty the size of the IWC assets protection environment. Although this questionnaire does not go into a great deal of detail, the CSO's rationale was to begin slowly and not ask for too many details too soon, as some information may not currently be collected.

In addition, the feedback on the questionnaire from the security managers at the various IWC locations gives a good indication of how much the security managers know about their own assets protection environment. For example, if they do not know how many of their facilities are protected by alarms due to the need-to-know (NTK) work being done in those areas, that suggests that they may not fully understand the extent of what is sensitive at their site, e.g., trade secret or proprietary information, processes, or equipment and how they are being protected.

The CSO will use the information not only to determine the size of the IWC assets protection environment, but also to help assess the job that the various security managers are doing.

Once the CSO implements an SMMP, the information required for properly managing an IWC assets protection program will be made more readily available.

EXAMPLES OF SOME METRICS CHARTS

The CSO has established a project and developed a project plan with the objective of identifying the IWC assets protection environment at all IWC locations. Through the assets protection questionnaire, discussions with the security staff, and others within IWC, such as the IWC audit department manager, the CSO established some metrics processes and subsequently developed some assets protection briefing charts so that the IWC executive management could be periodically briefed as to the progress toward meetings the assigned goals established for the CSO by the CEO and executive management.

The following metrics charts were developed to be used in the executive management briefings[3]:

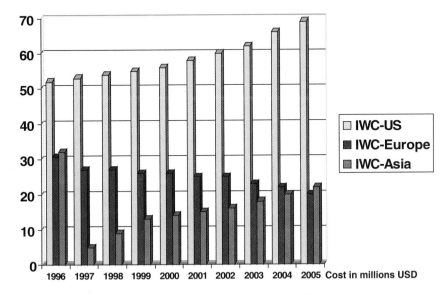

Figure 5-1 IWC security costs at all locations from 1996 through 2005.

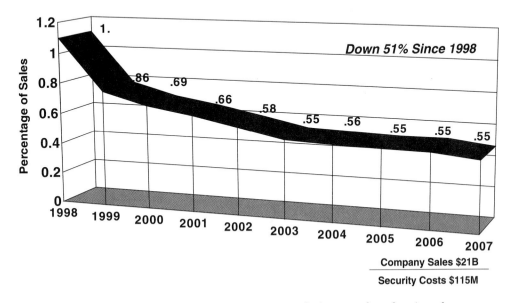

Figure 5-2 IWC security costs worldwide as a percentage of sales, actuals and projected.

---

[3] Dear reader, as stated in the preface, please do not try to analyze the numbers as they may or may not add up. The point is the use of such charts, the format, and not the detailed and bogus numbers.

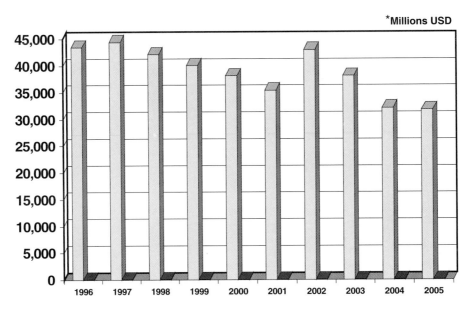

Figure 5-3   IWC security costs per employee between years 1996–2005.

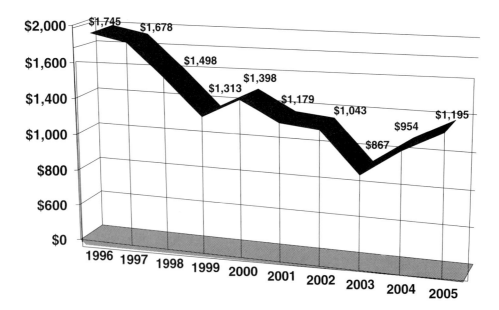

Figure 5-4   Another version of the IWC security costs per employee between years 1996–2005.

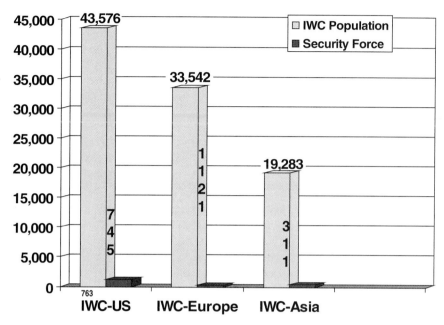

Figure 5-5   IWC security cost ratio by employee to security staff.

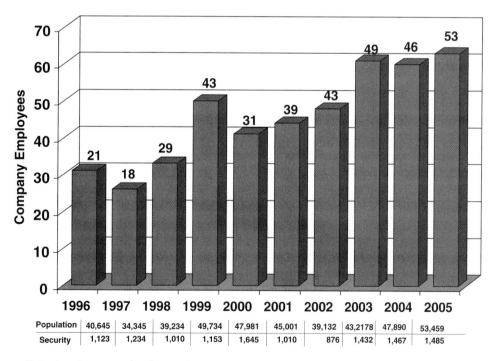

	1996	1997	1998	1999	2000	2001	2002	2003	2004	2005
Population	40,645	34,345	39,234	49,734	47,981	45,001	39,132	43,2178	47,890	53,459
Security	1,123	1,234	1,010	1,153	1,645	1,010	876	1,432	1,467	1,485

Figure 5-6   Another example of an IWC security cost ratio by employee to security staff.

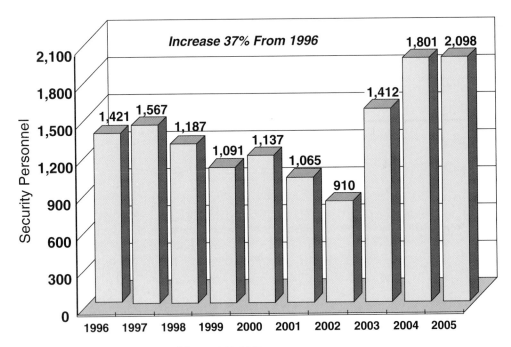

Figure 5-7   IWC-wide security workforce 1996-2005.

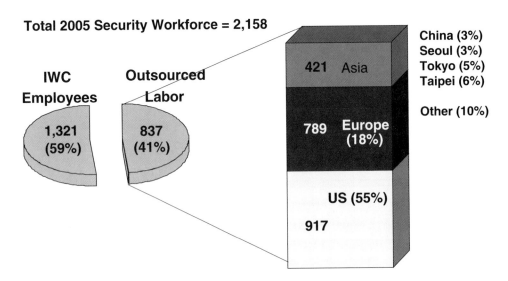

Figure 5-8   Composition of IWC security workforce.

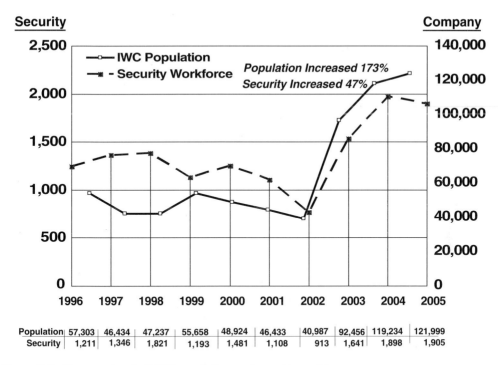

Population	57,303	46,434	47,237	55,658	48,924	46,433	40,987	92,456	119,234	121,999
Security	1,211	1,346	1,821	1,193	1,481	1,108	913	1,641	1,898	1,905

Figure 5-9   Ten-year trend of IWC population and security workforce.

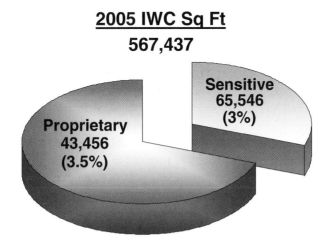

Figure 5-10   IWC facilities' utilization for proprietary and trade secret work.

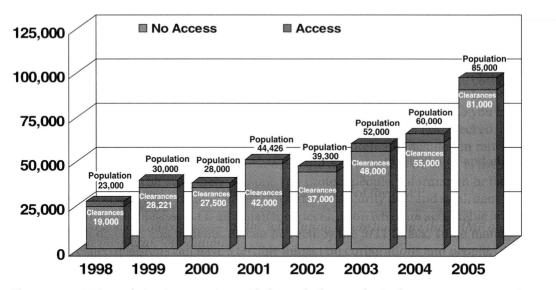

Figure 5-11   IWC population in comparison with those who have authorized access to sensitive IWC information and those that do not.

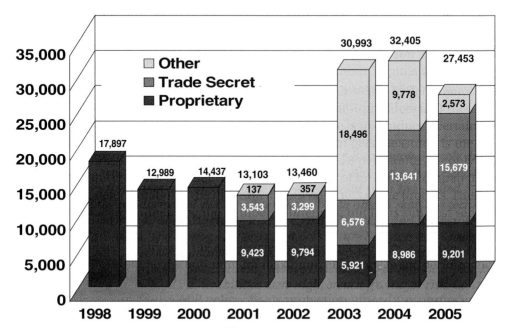

Figure 5-12   Those that have access to trade secret and proprietary information compared to the rest of the IWC population.

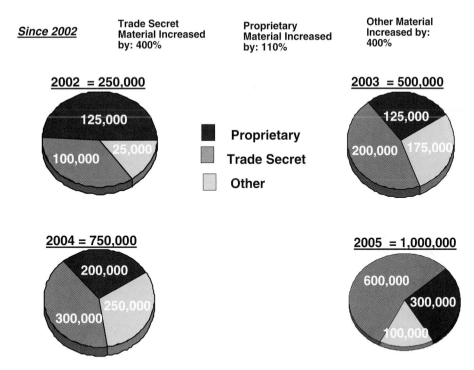

Figure 5-13 IWC's holdings of various types of sensitive information over a four-year period.

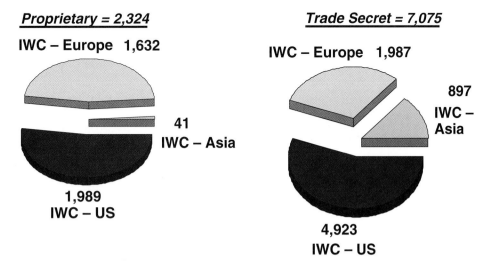

Figure 5-14 The number of personnel who have access to sensitive areas by regions.

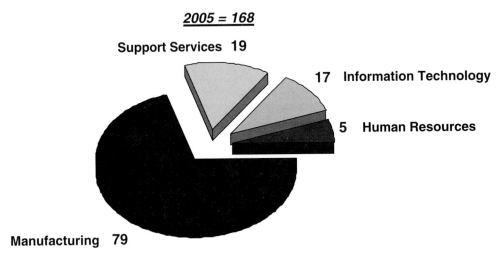

Figure 5-15   The number of workers and where they work in the IWC—US facilities.

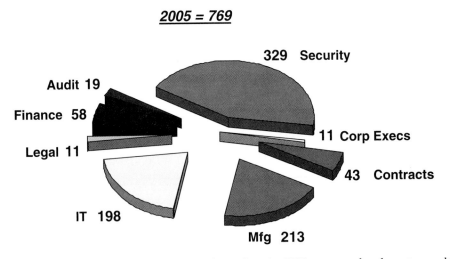

Figure 5-16   The number of nonforeign nationals employed at IWC corporate headquarters and in what departments they are assigned.

2005 = 593

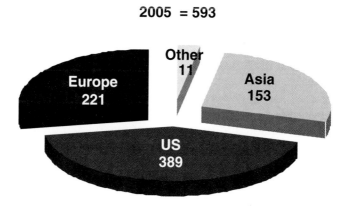

Figure 5-17   Numbers of expatriates and dependents assigned by region.

2005 Average Travelers Per Month = 1,218

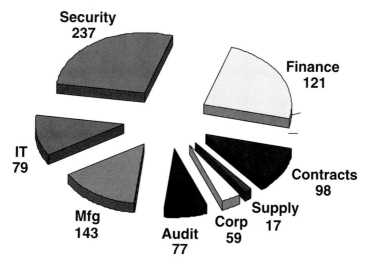

Figure 5-18   Monthly average number of IWC employees traveling to other IWC locations (needed for ensuring all briefed on travel dangers).

All the information compiled and analyzed provides the CSO with a picture, albeit a somewhat hazy picture at this time, of the basic environment of IWC at all worldwide locations, as well as some information that will be useful when it comes to compiling and analyzing additional information by individual security functions. For example, with all the IWC employees traveling around the world, providing information to the travelers on how to travel safely is needed and should already be in place. If so, then its usefulness and costs should be measured.[4]

One reason for compiling data on all aspects of a CAPP and security functions is that it helps to focus on the priorities, as well as what impacts the costs and schedules of IWC projects and employees.

SUMMARY

The information presented in this chapter provides some guidance as how to start to collect assets-protection-related and security-functions related data. When a new CSO is assigned, it is important to get an understanding of the size and needs of an assets protection program. This can often be done by using a questionnaire coupled with interviews of the security staff and others at IWC.

Once that information and data is collected, much of it can be compiled into data collection processes and incorporated into security metrics management charts to be used by the CSO to help manage the security department—analyze trend data and the CAPP—as well as brief executive management with those and other charts.

Remember the basic information shown on this chapter's charts helps the CSO "size the elephant." A CSO must have a clear understanding of the corporate environment world-wide prior to developing a meaningful CAPP and SMMP.

---

[4] When looking at the sample charts, see if you can identify the pros and cons of the format, fonts used, etc. You should always analyze your charts to be sure that they do provide for trend analyses and also project the objective of the chart as you see it. In other words, when you see it, what is the immediate message that it conveys and is that the message you want the chart to convey? Does it meet your management needs as a CSO? In addition, is each chart easy to see from the back of the room, assuming you would use it also as a briefing chart?

Chapter 6

Case Study: Six Sigma

INTRODUCTION

There are various methods used to measure processes. One of those is the Six Sigma approach. This chapter is a case study on the use of Six Sigma at Motorola Corporation.

A CASE STUDY—ANOTHER APPROACH TO SECURITY METRICS MANAGEMENT

William C. Boni is the Chief Information Security Officer and Corporate Vice President at Motorola Corporation. At Motorola, he uses a process known as "Six Sigma," a management metrics-related system. He provided the information below on that program.

What the Security Officer Needs to Know about Six Sigma

Managing an information security or protection organization has never been a simple or an easy responsibility. From the beginning of modern security organizations in the mid- to late 20th century, the profession has faced recurring challenges to its legitimacy, standing, focus, results, and therefore to budgets and headcount allocations.

If it ever was easy, then the general economic decline following the bursting of the global "dot com" (or was that the "dot bomb") bubble in early 2000, which dragged spending on information technology and associated areas (like information security) precipitously down, ended that.

There was a temporary upsurge in general management support for security following the terrorist attacks of September 11, 2001. For a brief albeit heady moment, many organizations threw off the budget restraints and invested in a range of then-new technologies like vulnerability management systems, intrusion detection sensors, and so on.

However, that passed quickly in the fortunate absence of additional attacks, as some security organizations failed to develop momentum for their programs. Often the reasons are multiple, but very often there is the sense by senior managers that security professionals, regardless of the background experience and educations are not really managers. In a time when perception quickly becomes accepted reality, it's vitally important that security professionals master the various tools of effective management and their direct application to the protection disciplines.

So Why Six Sigma?

Six Sigma (hereafter abbreviated as 6S) has proven itself a very capable tool with wide applicability in a number of disciplines including engineering, operations, and systems management. On the face of it, it would seem that it should be a comfortable and convenient resource for information security practitioners. After all, most information security managers came up through the ranks of one or more information technology (IT) functional areas such as applications, networks operations, and systems administration before transitioning into the security role.

What Is It?

Motorola originated 6S in the mid-1980s as a response to severe quality challenges to the company's products. The original goal was to reduce defects and variability in processes—to achieve circumstances where products are 99.999% defect free or, to put it another way, to assure that the company's products were designed, manufactured, and operated with this level of limited flaws. Other elements include understanding customer requirements, continuous process improvements and use of statistical analysis to drive fact-based decision making. It is now an overall business improvement methodology.

6S measures results against pre-established goals in the area of process improvement, financial gains, customer satisfaction, innovation and growth. It is much more than simply another name for total quality management (TQM).

Key elements of 6S when used as an overall improvement methodology include:

Alignment—Link customer requirements to business strategy and core business processes. Create appropriate measures to provide sustainable, measurable results that drive business goal achievement.

Mobilization—Teams drive improvements using projects selected by executives, project management methodology and 6S tools. Teams organized with clear charters, success criteria and rigorous reviews.

Accelerate—Action learning methodology that combines formal training and coaching to get from learning to doing fast.

Governance—Drive execution of strategy by managing scorecard metrics. Structure review processes by reviewing dashboards of results. Drill into process and projects to manage deviations from time, budget, schedule or results.

The key best practices of 6S include:

Voice of customer—Takes customer expectations and translates them into concrete specifications and organizational requirements. Management uses this data to determine and direct the strategic goals and processes of the organization so it can deliver value.

Balanced scorecard—Executive teams build scorecards to align on organization vision, mission, strategic objectives, breakthrough initiatives and metrics to monitor/track/report progress. The scorecard itself provides a clear and concise means of communicating these elements to the entire organization. Cascading the scorecard down and up the entire organization at all levels helps assure alignment.

Six Sigma black belt teams—Employed on highly complex projects that require advanced statistical tools. Typically used when process improvement, process development, product or service improvement, product or service development are the expected deliverables.

The intended results of 6S were to improve quality as well as reduce cost and cycle time in products. The results as originally executed were spectacular; in 1988 Motorola was awarded the first Malcolm Baldridge National Quality Award by the US government. Based on this initial success and many others, 6S has become a well-accepted tool for helping managements develop and deliver.

CASE STUDY—PATCH MANAGEMENT

The information security team at Motorola in the years from 2001–2004 faced challenges common to many companies. Patch management for over 100,000 Windows® systems became a major issue. In 2003 it became obvious that IT processes for patching Windows system were simply not keeping pace with the rapid increase in the number and complexity of patches. The number of Microsoft-issued patches increased dramatically in 2003.

This became urgent as the nature of the problems also changed dramatically. Over the preceding 3 years the time between the identification of vulnerabilities and release of an exploit decreased from about 6 months in 2001, to 30 days in 2002, 15 days in 2003, and reached 5.8 days in mid-2004.

We received another rude surprise when the "Slammer" worm was released in early 2003. Previously we had found that patching 90% or more of vulnerable systems was a very significant deterrent to significant disruptions of network and system availability. When the Slammer worm was released, there were only about 1500 vulnerable systems out of a population of 100,000 Windows devices on the company network. This means we had only about 1.5% at risk, so 98.5% of our systems were already patched or not vulnerable.

However, in spite of this relatively small number of "at risk" systems, within 15 minutes of the worm's Internet release, about 150 of the 1500 vulnerable systems became infected with the worm. This very small percentage of total systems nonetheless resulted in network outages due to bandwidth consumption. The network was not available for about 8 hours.

Our post-incident analysis revealed all this and it was obvious that we not only needed to be faster in applying patches to Windows systems, we also needed to increase coverage of the system population….anything less than 99% or better was no longer adequate. The speed of the worms and promiscuous nature of their attack vectors meant that any release inside the network was likely to be very disruptive. Past practices achieved reasonable results but were no longer sufficient. So in June 2004, the Security team initiated a Six Sigma team to determine how to improve our overall patch management process. Since our objective was process improvement, we selected the "Define Measure Analyze Improve Control" (hereafter abbreviated as DMAIC) process as our primary approach.

The Five Steps of DMAIC

The five steps of DMAIC are described below.

Define

The initial step of the process is to understand what is important. Here is where we set the target objective of the project; this is arguably the most important step in any new project. We answer the question: "What is the business opportunity at hand?" In the case of patch management, we needed to significantly improve both the time needed to deliver effective protection to Windows workstations/servers through patches, as well as also increase our overall coverage to a higher threshold. Our previous standard had been 90% or more systems patched in 30 days or less. A new target would ultimately emerge based on the results of the project.

The objective of the define stage of any DMAIC project is to validate or refine the business opportunity, document the existing business processes, and define specific customer requirements, as well as assemble an effective cross-functional team. This last is an especially important aspect in this case study. The security organization itself and alone would be wholly insufficient to accomplish improvements in the patch process. We needed the active involvement and support of the internal IT staff and management and as importantly the outsourced IT infrastructure provider. The security team did not manage operational elements of the patching process, and did not actually install or deploy patches that remain the responsibility of the outsourced infrastructure team and of retained IT staff in areas like manufacturing and selected engineering functions.

In this first stage the most important activity is to map the actual business process and conduct formal collection of the "voice of the customers" expectations, and then to translate that into specific objectives that must be achieved. As a result, at the end of this stage the team had been chartered by their respective managements, the current processes mapped, customer requirements documented, and a formal project plan for the work created.

Measure

The activities in this stage are intended to answer the question: "How are we doing?"

One of the perennial challenges in business is that urgent problems typically lead to urgent response. Too often managers and staff, operating from their personal and limited perspective, begin to take actions intended to "fix the problem" as soon as it becomes apparent a problem exists. This is unfortunate, because if they fail to take time up front to document the empirical basis of the current performance, it's unlikely that even the best-intentioned efforts will self-evidently improve the situation. In fact, the failure to know how we're doing and to have an effective measurement plan often leads to situation where the failure to address the root causes may actually cause the situation to become worse. So, in order to be able to prove the situation is "better" we must first have a starting baseline that will allow us to collect critical measures and make sure we know when and by how much we're doing better.

During this stage the activities of the team will include stating operational definitions and developing a specific measurement plan after identifying input, process and output indicators. When these aspects are documented, then the team must evaluate baseline performance so as to have a well-defined starting point description.

Analyze

This is the stage where the team starts to reap the benefits of the set-up work done in prior stages. At this point we are answering the question "What is wrong?" The team will be reviewing the process and customer requirements, understanding where there is a gap and identifying and validating the root causes of poor performance. In this stage, we also look to determine the sources of variation and the potential failure modes that can lead to customer dissatisfaction. This is when various statistical tools such as regression analysis, control charts, etc. are used by "green belt" trained staff under the direction of Six Sigma Master Black Belt specialists to achieve a rigorous factual basis for conclusions. The results of this stage will include both validated root causes of customer dissatisfaction but also potential solutions.

Improve

This is the stage where the team digs into the circumstances and answers the question "What must be done?" There are two key steps in this effort:

- First, we must be sure the correct or best improvements are selected. We're typically looking for the biggest result for the efforts.
- Second, is to prepare a formal change management approach that will help the organization deal with necessary changes that will arise from solution implementation. The activities in this stage will include generating a prioritized list of recommended solutions, validation steps, and both communication and implementation plans.

Control

In the final stage of the DMAIC, the team must answer the question "How do we assure performance in a way that will sustain the anticipated or achieved gains?"

During this stage, the team will actually implement the solutions as well as develop a plan to maintain the gains. Actions taken by the team will include implementation, steps to verify the beneficial results of the solution, and efforts needed to integrate the solution/changes into the normal operational work flow/processes. It is at this point as well that the team will close/end activities as a special 6S project team. However, one of the final tasks will be to assess whether there are opportunities to replicate the results of this project in other areas.

Results

The results were very significant. After only 3 months under the new 6S enhanced processes, the time to patch Windows workstations had been reduced and the total number of workstations patched increased. In addition, management was presented with specific recommendations for additional tools and process improvements that are expected, when implemented in the next year's budget, to result in consistently patching 99% of the systems in seven days or less...which will be an order of magnitude improvement in time/coverage.

CONCLUSION

6S is a wonderful tool for assisting security teams in aligning their efforts with what is most important to the organization. It can assure that changes are well documented, proven and result in measurable improvements to the protection program. As security managers consider how to meet the challenges of doing ever more work with limited or declining resources, the 6S DMAIC process and similar statistical tools should be used whenever possible. They offer a proven, flexible methodology that will improve both the quality and effectiveness of management decisions.

Section II

Administrative Security Metrics

...Key performance indicators are tracked by period, quarter, year-over-year and five years running...That enables cost and benefit impact assessments, risk-gap closure analysis as well as return on funds spent...Francis D'addario, Starbuck's vice president of partner and assets protection...[1]

This section includes Chapters 7–13. Within this section, we discuss the security functions we place under the umbrella of "administrative security." These security functions and subfunctions include:

- Chapter 7: Information Security
- Chapter 8: Personnel Security
- Chapter 9: Security Education and Awareness Training
- Chapter 10: Security Compliance Audits
- Chapter 11: Surveys and Risk Management
- Chapter 12: Corporate Assets Protection Program
- Chapter 13: Contingency Planning

Throughout Section II and also in Sections III and IV, we will continue to use a fictitious international corporation, The International Widget Corporation (IWC), as a model for our application of measurement to the many security functions and processes any business or government security organization may use. The IWC is structured with both domestic and international offices[2] (see Figure Section II-1 and Figure Section II-2). All functions identified in the organizational charts below will be addressed vis-à-vis security metrics measurement.

NOTE: You will find some redundancies throughout each of these chapters. This was intentionally done so the reader can view each chapter as a complete, stand-alone security function. That way, those functions that do not apply to your particular needs can be ignored. Moreover, with this approach you are less likely to miss some of the material that is related to your particular security function and that may have only been stated in one of the other chapters as applying to all the chapters. Confused? No need to worry. It will be clearer as you read through this section.

Furthermore, a certain amount of redundancy, we believe, will help you become more familiar with this security measurement process and management program and make it easier for you to apply it in your own security environment.

---

[1]   Quoted from CSOONLINE.COM, "Where the Metrics Are" article, February 2005 issue.

[2]   The figures identified are taken from the authors' book, *The Manager's Handbook for Corporate Security: Establishing and Managing a Successful Assets Protection Program*, published by Butterworth-Heinemann, 2003, for which the Security Metrics Management book can be considered a supplemental book.

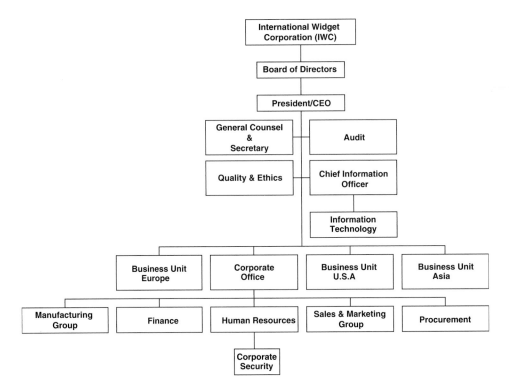

Figure Section II-1   The international corporation organizational structure.

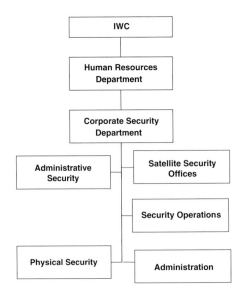

Figure Section II-2   The security department of the international corporation.

Throughout this section, we will show various charts using different formats. That does not mean one chart is necessarily better than the other. Sometimes it is matter of complying with the standards set within a corporation or a personal preference. If you have the option of choosing the type of chart that you prefer, then do so with the caveat that the format you choose is the best to depict the information that you choose to depict, in order to make the point that you want to make with that particular set of data.

Chapter 7

Information Security

This chapter will discuss the function of information security. Further, how to apply the process of metrics management to the function of information security will be examined in order to determine its costs, benefits, successes and failures.

INTRODUCTION

Since information is one of today's most valuable assets for any organization, business or government, and is one of the "triad" of valuable assets—(1) people, (2) information and (3) physical property such as facilities and equipment—it must be protected.

The protection of information in this age of electronic and digital information is more important, and more complex, than ever before. The loss or theft of information critical to a corporation's products, methods or processes may be devastating. In this age of global competition, the importance of implementing a comprehensive program for information protection is critical and cannot be overstated.

Information[1]

1. *knowledge: definite knowledge acquired or supplied about something or somebody*
2. *gathered facts: the collected facts and data about a particular subject*
3. *making facts known: the communication of facts and knowledge*
4. *computer data: computer data that has been organized and presented in a systematic fashion to clarify the underlying meaning*

---

[1] Definition taken from Microsoft's Encarta World English Dictionary
(See http://www.microsoft.com/encarta/)

When the Chief Security Officer (CSO) was hired by IWC, there wasn't a formal program in place to protect information at all of IWC's company locations, domestic and international. The only area where information was identified for protection was through the trade secret and proprietary information process "owned" and implemented by the IWC legal department. Very basic procedures were used for marking documents and locking them up in storage containers after normal working hours. There were no provisions for protection of information in a holistic and comprehensive manner across all the various IWC environments—that included automated information: that information stored, processed, displayed or transmitted by computerized systems, including cellular telephones, emails, faxes, personal digital assistants (PDAs) and other forms of information systems, as well as hardcopies.

> *Proprietary information is that information belonging to "…one who has the exclusive title to a thing; one that possesses or holds the title to a thing in his own right…*[2]*"*

The IWC security department has established the administrative security organization as a primary security organization and under that a function, information security, was established to deal with the protection of this valuable corporate asset. (See Figure 7-1.)

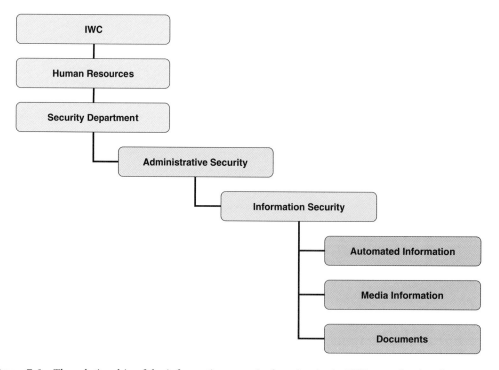

Figure 7-1   The relationship of the information security function in the IWC organizational structure.

The CSO determined that, because of the global marketplace where IWC had to compete for business using its proprietary formulas, computer programs, processes and

---

[2]   Black's Law Dictionary, Deluxe Edition.

proprietary widget parts, an all-encompassing program was required. The CSO decided that this was too important a project to delegate to a member of the security staff to lead. Therefore, the CSO formed a project team to address the issue across all regions—United States, Europe and Asia, as well as some minor marketing offices in Africa and the Middle East.

The CSO believed that, since information permeates throughout all of IWC, all the security organizations must be involved in one way or another in leading information assets protection. The CSO picked the project team members accordingly. For example, the manager for administrative security would be involved since plans, policies and procedures must be written and published relative to this function. The physical security manager was required to develop processes and security measures to ensure sensitive information did not leave any IWC facility except through the use of approved protection processes.

> *Trade secret information is: "...A plan or process, tool, mechanism, or compound known only to its owner and those of his employees to whom it is necessary to confide it...A secret formula or process not patented, but known only to certain individuals using it in compounding some article of trade having a commercial value...*[3]*"*

The CSO also decided that this was the best time to discuss information systems security and automated information systems protection with IWC's vice president of information technology (IT).[4] A meeting was held between the two. The CSO explained that, although assets protection was everyone's responsibility, the CSO and the security department were charged with leading the assets protection program for IWC—which includes the protection of information assets, which includes information systems. The CSO went on to say that information systems, other computer devices, telecommunications systems, and similar tools were some of IWC's most valuable assets. Therefore, under the IWC corporate assets protection program (CAPP), they must be protected and the IWC CSO was charged with developing, implementing and maintaining the CAPP and all related processes.

The vice president of IT agreed with the CSO's assertion but voiced a concern that the security department's staff might try to direct the IT staff to comply with information assets protection methods that could adversely impact the ability of the IT staff to provide the level of service that had been mandated by IWC's executive management. This is a classic conflict between a service provider and an assets protector. The service provider prefers to have nothing in the way of delivering the service. The protector (security department) must ensure some controls are in place to protect assets, which sometimes inhibit the delivery of these services.

The CSO provided the vice president of IT a summary of the philosophy and processes that are being used by the security staff and implemented throughout IWC, and how it would be used when dealing with the IT staff:

- All information assets protection policies were being coordinated across all IWC departments for comments and input prior to implementation. Therefore, any policies that may have an adverse impact on IT processes would be identified by the IT staff during that coordination process.

---

[3] Ibid.
[4] Chapter 22 will address Information Systems Security; however, it was also presented here to offer several views of this important topic.

- Corporate assets protection program (CAPP) serves as the implementation mechanism for compliance with the information assets protection policies that are to be established and documented; while the compliance procedures are to be written and implemented by the IT staff and coordinated with the security department as needed for clarification, interpretation, and assistance.
- The IWC audit department would be responsible for determining if the procedures in all IWC departments comply with the IWC information assets protection policies and procedures, including those of the IT department.
- If any conflicts occurred between the security and IT staff relative to how information assets are to be protected, a risk management survey led by the security staff would be conducted with IT representatives on the survey team as deemed appropriate by the vice president of IT. The results would be presented and based on those results, additional information assets protection measures would be implemented or the owner of the assets would be required to accept the additional risk, in writing.

The CSO further advised that the IT department would be responsible for compliance with CAPP policies. Like all other IWC departments where the assets in each department have a focal point, or assets custodian who is responsible for the day-to-day protection of assets, the IT department must have the same for its information assets. This includes protection of information systems and other computing devices and all other communications assets (e.g., cellular phones, company-owned PDAs, facsimile machines, etc.). The CSO further advised that an information systems security organization would be established within the security department and information systems security would be part of that organization. However, using a holistic approach, the security department's information assurance and protection philosophy will be based on IWC's high technology operating environment and its needs, vulnerabilities and threats.

The CSO advised that information systems requiring protection went well beyond LANS and WANs and items already identified. Included under the protection umbrella are the systems that run manufacturing robots, complex automated tools, telecommunications devices and other high technology-based equipment that processes, stores, displays and/or transmits IWC information. This environment is unique and has unique threats, vulnerabilities, risks, and thus unique protection requirements (see Figure 7-2).

The CSO explained that information that is considered sensitive—vital—to IWC must be protected at a level relative to its importance regardless of the environment or form that information took, whether hardcopy, voice, pictorial, or zeroes and ones. All IWC information is important for conducting business. However, some IWC information is more sensitive and critical to the mission and therefore requires a higher degree of protection.

A holistic approach must be used if IWC is to be successful in protecting its information assets. That is to say, information in all forms (hardcopy, electronic, spoken, even information that is in the form of ideas in the heads of employees) must be protected. If information were to be protected only when in hardcopy but someone attached a proprietary document to an email and sent it out to an unauthorized person, what good would it have done to only protect the hardcopy? The vice president of IT was still concerned but agreed with the CSO's approach. They further agreed that a senior IT representative would be identified and be the focal point for all information systems security-related matters on that portion of the CSO's project team dealing with matters that impact IT processes.

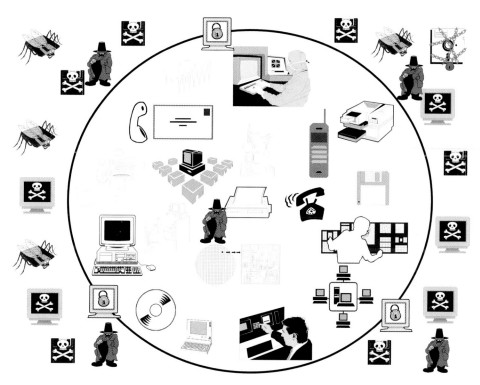

Figure 7-2   The IWC information environment and protection philosophy.

THREE BASIC CATEGORIES OF INFORMATION

IWC divided its information into three basic categories:

- Personal, private information;
- National security (both classified and unclassified) information;[5] and
- Business information.

Personal, private information is an individual matter, but also a matter for the government and businesses. A person may want to keep private such information about themselves as their age, weight, address, cellular phone number, salary, and their likes and dislikes. Many nation-states have laws that protect information under some type of "privacy act." In businesses and government agencies, it is a matter of policy to safeguard certain information about an employee such as their age, address, salary, etc. The IWC CSO understands that, although the information is personal to the individual, others may require that information. At the same time, IWC has an obligation to protect that information because it is considered to have value. Therefore, this information is categorized as a vital asset requiring protection under the CAPP.

---

[5]   National security information is discussed in Chapter 21 and will not be repeated here.

> *Privacy is: "…The right to be let alone, the right of a person to be free from unwarranted publicity…The right of an individual (or corporation) to withhold himself and his property from public scrutiny, if he so chooses. It is said to exist only so far as its assertion is consistent with law or public policy, and in a proper case equity will interfere, if there is no remedy in law, to prevent an injury threatened by the invasion of, or infringement upon, this right from motives or curiosity, gain, or malice…[6]"*

Business Information also requires protection based on its value. This information has been categorized at IWC as:

- IWC Internal Use Only;
- IWC Private;
- IWC Sensitive;
- IWC Proprietary; and
- IWC Trade Secret.

This information must be protected because it has value to IWC. The degree of protection required is also dependent on the value of the information during a specific period of time.

> *Generally, the types of information which have value to the business and which require protection include: All forms and types of financial, scientific, technical, economic, or engineering information including, but not limited to, data, plans, tools, mechanisms, compounds, formulas, designs, prototypes, processes, procedures, programs, codes, or commercial strategies, whether tangible or intangible, and whether stored, compiled or memorialized physically, electronically, graphically, photographically, or in writing. Examples of information requiring protection may include: research, proposals, plans, manufacturing processes, pricing, and product.*

AN INFORMATION PROTECTION PHILOSOPHY

The CSO advised the project team that the most difficult of all information protection tasks and a major milestone was determining how to classify (declare its sensitivity in a consistent and determined manner) information based on its protection needs and do so without developing a complicated and bureaucratic process so cumbersome that it was impractical and unworkable.

The CSO provided the information below to the project team. Although determining the value of corporate information is a very important task, it is one that is seldom done with any systematic, logical approach. The consequences of not properly classifying corporate information could lead to over-protection, which is costly, or under-protection, which could lead to the loss of that information and thus the competitive advantage and profits. If the information has value, it must be protected; ***protection is expensive***.

- One should only protect that information which requires protection;
- Only in the manner necessary based on the value of that information; and
- Only for the period required.

---

[6]   Ibid.

To determine the value of IWC information, one should first understand:

- what is meant by information;
- what is meant by value of information; and
- how to properly categorize and classify the information.

> *Value is defined in one Webster's dictionary as "....the worth of a thing in money or goods at a certain time; market price...; that quality of a thing according to which it is thought of as being more or less desirable, useful, important, etc...."*

One might ask, "Does all the corporate information have value?" If you were asked that question, how would you answer it? The follow-on question would be, "What information does *not* have value?" Is it that information which the receiver of the information determines has no value? When the originator of the information says so? Who determines if information has value?

There are two basic assumptions to consider in determining the value of information:

- All information costs some type of resource(s) to produce, whether money, hours, or use of equipment; and
- Not all information can cause damage if released outside protected channels.

BUSINESS INFORMATION TYPES AND EXAMPLES

This section provides some examples of the various classifications that the CSO and the project team are considering for use when classifying IWC information.

Types of IWC Internal Use Only Information:

- Not generally known outside the corporation;
- Not generally known through product inspection;
- Possibly useful to a competitor; and
- Provide some business advantage over competitors.

Examples are: Corporation telephone book, corporation policies and procedures, and corporation organizational charts.

Types of IWC Private Information:

- Technical or financial aspects of the corporation;
- Indicates corporation's future direction;
- Describes portions of the corporation business;
- Provides a competitive edge; and
- Identifies personal information of employees.

Examples are: Personnel medical records, salary information, cost data, short-term marketing plans, and dates for unannounced events.

Types of IWC Sensitive Information

- Provides significant competitive advantage;
- Could cause serious damage to the corporation; and
- Reveals long-term corporation direction.

Examples are: Critical corporation technologies, critical engineering processes, and critical cost data.

SECURITY DRIVERS

What are the security drivers that create the need to protect information assets? Information is a valuable asset as was stated earlier. However, not all information is considered an asset. Since information, as it is categorized at IWC as stated above, defines what is important, we can deduce that the information that requires protection is that information that is needed by IWC and which would cause harm to IWC if not properly protected, and became available to unauthorized people without the need-to-know (NTK).

> *Remember that information's value is time-dependent. Protecting it when it is no longer required is a waste of resources, such as protecting information related to a new product. However, when that new product is announced to the public, its protection is no longer required. Processes must be in place to avoid over-protection of information assets.*

Therefore, information assets that must be protected are those information assets which, if not adequately protected, would be in violation of laws, regulations, management direction, corporate policy, ethics, and otherwise would adversely impact IWC. These are the information assets protection drivers.

INFORMATION SECURITY PROCESS FLOWCHARTS

Information that requires protection must come from somewhere. There are two primary sources of information that requires protection:

- Information that is born from the brains of IWC employees who develop such information in the course of performing their IWC duties. That information then becomes the exclusive property of IWC and is to be protected and used as directed by IWC's CAPP.
- Information provided to IWC by customers, associates, contractors, and others with a stipulation that the information provided must be protected from unauthorized access, damage, modification, destruction or theft. It is to be used only as they direct its use. This information often is provided in writing in the form of contractual requirements.

The CSO's information security project team developed a high-level flowchart that is to be used to provide a "picture" of information flow. Based on that flowchart, metrics targets can then be identified (see Figure 7-3).

When looking at this flowchart, some concepts relative to security metrics management should become apparent. The process to categorize the information is time-consuming, as are the protection processes that follow. One has to be sure that infor-

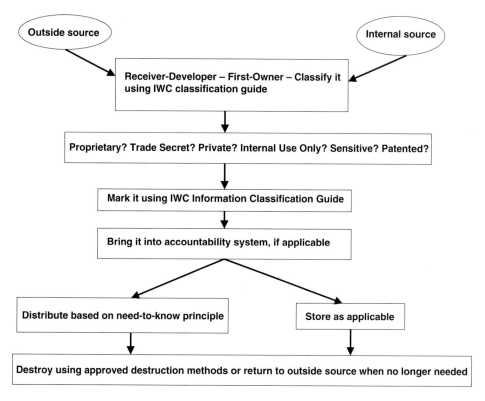

Figure 7-3   An overview of the information process flow for that information requiring protection as a valuable IWC asset.

mation is adequately protected, which means employees understand the sensitivity of information and they take actions such as locking documents in proper containers, maintaining an accountability record for the most important information such as proprietary research information, not discussing sensitive information with people who have no need-to-know, and many other measures.

And as previously noted, a process must be in place to provide a time limit for protecting information, to include a periodic review to determine if protection is still required, or if less protection can be implemented, which will save some resources—for example, safes or accountability controls. All information is perishable or has a "shelf life." It's important not to protect information for periods that are far too long or far too short.

So, in this case, the flowchart allows the CSO to analyze the information protection process from "cradle to grave." Of course, your flowcharts would be in much greater detail so that you can do an in-depth analysis.

One other thing to keep in mind is to try not to do too much at one time. Some tasks can be done by the project team in serial order and other tasks in parallel. For example, after you analyze the process supported by the flowchart, the next step would be to interview not only those that perform the information security duties but also the IWC employees who are affected by the information assets protection policies and procedures. You want to know if the IWC Information Classification Guide is useful. If not, why not? You may need a separate project to address that issue.

As the CSO, you want to know how much equipment is used throughout IWC to protect information. You want to break that down by location and type of equipment, such as safes, key-lock filing cabinets, or information system access control software, as well as costs. (See Chapter 16, Locks and Keys where that will be discussed.)

This process is the beginning of the security metrics management process for the information assets protection function:

- Identify the information assets protection drivers
- Develop and analyze the information assets protection processes flowchart
- Target areas for data collection with the ultimate goal to make the process more effective and efficient
- Develop a method for data collection
- Collect and collate that data
- Analyze the data
- Develop security metrics management charts as a management tool and also to brief executive management on the matter or as part of an overall CSO briefing to executive management
- Develop and implement projects to increase effectiveness and efficiencies of the processes and subprocesses

WHAT, WHEN, WHO, WHERE, HOW OF DATA COLLECTION

As part of this project, one must determine:

- What data will be collected?
- At what points in the process will the data be collected?
- Who will collect the data?
- When will they collect the data?
- How will they collect the data (manually or through an automated process)?

Once that is decided, a pilot subproject or major milestone task should be initiated under this project—to test the collection process. After all, you wouldn't want to establish the collection process and ignore it until the first data collection is completed after one month or more, and then find out that the data collected is not what you had in mind. So, not only is the data collection process to be tested but those involved in the collection process must understand what they are doing and why they are doing it. Furthermore, they *must* be directed to notify the data collection project lead, their manager, or you if they have any questions or the process is not working based on its objective.

As far as data collection from employees, one can send them a survey form to complete. Be sure it is clear why you want the data and provide them an easy process to report the survey—e.g., place it on line, send it out by email and have them reply by email.

Also, you must determine if the survey information is to be tabulated manually and input in a database, spreadsheet or if a program is written and placed on line that will allow for the automated collection of the data, ready for analysis. Remember, all this takes time and time is money.

> *Analysis is needed but caution: beware of analysis to the point of paralysis.*

NOTE: See Chapter 5 and the Appendix for examples of data collection questionnaires that include information assets inventory data, as well as some sample metrics charts relative to information assets protection.

SAMPLE METRICS CHARTS

The following security metrics management charts are just a few examples of the type that may be relevant when determining the costs in terms of money and time spent, not only by the security staff but also the IWC employees who use the process.

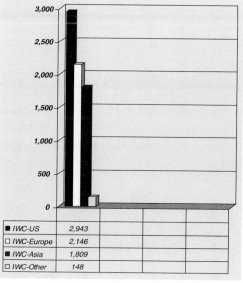

- There are a total of 7,046 proprietary documents and other media, i.e., CDs, being stored throughout IWC facilities worldwide.
- The estimated cost of storing each information media per month, at all locations, includes labor, secure containers, and excluding processing time to take it in and out of storage, e.g., unlock the container, sign the container open-close sheet as open, lock the container, and sign it as closed, and other information assets handling procedures.
- The cost is approximately $15 per month per document or $45 per quarter.
- Total cost per month at all locations is approximately $105,690 and $1,268,280 per year.

■ IWC-US	2,943
□ IWC-Europe	2,146
■ IWC-Asia	1,809
□ IWC-Other	148

Figure 7-4 Inventory of "accountable" (proprietary and trade secret) information. That is, the information most sensitive to IWC that therefore requires that strict controlling and handling processes be in place.

How can you use this chart to help you identify costs and productivity losses in time? One way is to identify the costs of storing a proprietary document. That includes security staff and other labor costs, security container costs, and all related resources necessary for the protection of that document. Then, multiply that number by the number of proprietary documents being stored. This will give you a general idea as to the costs of this phase of protecting these information assets. Yes, this is a very simplistic example, but hopefully you get the idea.

You would undoubtedly want to present your charts in color and probably view them online at your desk. However, remember that they may be reproduced as black-and-white charts. So, always be sure to check them not only for accuracy and to understand what they are showing, but maybe just as important, are they clear to the viewer?

As the CSO, you will probably be responsible for providing the handouts and, as cheap as color printing has gotten, colored handouts would not only look more professional but also allow easier viewing of the data.[7]

---

[7] It is hoped that you critique the charts not only in this chapter but throughout the book, as we have made many of them—shall we say, not as good as they could have been. You should be very critical and view them as a CEO and "attendee" at a CSO briefing. Ask yourself the questions that the charts may elicit. Hopefully, that will help you design better charts.

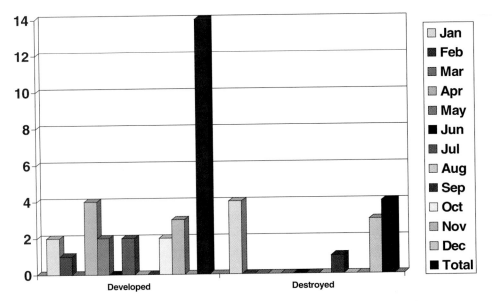

Figure 7-5   Depiction of the number of trade secret documents created and destroyed.

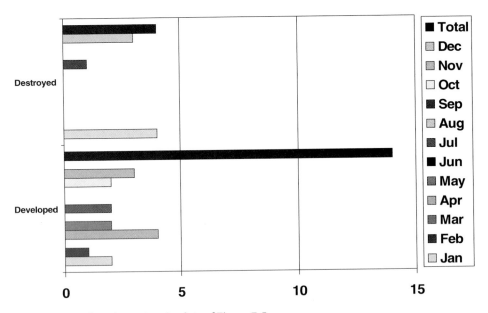

Figure 7-6   Another view using the data of Figure 7-5.

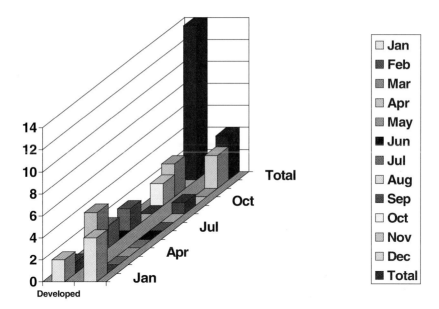

Figure 7-7   Another view using the data of Figure 7-5.

Compare the views presented in the previous charts. Which is better? Why? Would you choose another style? If so, ask yourself why? Always ask yourself why you chose the chart style you have over all the others.

A CASE STUDY

If you recall, the CSO found that IWC had five different types of business information. They were:

- IWC Internal Use Only;
- IWC Private;
- IWC Sensitive;
- IWC Proprietary; and
- IWC Trade Secret.

He also knew that this information must be protected because it has value to IWC. The degree of protection required is also dependent on the value of the information during a specific period of time. So, although each category requires some degree of protection, that is dependent on the information assets protection policy. No matter the category, the information assets that are being protected are all to be protected from those who do not have a need-to-know for that type of information.

So, the logic is that the degree of protection mitigates to various degrees the risks to the information asset being protected. But still, the goal is not to give unauthorized personnel access to it, regardless of its classification.[8]

---

[8]   Excluding the requirements established by government agencies for their (national security) information which corporations use under their contracts with government agencies. This information must be protected as directed by the government customer, as spelled out in the contract.

If you were the CSO, what would you do to lower the costs of information assets protection? Yes, there are many possibilities; however, there is one basic possibility that may be the easiest to deal with and that is eliminating some of the information classifications. Review the categories of information and that information that is not sensitive, or may be only somewhat sensitive for a very short period of time, could be protected as routine information requiring no additional controls. In essence, the universe of information requiring protection would be shrunk to include only the most sensitive information. Yes, there may be a slightly increased risk of exposure to some information, but that may be offset by the economic savings of reducing the amount of information requiring additional (and continuous) protection. If you were the CSO and wanted to look at that possibility, how would you go about doing that and in what order?

Here's one possible scenario:

- Initiate a project plan for tasks that have an objective, beginning and ending date and are classified as projects
- Identify project team members
- Brief them on the objective of the project
- The goal is to find enough commonality among the categories to reduce the five to two—one for sensitive, trade secret and proprietary information, and one for all other IWC information that is not to be released to unauthorized personnel
- Get their input
- Identify tasks and assign them
- Identify the policies, procedures and processes used for each category of information assets being protected
- Identify commonalities of protection among the five categories
- Identify the costs of that protection (for each category of information)
- Identify the different types of physical containers approved and used to protect each category of information
- Determine how many containers there are within each IWC department and compile by region and then total
- Determine if there are any security drivers external to IWC that require the classification (naming convention) of certain information
- Determine if there are any security drivers external to IWC that mandate specific protection mechanisms
- Based on the data collected as to the costs for protecting certain information in a certain way determine if you could reduce those categories to two and recalculate the protective measures costs, assuming that the minimum protection requirements will be used
- Brief management using the security metrics management charts
- Gain their approval
- Establish an implementation plan
- Implement the plan
- Monitor the process and costs thereafter using the security metrics management tools

SUMMARY

Information assets are one of the three types of assets requiring protection. Like all other types of security functions, information assets protection is costly and some of the costs are unknown.

Even information that requires protection today may not require protection tomorrow, as information is time-sensitive. If you protect information no longer requiring protection, you are wasting valuable corporate resources. If you misclassify information, you may not be protecting it as you should or over protecting it. Either way, it is costly.

Using security metrics management techniques:

- identify security drivers
- identify information assets protection processes
- flowchart the processes
- identify target areas of opportunity to reduce costs in terms of money and time
- establish projects to quantify costs, analyze the processes and develop modifications to the processes that will make them more effective and efficient

Chapter 8

Personnel Security

This chapter introduces the function of personnel security and the process of personnel security metrics management identification and establishment to determine costs, benefits, successes and failures.

INTRODUCTION

The personnel security function under the administrative security organization has two primary responsibilities:

- Pre-employment and Background Investigations (BIs)
- Workplace Violence Prevention Program Support

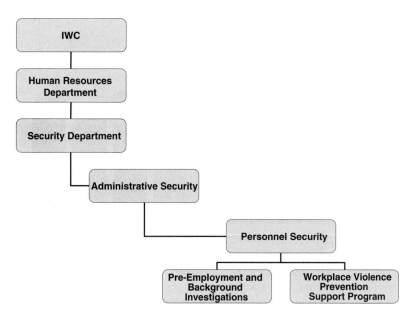

Figure 8-1 Shows where the personnel security function fits into the IWC security department.

These are both vital functions that are an integral part of any corporate assets protection program (CAPP). You may not agree with some of the criteria used to screen out potential employees—such as convicted felons who have served time and paid their debt to society, or someone who had filed for, or still is in, bankruptcy. However, establishing the criteria is the prerogative of the company, in this case IWC, and must be done in accordance with all applicable laws and regulations, company policy, and values. IWC must establish its own threshold for risk in regards to the suitability of employees.

Remember that the screening process is done to try to hire only the most qualified, honest and capable employees. Only the most suitable for IWC should be hired. Employees must be suitable for the work environment and they must be trustworthy. After all, much will be expected of any IWC employee and they must be capable of delivering. That delivery includes the ability and willingness to protect corporate assets.

PRE-EMPLOYMENT AND BACKGROUND INVESTIGATIONS

Every company wants to employ competent and trustworthy people and IWC is no exception. IWC cannot afford to have employees who are incompetent or untrustworthy. This is a recipe for problems at best and disaster at worst. Incompetent employees are not capable of producing the best products and services.

Untrustworthy employees can harm a company in many ways. Theft of assets such as IWC proprietary information or fraudulent and unethical behavior are some of the ways untrustworthy employees can damage a company. IWC is not immune from the bad employee. Every company has them. The goal is to have none, but the key is to have as few as possible. Measures can be taken to reduce the probability of hiring untrustworthy employees, thereby reducing the risk of harm to the corporate assets.

Screening out the potentially bad employee prior to hiring is a much more effective and painless process than trying to get rid of an employee who has just been determined to be untrustworthy.

Whatever screening process is employed, there are no guarantees that all new hires will be trustworthy. However, the CSO reasoned that if IWC has a comprehensive, consistent and thorough pre-employment background investigation process, the probability of hiring untrustworthy people will be reduced. Moreover, incidents of workplace violence that can lead to legal action against IWC should also be reduced.

If no such process is in place at IWC, it cannot demonstrate that reasonable steps were taken to maintain a safe and secure work environment. One reasonable step is to have a process that tries to ensure that only the most trustworthy people are hired as employees. This requires an evaluation of all prospective new hires, which consists of gathering relevant information, assessing that information in the context of how it relates to the specific job and the needs of IWC, and making a judgment to hire or not hire.

Having a pre-employment background investigation process improves the odds that only trustworthy people will be hired. However, it can also be problematic. In certain types of environments, the pool of potential candidates may be small. High-technology positions or positions that require highly skilled workers already have a limited pool of potential candidates. Adding a screening process to filter out the potentially untrustworthy candidates reduces this pool even further. Generally, this will not make the hiring manager or the staffing person in the human resources organization happy since it will cause them to do more work in developing a larger pool of candidates. In the bigger picture, screening out potentially untrustworthy employees is always worth the inconvenience and effort. It's like the old commercial says, "Pay me now or pay me later."

BASICS OF PRE-EMPLOYMENT CHECKS

The pre-employment background investigation process is meant to augment other screening methods. All pre-hire interviews, either with the hiring manager or the human resources staff, are opportunities to look for indicators of untrustworthiness. Generally, conducting the background investigation provides additional information to support the hiring decision.

WHAT ARE PRE-EMPLOYMENT BACKGROUND INVESTIGATIONS?

Pre-employment background investigations are investigations conducted to gather necessary background information on a potential employment candidate or contract labor person. These investigations can be conducted directly by the hiring company, or by a contract with a service provider. The information is then used to assist management, human resources and the CSO's security managers in making an assessment as to the trustworthiness of the potential candidate and then making a determination to hire or not hire.

> *Pre-employment background investigations are part of the overall evaluation process for future employees.*

Background investigations are sometimes necessary for current employees. At IWC, this need usually occurs as a result of a promotion opportunity or a significant change in responsibility. For example, at IWC, a person being promoted to the position of Chief Financial Officer should be subject to a background investigation with a particular emphasis on the individual's financial condition.

PRE-EMPLOYMENT AND BACKGROUND INVESTIGATIONS DRIVERS AND FLOWCHARTS

As with each security function, the security drivers should first be identified. Why have the functions at all? If it is found to be a necessary function, then the next question should be, "Why do it the way we are doing it?" And please don't ever accept an answer from anyone who says, "We've always done it this way." If you hear that reply, you have almost a guaranteed certainty that no one has ever looked into the process in any detail to see if it is being performed as effectively and efficiently as possible.

The overall security driver is of course, the need to protect the assets of the IWC owners—the stockholders—as required by laws, regulations and owner expectations. By screening potential employees and hiring only the most suitable persons, the risk to IWC assets should be decreased—at least that is the theory. However, neither process nor person is perfect, but one does the best one can. It is much better than not screening potential employees.

If you are the CSO or other security professional responsible for a security organization or function, regardless of how long you have been in the security business, never, and we mean never, accept that a particular function must be performed, unless it is backed up by valid security drivers. Once that is established, the next task for the CSO is to do what?

If you answered "Develop a personnel security functional flowchart," you are absolutely—wrong. The next step is to establish a project and a project team with the objective of determining how best to perform this function in the most effective and efficient way.

Of course, the project "team" may consist of primarily one person; however, even that one person will need assistance from time to time. Once the project is activated and the security drivers specific to that function are documented and validated, then the next step would be to develop a personnel security flowchart or charts.

In this case, separate flowcharts are developed due to major differences between the two functions of investigations and workplace violence prevention. They are connected in some ways; for example, if an employee threatens to or actually performs acts of violence, one of the after-action tasks must be to determine how the individual made it through the pre-screening process (see Figures 8-2 and 8-3).

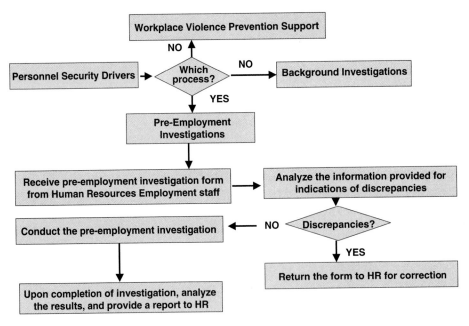

Figure 8-2   Example of the overall personnel security flowchart.

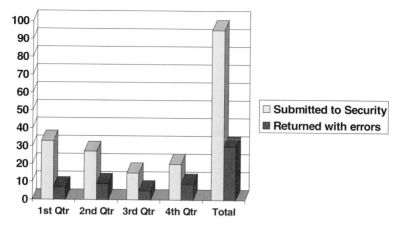

Figure 8-3 Example of a more detailed flowchart relative to the function of pre-employment and background investigations.

SAMPLE PRE-EMPLOYMENT AND BACKGROUND INVESTIGATIONS METRICS CHARTS

Based on the flowcharts, the CSO targeted several areas for security metrics management. This was done *not* to determine if the process was operating as effectively and efficiently as possible. That would be premature. Based on targeted areas identified by analyzing the process as shown in the flowcharts, the CSO wanted first to determine the quality of the process (how well it was being performed) and the number of background investigations being performed. This would size the statement of work. Furthermore, the CSO needed to understand what all of this was costing the company.

> *Before trying to make changes to a process with the goal of making it more effective and/or efficient, it is first necessary to have something to compare it with. The purpose of any measurement is to be able to use that metric as a point of comparison. That comparison may be against past performance (trend), or a comparison of output against money spent (efficiency). For example: doing the same amount of work from one year compared to another but at a lower cost. This suggests an improvement in efficiency.*

The first thing the CSO noticed on the flowchart was some prescreening forms that were filled out by the applicant and checked by the human resources (HR) employment office staff were sometimes returned by the security staff to HR due to errors, such as incomplete information, time gaps in applicant background (education and employment), or a failure to obtain the privacy waiver signature of the applicant, etc. (see Figure 8-4). This failure causes a delay in the start of the process. Implementing a quality check early in the process should prevent these errors and eliminate the interruption to the start of the process.

This simple tracking tool allows the security professional or process owner to immediately see a problem with the process. Continuing with this part of the process, what would you, the CSO, like to see as a follow-up chart?

Remember, your goal is to make this entire process as effective and efficient as possible. With that goal in mind, wouldn't it be nice to know how long it takes for the pre-employment form to be corrected and returned to personnel security for processing? Of

Pre-Employment Metrics Data

Date Received		
Name of HR sender		
Name of applicant		
Department		
Returned to HR-Errors	Yes	No
Identify Error		
Date Investigation Started		
Date Investigation Completed		
Derogatory Information	Yes	No
Returned to HR		

Figure 8-4   The number of pre-employment forms submitted to the personnel security staff and those that were returned for corrections.

course it would, and why is that important? It is important because the potential employee has been identified and the longer it takes to process the pre-employment investigation the longer it may take to get that applicant on-board with IWC as an employee. This delay translates to work not being done and the organization being less productive.

It may very well be that others are required to take up the workload due to a shortage of staff, which in the long run adversely affects employee morale. Poor employee morale is one of many conditions adversely affecting employee productivity. Add the problem of increased workload leading to additional errors, and the problem becomes worse.

What does all this mean? The cascading effect of the lack of quality control in properly completing the forms—"doing it right the first time"—can be very costly (see Figure 8-5).

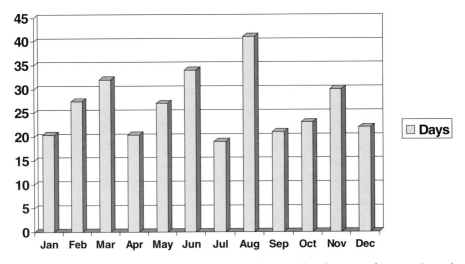

Figure 8-5   The average turn-around time of improperly completed pre-employment investigations forms.

Once you identified this problem, you may want to identify the costs associated with it. For example, determine the starting salary of the new employee and multiply that by the number of days the form is delayed in the process. That will provide an estimated cost in productivity loss for that new employee, assuming the person was hired based on an investigation indicating no employment-related issues.

You may think that is stretching this thought process a little, but it really isn't. That is because IWC needs this employee to work as soon as possible and is willing to pay a certain wage for the productivity of that employee. So, it makes sense to address the issue from this point of view.

One can also take this analysis further and interview personnel in the organization to which the new employee would be assigned and determine how they are meeting their goals without this or several new employees. However, that may be far too time-consuming (and only provide a greater level understanding of an already known problem) and at this point in the security metrics management application to this issue, it is unnecessary since the primary goal is not the impact on the other employees but eventually providing a more efficient and effective process.

So, as the CSO monitoring these metrics, what would you do to correct the problem, or at least get the rejection numbers lowered?

You can go to your boss, the vice president, HR, and explain the issue. However, is that really necessary at this point? Were you not hired to solve problems like this yourself? Part of your role as the CSO it to identify problems and find solutions. The best course of action is to meet with the HR manager responsible for that part of the process and explain the problem. When doing so, do not come across as complaining but as one who says that "we" have a problem. Explain the problem using your security metrics charts and then propose a solution. Why should you propose a solution? Because you own this problem, as this process is in place as part of the CAPP and you are responsible for leading the CAPP and that means all its policies, procedures, plans and processes. The HR manager is just following IWC and CAPP policies by being part of the pre-employment investigative process.

The problem, according to the HR manager, may be that there are several new employees involved in this process and they are learning on the job. However, it may very well be that they are understaffed so the three people handling all these applications instead of the usual five are overworked and producing lower quality results. As the CSO, you may not want to ask the HR manager why more HR specialists are not hired. The reply may be that they are awaiting the completion of the pre-employment investigation! What would be your proposed solution?

The immediate solution may be to hold a training class for all personnel involved in the process. The pre-employment investigation form could be reviewed, explained and discussed step-by-step or even revised. The HR and security personnel involved would also get to know each other better and identify where the people working the process see issues. Parts of the form may be vague and they may agree that some changes to the form would be helpful. Also, they may be able to change their daily approach to problem solving by engaging others working on the process in a productive way (a phone call from the personnel security specialist would help speed up the process instead of just mailing the form back to HR with a form letter on top saying why it is being returned).

Once any form changes were completed and the training session completed, would you drop the security metrics management of this process? As the CSO, you would not want to eliminate this metrics because it is important to see if the problems identified and allegedly corrected are in fact the systemic problems that caused the process to be ineffective in the first place. Moreover, the process needs to be monitored to determine if the changes made were effective and what is the cost of the process.

Keep in mind, the purpose of measuring any process is to have a means of evaluating the performance of that process. Knowing about a problem or change early will lead to early corrective action, thereby reducing the amount of lost time and money.

One important aspect of this issue has not been discussed and that is, how do you collect the data to begin with? The data should be collected where the problem was identified, In this case, it would be collected by the personnel security staff that check the form and begin the pre-employment investigative process.

So, once the "data collectors" are identified, how is the data to be collected? The easiest way is to use a manual log or computerized database or spreadsheet. Using a database or spreadsheet to input the data may work the best, as that may make it easier to compile the data for analyses and also for making out metrics charts to show that compiled data in a meaningful format for analyses and briefings.

As the CSO, what data would you like to have collected? Well, in order to provide the data that will serve the most good for targeting the problem, the data collected should at a minimum be:

- Time delays in processing the forms
- Persons involved in the process (to identify those making the errors as candidates for additional training)
- Name of the applicant
- Future organization of the employment applicant to determine which departments are most affected. Possibly their needs might be prioritized as far as which investigations get done first (see Figure 8-4). Figure 8-4 is an example of a spreadsheet that can be used to track the receipt and status of all pre-employment investigations (see also Figure 8-6).

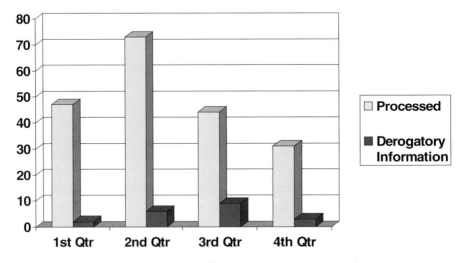

Figure 8-6 Comparison of the total number of investigations with those where derogatory information was produced.

Using this spreadsheet, data such as average dates of processing time within the personnel security department, number of requests processed, how many from each department, whether or not derogatory information was found, and so forth, can all be compiled, analyzed, charted, and reported from this one form. It can also be used to identify the costs of this entire process, as well as portions of the process.

Key Process: *Pre-employment investigations*
Product or Performance-to-Target Metric: *Percent of investigations completed within the established time frame.*
Predictive or Process Metric: *Cycle time (trend analysis; goal is decreasing cycle time).*

This metric allows for the development of an average expectation of the percent of investigations that produce derogatory information about a potential candidate. This metric will be useful to view as a trend. If it changes significantly, it may indicate the applicant pool needs to be reviewed or changed. It may also lead to further analysis. As the CSO, what other relevant metrics would you like to have available?

Once the data is collected on the time it takes to conduct a pre-employment investigation (from the time the correct pre-employment investigation form is received by the personnel security office staff to the time the investigation is completed and the results forwarded to the HR staff—the total time spent conducting the investigation) and reporting the finding cannot only be tracked but the time spent by the personnel security staff can be converted to costs (see Figure 8-7). In addition, the data collection should be in such detail as to track all the tasks associated with that process:

- Time it takes from receipt of the form to the time it is assigned to an investigator.
- The time it takes the investigator to conduct the investigation.
- From the time the investigation is completed until the time the report is produced.
- From the time the report is produced until the time it leaves the personnel security office.
- From the time it leaves the personnel security office to the time it reaches HR.

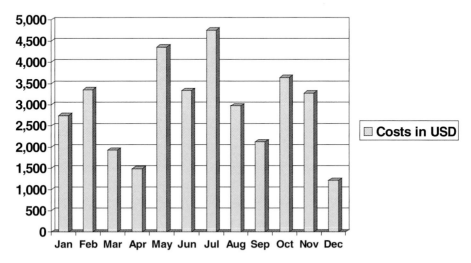

Figure 8-7   One example of the use of metrics to chart the costs of an investigation throughout the process. Depending upon your specific needs, other metrics may be useful.

NOTE: Each detailed step in the process can also be equated to time spent and all time spent can be converted into costs.

As the IWC CSO, can you identify other security metrics management data showing costs that you would like to have charted for analyses and executive management briefings?

Here are examples of other costs that could be identified for further analyses and use in analyzing the process and identifying more efficient and effective pre-employment investigative methods and measures:

- Average cost for each investigation.
- Individual total costs for completing each standard investigative step, e.g., credit bureau check, reference interviews, public database check, etc.
- Average costs for completing each standard investigative step, e.g., credit bureau check, reference interviews, public database check, etc.
- Average cost (time and USD) of the personnel security staff effort in the total process of an investigation.
- Total costs (time and USD) of the personnel security staff effort in the total process of an investigation.
- Average costs (time and USD) for each detailed step in the pre-employment investigative process.
- Total costs (time and USD) for each detailed step in the pre-employment investigative process.

Each of the steps in the process could be identified in a detailed flowchart and subject to further analysis to include measurement. The reason is that each step in the process could be made more efficient. For example: The investigator conducts the checks required, makes notes accordingly, and when investigative work is complete, prepares a final report of the results of the investigation. Suppose that the investigator used a digital recorder for use on the road when conducting the investigation and also had a voice recognition software program on the office computer.

The investigator could dictate the results into the recorder and, through the USB port, have it downloaded to the office computer and automatically typed. In addition, using the computer microphone, the investigator could also dictate the investigative results as the investigation was progressing. This would also be automatically typed—without mistakes and with the potential for greater speed and accuracy. This is an example of using technology—information technology—to produce a better and more efficient process.

This method may be cost-beneficial by shortening the time it took to conduct and report the investigative results back to HR. However, this is a possible solution that should only be considered as part of a project plan to identify and analyze the time spent conducting investigations. The reason that this should not be prematurely considered is that you may not have examined all aspects of this process in sufficient detail and prematurely identified the problem; however, it may have been more of a symptom and not the systemic problem. You would have implemented a solution costing a considerable sum of money to purchase the software and hardware and train the staff, only to find out that the time it took to conduct the investigations and report the findings were the same or on average may have taken longer.

It is not uncommon for project teams to look for quick solutions, using technology, but end up with a costly change producing little or no improvement.

> *Understand the process and its weaknesses before making changes.*

We want you to avoid that unwanted condition of "getting your daily exercise by jumping to conclusions." This may be such a case, so caution is warranted.

WORKPLACE VIOLENCE

Workplace violence can be perpetrated by employees, visitors, customers or those who choose to engage in criminal behavior. A situation where two employees engage in a fist-fight in the IWC parking lot is also an act of workplace violence. Workplace violence is not limited to acts of physical violence alone. Threats of violence or the fear that one may be subjected to violence is a form of workplace violence. A threatening environment can be just as disruptive and damaging as any acts of physical violence. Conditions that create an environment of fear can be as damaging to the workforce and individuals as actual acts of physical violence.

> *The American Heritage Dictionary*[1] *defines* violence *in the following way: 1) Physical force exerted for the purpose of violating, damaging, or abusing. 2) An act or instance of violent action or behavior. 4) The abusive or unjust exercise of power; an outrage; a wrong. 6) Vehemence of feeling or expression; fervor; fanaticism.*

Employees have a right to work under conditions free from the threat of workplace violence. That is to say, employees have the right to work in a safe environment. IWC therefore has an obligation to provide a safe and secure workplace for its employees. Furthermore, it is to IWC's advantage to provide a safe and secure work environment. Disruptions from the threat of violence or from actual physical violence adversely affects the productivity of the workforce. In any event, nothing good comes from workplace violence. Therefore, any conditions or behavior that creates an abusive or violent environment must be prohibited.

As part of providing a safe workplace for employees and visitors and maintaining compliance with applicable government laws and regulations, IWC has a policy concerning the prevention of workplace violence. The foundation of this policy is a zero tolerance position. Any threats or acts of violence against employees or visitors will not be tolerated. Any violation of this policy will lead to the termination of employment for the violator. IWC management is committed to furnishing a work environment that is free of acts of violence, the threat of violence, or employee intimidation. Moreover, they must act when incidents of workplace violence occur.

To best achieve this workplace violence-free condition, a workplace violence prevention program should be developed, implemented and monitored. Paramount for this program is the following:

- Protection of employees
- Protection of customers, visitors and suppliers
- Prevention of business disruption
- Preservation of the good company reputation

---

[1]   Morris, William, Editor, *The American Heritage Dictionary of the English Language.* (Boston, Massachusetts: Houghton Mifflin Company, 1981), p. 1431.

Although the odds of occurrence of acts of workplace violence are low, the greatest threat comes from current employees. Having a security awareness training program for the prevention of workplace violence along with an effective pre-employment background investigation process helps to create an environment where employees are less likely to engage in acts of workplace violence. Moreover, having an intervention strategy, focused on identifying potential problems and interceding where and when necessary, can keep incidents of workplace at a nonexistent level, or at least to an absolute minimum.

Part of an intervention strategy used at IWC is the use of Employee Assistance Programs (EAP). EAP are designed to support employees with problems or experiencing adverse conditions. Employee performance may decline due to a crisis situation, emotional stress, untreated personnel problem, or a medical problem, such as alcoholism or drug dependency. Such problems can often be prevented or treated successfully through education, training, and supportive intervention. If left untreated, these problems have the potential of manifesting into larger problems or situations of potential or actual workplace violence. At IWC, an EAP was established to help meet the needs of employees experiencing any of the prior stated conditions. An EAP program will go a long way in serving to prevent workplace violence

WORKPLACE VIOLENCE PREVENTION PROGRAM

Having a workplace violence prevention program (WPVPP) in place helped mitigate the situation. The following are elements of a sound and effective WPVPP and should be incorporated into a CAPP:

* *Policy*—Have a zero tolerance policy on threats or acts of violence in the workplace. In other words, threats of violence or acts of violence should result in disciplinary action up to and including termination of employment.
* *Pre-employment background investigation process*—Having a process in place ensures some level of screening occurs prior to hiring, thereby reducing the chances of hiring potentially violent people.
* *Grievance procedures*—Having a formal grievance process for all employees to use allows for employees to be heard. Often, employees are only looking for the chance to have their issue or perspective heard and be assured that management will address issues promptly and fairly.
* *Conduct formal and recurring training*—In workplace violence prevention methods for all management and employees including newly hired personnel. This will create a company-wide consciousness and individual awareness.
* *Employee Assistance Program*—Offer employees a discreet and confidential means of receiving guidance or counseling on dealing with serious personal problems.
* *Out-placement Services*—When employees are forced to leave the company through lay-off or restructuring, having an out-placement service available to them can make the transition easier and less stressful.

As the CSO at IWC, you are interested in using security metrics management techniques to determine not only the costs of the IWC WPVPP (at least the costs to the security department), but also the costs of violence in the IWC workplace in terms of lawsuits, lost productivity due to disruptions in the workforce, the time it takes for additional training following an incident, and the cost of an employee being terminated and cost of hiring a new employee. Workplace violence incidents have an adverse impact on any company in many different ways.

In the effort to better understand the effectiveness of a WPVPP, what types of data would you collect and what measures would you use to help you better understand the process and be able to do analysis work?

- What data is needed?
- What do you want to know?
- How often would the data be collected?
- Who would collect the data?
- When would they collect the data?
- Where in the process should the data be collected?
- How is the data to be compiled and reported?

Since workplace violence is often a product of a hostile, unsafe or unfair work environment, identifying the various indicators of a hostile, unsafe or unfair workplace is the best place to start.[2]

Assessing the condition of the workplace can be accomplished by conducting workplace climate surveys. The CSO must work with HR to develop and administer such a survey. How employees respond to questions related to fairness (usually in terms of how they are treated by management and other employees) workplace safety, and working conditions, will produce enough information to make a determination of the general conditions of the workplace. Should there be negative indicators developed during the survey, senior management must be engaged and a plan developed to address the identified issues and change the negative workplace climate.

The most obvious measure for assessing the effectiveness of workplace violence prevention is by measuring the number of incidents. This analysis can be taken further by measuring the number of averted incidents through use of a referral to EAP process. When management and employees are sufficiently trained to recognize indicators in behavior as having the potential for violence and they intervene during the early stages of behavior change, it can be assumed that a potential WPV situation was averted. As complicated as this may sound, the CSO working with HR and EAP professionals should be able to develop a training program for managers and employees and a means of measuring the effectiveness of a referral process in terms of WPV prevention.

CASE STUDY

The IWC CSO was concerned with the security department's share of the costs of the WPVPP when he found out that this was a recently started program brought on by an assault incident when an employee subjected to a layoff, as a result of a reduction in force, acted out violently. The employee later sued not only for wrongful discharge but also because IWC had not prepared him for such an event and if it had, he never would have assaulted his boss. The employee believed that IWC did nothing to assist the employee in the transition from IWC to another job opportunity. In essence, the employee claimed there was no support structure in place to assist employees affected by work force reductions.

As the IWC CSO, do you think the workplace environment was as good as it could be during this difficult period? Could IWC have taken actions to mitigate the pain and

---

[2] Remember to identify the drivers and flowchart the security-owned processes prior to getting into data collection.

suffering experienced by employees being terminated? Perhaps the affected employee felt mistreated, with dignity damaged and resentment of the perceived callous attitude on the part of the company so, under frustrating circumstances, lashed out.

Ater this incident, IWC's executive management immediately wanted a total program review to assess the workplace environment and determine what needed to be done to improve IWC's ability to prevent incidents of WPV. Naturally, this effort will cost time and money.

Although the CSO understood the need and the urgency, budget was a factor. Therefore, the CSO implemented a project to identify and track the security department's costs so that during the next budget cycle, the CSO could use the security metrics management program and its associated metrics charts to justify the new security budget. Of course, the metrics charts relative to the WPVPP would be included.

Beginning with a high-level flowchart (see Figure 8-8), the CSO's analysis concluded that for several key targeted areas, metrics compilation and charting would be completed in time for the new budget talks in approximately six months (see Figures 8-9 through 8-11).

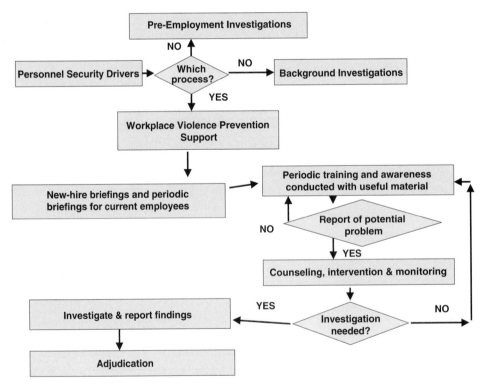

Figure 8-8   High-level flowchart of IWC's overall WPVPP.

However, not waiting for the budget talks, the CSO took a look at the requirements and then talked to the manager responsible for the new-hire orientation. They reached agreement that the security briefer would train several of the HR personnel who were responsible for providing other briefings during the new-hire orientation day, as well as provide them pamphlets on the WPVPP and the briefing slides that were used by the security briefer. HR would then do the security orientation briefing, including the WPVPP.

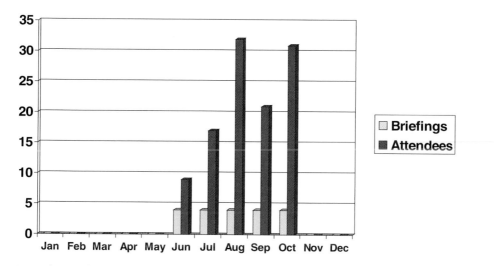

Figure 8-9 The number of new hire WPVPP briefings held per month and the number of attendees.

The security department thus saves the one-hour briefing time per week, as well as the prep time and time needed to get to the briefing room, a total of two hours per week. This savings was calculated as: two hours per week × 50 weeks a year = 100 hours a year of time saved and at $20 per hour including benefits = $2000 USD. Yes, this may be considered a transfer of costs and not a savings per se, but it does help the CSO and still gets the job done.

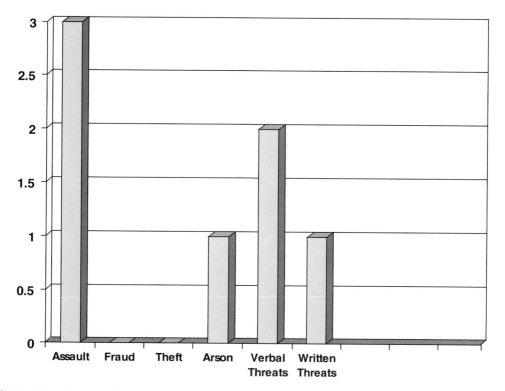

Figure 8-10 The type of workplace violence investigations conducted.

This metrics chart shows what type of workplace violence incidents may be occurring. This will help direct the intervention and training program for WPVPP to emphasize those areas which may help minimize the probability for such incidents. Furthermore, IWC managers could be further briefed on what indicators to be alert for in any employee that may be indicative of such contact so that it could be prevented through intervention by management with the employee before escalation. Prevention is the key.

Follow-up metrics would include one showing the time spent per investigation. Another would show the action taken by HR based on the investigative findings, as well as costs throughout the process.

Such a chart, as shown in Figure 8-11, is helpful as an indication of the workplace climate. Is there a trend developing? Are acts of hostility increasing? Is there a behavior change taking place in the workforce? All are questions that must be asked when the number of incidents or threat of incidents increases.

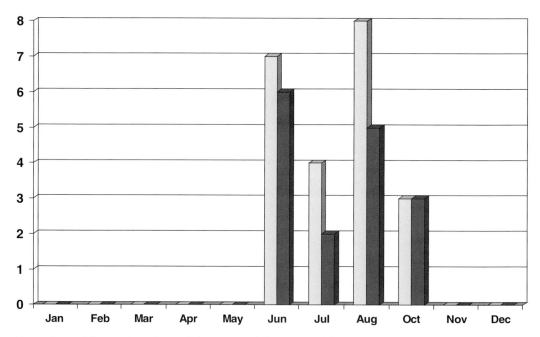

Figure 8-11 The number of complaints received that were valid and those that were not.

Regardless of the type of incident, an SMMP will assist in determining changes and trends. In addition—and somewhat of an unfortunate reality—the security investigators can prepare for the additional workload.

SUMMARY

Under administrative security is the function of personnel security. Personnel security has two primary functions: Pre-employment and background investigations, and workplace violence prevention program support.

Using security metrics management, the effectiveness of both programs can be assessed. Moreover, the cost of preventive measures can be measured, as well as the consequences of having and not having effective preventive measures in place.

Chapter 9

Security Education and Awareness Training

This chapter will discuss the security education and awareness training program (SEATP) security function and the process of using a security metrics management program (SMMP) to measure and manage its costs, benefits, successes and failures.

INTRODUCTION

The SEATP mission is to ensure all IWC employees and support personnel (e.g., in-house contractors, suppliers, and partners) are aware of their responsibilities to protect IWC assets. Another objective of the SEATP is to teach them how to protect those assets. Through periodic security briefings, reinforced with the development and distribution of security awareness materials, the Chief Security Officer (CSO) must continue to work to raise the level of security consciousness within IWC.

In addition, the IWC CSO has charged the security staff supporting the SEATP to manage this function as efficiently and effectively as possible. This includes ensuring the security staff is well prepared to develop and deliver security training materials specific to the needs of IWC. However, for our purposes in this chapter, we will concentrate on the two functions, security awareness and how to protect assets.

Once all the administrative security tasks, such as policies, procedures, plans and processes, are in place, those that are expected to comply with them must know about them. After all, they would be useless if IWC employees and other personnel did not know that these policies, procedures, plans and processes even existed or what the employees and others need to do to comply with them.

The entire IWC corporate assets protection program (CAPP) consists of security or assets protection "layers." One of the "foundation" layers is employee vigilance and understanding as to how to protect corporate assets. That understanding and hopefully the motivation to protect corporate assets are learned and developed through the use of SEATP tools (briefings, videos, pamphlets and other security training and awareness material).

> *What is "education"? Basically, we are talking about acquiring information and knowledge through some form of teaching and learning experience.*

The SEATP is used to make the IWC employees aware of explicit assets protection policies, procedures and how to comply with them. The objective, of course, is for everyone at IWC to protect corporate assets, supported by the employees having a clear awareness as to why and how to properly protect the IWC assets.

The IWC SEATP is based on effective communications (see Figure 9-1) with constant feedback, supported by measurement (SMMP), to determine if the SEATP is meeting its established goal of lowering assets' threats, vulnerabilities, risks and losses through an informed and supportive IWC employees and a robust CAPP.

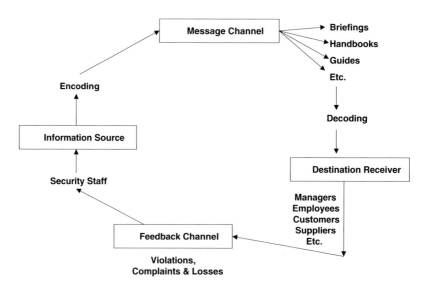

Figure 9-1   A basic SEATP communications feedback loop.

SEATP ORGANIZATION

The SEATP is one of the primary functions performed under the administrative security organization. It is a crucial security function and it makes sense that it should be a function of the International Widget Corporation's (IWC) administrative security organization (see Figure 9-2).

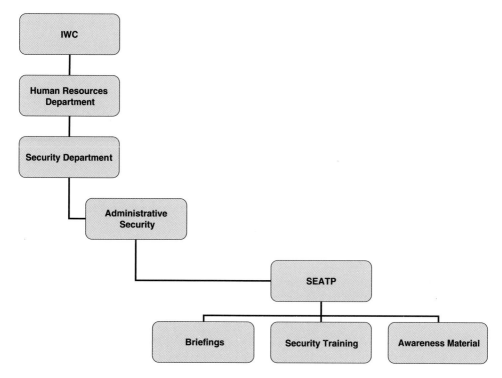

Figure 9-2 The SEATP in relationship to other security functions.

SEATP DRIVERS AND FLOWCHARTS

United States' court decisions have shown that, if a corporation does not adequately protect its assets *and* the employees don't know and understand their responsibilities relative to the protection of those assets, it is highly unlikely that a corporation will have a successful lawsuit against an employee for such things as theft of corporate property. If a complaint is accepted and the employee is prosecuted, the judge is likely to find that, if the employee was unaware of "the rules," how could the employee be expected to follow them? In addition, judges have ruled that if a corporation does not do a proper job of protecting its assets, it should not rely on the court to do it for them.

After gathering the information needed, one first has to look at security drivers, specifically the drivers for any corporation, in this case IWC, to protect assets. In other words, why is a SEATP needed in the first place? The security drivers identified are:

- Need to comply with federal, state, and local laws, and government regulations
- Comply with the laws of the nation-states where IWC does business
- Comply with IWC internal policies, procedures and directives
- Comply with contractual requirements related to IWC assets used by others and the use of others' assets by IWC
- Loss of IWC's valuable assets would adversely impact IWC's ability to successfully compete in the global marketplace

Based on the drivers, the SEATP was developed (see Figure 9-3).

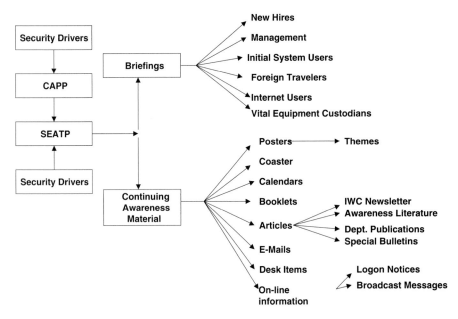

Figure 9-3 High-level flowchart of the SEATP function and tasks. It also depicts the scope of education and awareness tool developed and used to educate employees and create a higher level of security consciousness.

SEATP METRICS

How does a CSO really know the impact of a SEATP on the company? Is the SEATP effective? To learn this, it will be necessary to measure the program in some way.

There must be measures put in place to track the costs, benefits, cause and effects of a SEATP on the protection of IWC assets, as well as the time spent (potential productivity loss) by employees because they spend time attending training or awareness sessions that take them away from doing the "hands-on" job they were hired to do.

Every lost hour (time not spent producing goods or services of the corporation) by workers has an adverse impact on total productivity, and thus profits. If the SEATP adversely affects the productivity of workers, it must be able to demonstrate how it contributes to the protection of company assets, offsetting that loss of productivity—in essence, it must justify itself. Security metrics management program (SMMP) techniques can assist in doing that.

One of the SEATP goals is to provide all briefings and training required to all applicable employees. The goal is, at the end of the year, to have reached 100% of the employees and support personnel. The effectiveness of training is measured by the correlation analysis of hours of training/employee at each site to all applicable assets protection policies and procedures at each location (measures effectiveness of training). The goal is a positive downward trend of the loss (theft, damage, or destruction, etc.) of corporate assets. A reduction of security violations throughout the corporation is another potential indicator of success.

Each of the subfunctions and their products' development processes should be analyzed to determine their costs in terms of labor and materials. A useful tool to begin to accomplish this is— hopefully you guessed it—to flowchart the process.[1] In that way, each step in that process can be understood in the necessary detail to help determine its value. This will assist the CSO in developing an understanding of the real costs involved in the development of security products and assess the cost-benefits of each part of the SEATP. For example:

- What is the cost and benefit of developing and distributing awareness material such as posters displayed throughout the company containing a security message?
- Do the use of these and other SEATP products cause the employees to better protect the IWC assets?
- If not, what other purpose do they serve?
- Are they just a "nice-to-have" item with no visible return on investments? If so, eliminate them.

An SMMP will help the CSO make this determination. In times of corporate frugality, such products may be seen as too expensive and the CSO, when placing much reliance on them, may be looked upon as not understanding the business world of costs and profits. After all, a good business person must be able to demonstrate a return on investment. Using the tested measurement process, the CSO can demonstrate the value of the program. If the program has little value, the CSO must change or eliminate it. If the program demonstrated more of a benefit than it costs, the CSO should continue the program but also continue to strive to make it more effective and efficient.

Other considerations for the CSO include the effectiveness of the employee awareness briefings. Are they being accomplished cost-effectively? Are the security specialists conducting the briefings doing them for large audiences and thereby operating more cost-effectively by providing fewer briefings? By providing fewer briefings for more attendees per session, the security specialist frees up some of his or her time. That is time that can be used to perform other duties, contributing to the security program in other ways or making up for a shortage of security resources in other areas.

SAMPLE SEATP METRICS CHARTS

As with all security functions, there are numerous types and formats of data collection methods and chart development processes to support a CSO's assets protection analyses and decision-making processes. The following are a few examples of such SMMP-related charts.

Looking at the data in the sample charts below, what questions might the CSO ask? Should there be concern about the uneven distribution of work between most months? Could there be a better way to deliver security awareness briefings? For instance, could there be a more efficient approach?

Graphic depictions of data should tell a story. They should also cause the viewer, in this case the IWC CSO, to see patterns, trends or anomalies leading to questions about how this work can be accomplished more efficiently.

---

[1] Remember all initial establishments of a functional or subfunctional SMMP should be through a project plan to ensure an organized, formal way of working this issue.

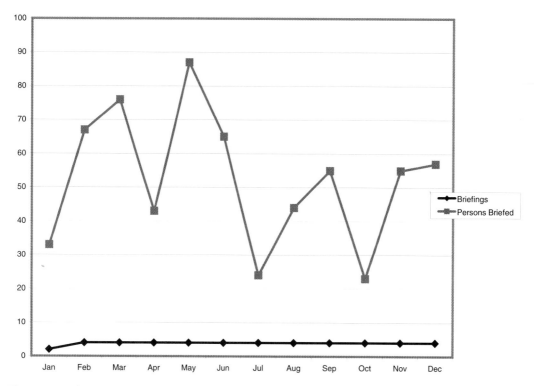

Figure 9-4   The number of persons briefed and the number of briefings conducted each month over a period of one year.

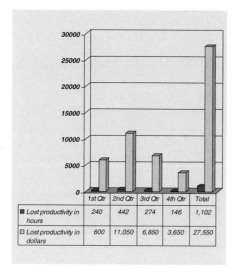

- The FW&A briefing project was launched per CEO direction based on new federal law requiring FW&A briefings to all employees within 90 days and annually thereafter. Proof of compliance must be available.

- During the first year of annual briefings all 551 IWC corporate employees were briefed. Similar briefings were held at all IWC U.S. locations.

- Total cost in lost productivity to IWC Corporate Office was $44,300 for one year.

- Productivity lost based on one hour briefing, one hour round trip to briefing site and back, and average IWC wage with benefits of $50.00 per hour.

Figure 9-5   The cost of briefing employees in terms of lost productivity for Fraud Waste & Abuse (FW&A) briefings.

In this case, the briefings are conducted in order for IWC to come into compliance with federal law. There are many reasons to use the briefing process to increase employee awareness. In all cases there is a cost. However, that cost may be offset by adverse consequences. In this example, the consequence would be not complying with federal law. Consequences differ from situation to situation and requirement to requirement. How each is handled is very much related to how much risk management is willing to accept.

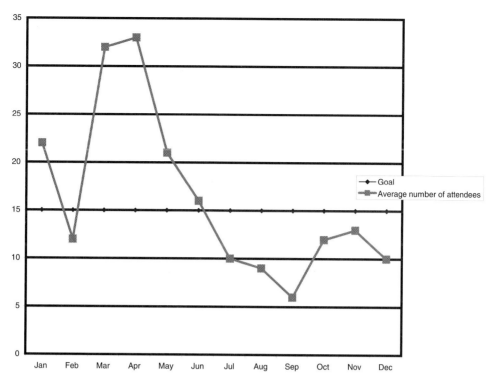

Figure 9-6   The actual number of people who attended briefing sessions as compared with the target number or goal.

Figure 9-6 allows the CSO to see how close actual performance came to the goal. Measuring actual performance to established goals is essential. What would be the purpose of having goals if achieving them is not measured and determined to be successfully accomplished?

Figure 9-7 shows the results of another metric which relates SEATP to CAPP policy changes and increased assets protection, and "proving that an SEATP" is cost-effective.

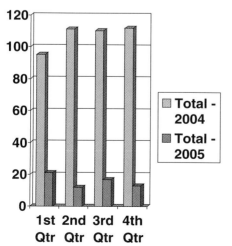

- High-value assets losses in 2004 to include cell phones, PDAs and notebook computers containing sensitive IWC information. None were recovered.
- In 2005, change in CAPP policy requiring employees' pay for items if negligence shown.
- Awareness briefings and materials modified to emphasize need to protect these assets and consequences of not protecting them.
- A downward trend in losses occurred as the result of an investment in awareness material and briefings. This action contributed to an overall savings as the cost of past losses was greater than the cost of awareness briefings.

Figure 9-7   How high-value loss briefings contributed to assets protection.

As shown by these basic metrics charts, one of the primary metrics that should be used to manage a SEATP is the relationship to costs and productivity losses of employees attending the briefings, as well as the success of a CAPP or portion thereof.

It is important for the CSO to know how much it costs to develop and provide security awareness briefings, and what the impact is to company productivity, as well as assets protection. Furthermore, the CSO needs to be thinking about how effective those briefings are. Did employee awareness increase? If so, how do you know? One potential metric is to track the number of security violations committed and compare that to the number of persons briefed. If all company employees were briefed on their security responsibilities, did the number of security violations decrease or increase?

DATA COLLECTION AND METRICS MANAGEMENT

Some of the questions that may be asked by a CSO or a CSO's staff responsible for the SEATP are:

Who should track the functional metrics input data? As with all security functions, the tracking of the data should be done by the person at the lowest level who is responsible for the day-to-day SEATP activity.

What to track? To begin with, all major tasks should be tracked and, gradually, data collected in more detail as one moves through the work breakdown structure of the SEATP. To start, the tracking and data collection should be basic. The number of briefings and number of attendees at those briefings and the associated costs will provide a baseline of information to work with; the type, number and costs of all awareness material, and the costs of meeting all requirements (remember the security drivers) mandated action (e.g., laws and regulations) will also help establish an SMMP baseline.

Why track it? First and foremost, it is difficult at best to manage what you don't know. Therefore, tracking data and measuring performance is essential to know the basics about a process and what it does. Any process of high cost or frequency must be tracked as it is likely to get much attention. Once these factors can be quantified and qualified, then the process of analysis can begin to determine more cost-effective ways of providing the SEATP service and support to the CAPP and thus IWC.

How to track it? It's actually a simple process. To begin with, the tracking of costs and lost productivity of workers can be accomplished by maintaining a record of attendees (having a sign-in log for those attending the briefings) and the amount of time each spent at the presentation. This can then be entered into a spreadsheet and the total time spent at the briefing can be calculated, as well as the average time spent by each employee. This time can then be added to the average time it takes for an employee to get to the briefing and return to work.Multiply that time by the average employee pay rate plus benefits and you will have the total time of lost productivity due to attending SEATP briefings.

Of course, the next thing to do would be to quantify the value of the briefings. This is a more difficult task. As the IWC CSO, how would you go about doing that? (See the case study, towards the end of this chapter.)

When to track it? The tracking of various data from the processes making up the SEATP can be done at different intervals beginning with each occurrence and compiled— monthly, weekly, bi-monthly, etc.—and should be done in a way consistent with your organizational needs. Again, the criteria that should be used are how often the data is needed for analyses along with special actions and follow-up for CSO assignments and projects. To keep the process as simple as possible, data collection should occur as often as briefings are conducted and as often as awareness materials are distributed.

For distributed awareness material, the cost in time and other resources should be collected as awareness materials are developed. Added to that would be the publication and distribution cost, including material, labor and other resources. So, for awareness material, the data would be collected at the end of each project. The total costs of all projects relative to the development of awareness materials would be summed on a monthly basis, again on a quarterly basis, and also on an annual basis; or, whatever your specific need happens to be.

> *The use of awareness material such as security calendars, pamphlets and brochures, and other related items is a common approach to enhancing security education efforts often used by corporations and government agencies. However, if they can't be qualified or quantified in terms of their value and benefits to the SEATP and ultimately to employee security consciousness and the protection of assets, then you should consider eliminating them. Using a tool for which the benefit cannot be derived is a luxury that can't be afforded in these times of global competition.*

Where to track it in the functional process? Each briefing's data would be collected at the end of each briefing, and entered into the spreadsheet or database. Each awareness material development, production and distribution would be collected at the end of the project for each awareness material project.

In analyzing these SEATP charts, the CSO can see if the ratio of attendees to briefings is cost-effective. Changes can be implemented on a trial basis to see if it has a positive impact, resulting in a more cost-effective briefing program. If so, excellent! If not, make another adjustment. The beauty of measurement is that it helps the CSO or security professional manage change, track results and continue to make positive adjustments in the process working toward the most effective and efficient processes possible.

Another measure the CSO can use is the cost of lost productivity, because each employee must attend an annual briefing in person, therefore they are not spending that time being productive (in terms of their normal assignment and responsibilities). Assume an average wage of $50 an hour per IWC employee, which includes benefits as a part of that average wage. Then assume that it takes about 30 minutes for each employee to shut down their work and go to the briefing location and another 30 minutes to get back to the office and return to their primary duties. That means if you multiply the number of attendees by $50, you can estimate the cost factor of the employee's "travel" time alone. Now factor in another hour each at $50 an hour for listening to the one-hour briefing.

> *Learning can be expensive. The most critical point is what you get for that "learning."*

Suppose that you, as the CSO, learn employee security awareness must be achieved to a minimum standard in order to ensure all employees understand their responsibility to protect corporation assets. Essentially, your security awareness briefings are now required by federal law. What does this mean to you?

The law requiring that the employees be made aware of their duties and responsibilities for IWC assets protection may be interpreted (here you want to get a representative of the legal staff to provide guidance to you, the CSO) to mean that a briefing can be through a simple distribution of a security awareness pamphlet or an online briefing where employees can acknowledge their responsibilities as they go through charts and take a simple test to demonstrate they have learned the basic information. Which to choose? Keep in mind, your goal should be to determine which is most efficient and effective.

By placing the briefing online, there are advantages. It can be rapidly updated and tied to security software—used to collect data—so the relevant data can be collected in a centralized database for later metrics analyses. Furthermore, the travel time is eliminated so a savings of $50 per employee per briefing can be claimed as a savings and increase the employees' productivity.[2]

There is of course the unknown factor and that is: By attending the briefings in any format, does that make the employees more aware of their assets protection responsibilities and are they then more apt to comply with the IWC CAPP and properly protect the IWC assets? If so, how do you know? One way to know is to look at the metrics of violations of the CAPP. (See Chapter 20 for more on this metric.)

SEATP CASE STUDY

The IWC CSO met with the security department's investigations manager who stated that there was an ongoing security problem in IWC. That problem is the theft of IWC's information technology's assets used by employees, specifically theft of notebook computers out of the vehicles of IWC employees when the employees were out on business trips. It became particularly problematic when it was discovered that many of these stolen notebooks contained sensitive IWC information, information that was in many cases considered to be competitive-sensitive. That is to say, if IWC competitors were to obtain that information, IWC could see their competitive advantage negatively affected.

As the CSO, what would be your plan of action to eliminate the thefts and losses of these valuable IWC assets and the information they contained?

Of course, you should know by now that this calls for action managed through a project plan. In this case, the project plan consisted of the following tasks[3]:

* Collect and analyze all investigative report data on the losses to include the usual who, how, where, when, why, and what (see Figure 9-8), using a spreadsheet format.
* Coordinate the results with the SEATP security specialist.

---

[2] We use the word "potential" here recognizing that, realistically, one can usually not count on a 100% productivity increase as one never knows what the employee will do before or after the briefing. However, it would be realistic to assume that time savings are cost savings and a gain in employees' productivity, e.g., they are available for working their primary duties instead of traveling to and from a briefing.

[3] Of course a more detailed list of tasks can and should be developed. This case study just shows an example of what would be included.

- Develop an IWC-wide communication (it may be as simple as a corporate-wide email notice) advising all employees of the problem and how to eliminate it.
- Update the new-hire and annual employees' CAPP briefings to emphasize the problem and solution.
- Update the CAPP policy to include a statement that all losses of notebooks and other valuable assets due to the employee being negligent in their duty to protect company assets would require them to pay for the loss (at least the equipment as its value is easily quantified) out of their salary, This will be an unpopular "pill to swallow" but it may get employee attention (of course, this must be coordinated with and approved by the legal and HR staffs). No employee would be authorized the use of a notebook computer or other assets, such as PDAs or cell phones, unless they signed a statement acknowledging their obligations to protect these valuable assets and having an understanding of the consequences. Failure to agree to such a practice will result in a restriction imposed on them to not remove any such assets from the facility.
- Develop and implement a useful security metric as a means of graphically depicting the future loss trends. Keep in mind that the goal is to drive down the number of losses and eliminate that asset protection problem. (See Figures 9-8 and 9-9.)

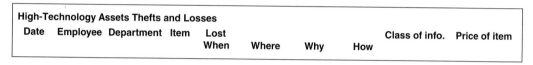

High-Technology Assets Thefts and Losses									
Date	Employee	Department	Item	Lost When	Where	Why	How	Class of info.	Price of item

Figure 9-8   The spreadsheet used to collect data. This spreadsheet method is a simple but effective way to collect data.

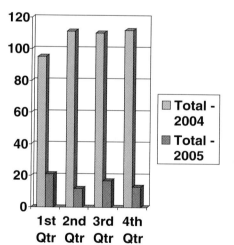

- High-technology assets losses in 2004 to include cell phones, PDAs and notebook computers containing sensitive IWC information. None were recovered.
- In 2005, change in CAPP policy requiring employees' pay for items if negligence shown.
- Awareness briefings and materials modified to emphasize need to protect these assets and consequences of not protecting them.
- A downward trend in losses resulted in a cost of awareness material of $327 and briefing change at a cost of $43 for $370 which contributed to a net saving of $37,872

Figure 9-9   Trend chart of notebook and other high-value information technology assets lost or stolen.

Assume you are the CSO and are to analyze the charts above and supporting data as well as provide a briefing to executive management personnel related to this problem. You must be prepared to clearly, convincingly and concisely present your "story." Your graphic depiction of security metrics will support you in doing this.

Always ensure that you have detailed charts and related documents to back up your overview charts and triple check them for accuracy, as any errors would detract from your reporting. Be sure you never present charts with inaccurate or inconsistent data. The integrity and quality of your charts are a reflection on you, the CSO. Bad charts equal a bad presentation with your message possibly being lost—or worse yet, not believed—at least in the minds of those subjected to your poor performance.

The metrics trend chart shown in Figure 9-9 should be followed by several other charts to include charts that show:

- Losses by items, e.g., notebooks, PDAs, cell phones
- Value of lost items
- Impact to IWC as a result of the item being lost or stolen
- Identify sources of losses, e.g., each department name

By depicting the losses by department, the CSO may generate a little competition between departments as they do their best to have the fewest losses in IWC. No one, particularly senior executives, wants to look bad in front of their peers or the CEO.

One way for a manager to eliminate the problem of lost high-value equipment may be to be sure that the losses are not reported (Gee, would a department manager actually not report a loss? Game the system? Yes!). However, this can be mitigated by regular assets inventories of certain types of high-value equipment.

SUMMARY

The SEATP is an important subfunction under the administrative security function. It is primarily responsible for awareness briefings, development and distribution of awareness material and also for administratively managing the security departments' security professionals' training program.

The SEATP costs in terms of lost productivity and the loss of other resources can be measured and should be measured using a security metrics management approach. In addition, it can be used to help eliminate a trend of assets losses by emphasizing the problem and solution through awareness materials and briefings monitored through metrics trend charts in conjunction with other protective measures.

Security metrics charts, such as the ratio of briefings to employees attending, lost productivity caused by attending briefings, costs and benefits of awareness materials, and cost-saving in terms of identifying assets protection loss trends and mitigating those losses through enhanced awareness materials and briefings, are the basis for a SEATP supported by an SMMP.

Chapter 10

Security Compliance Audits

This chapter will address the administrative security organization's security compliance audit (SCA) function and the process of using security metrics to measure and manage its costs, benefits, successes and failures.

INTRODUCTION

The SCA function is an integral part of the administrative security's organization. Some may see this as a conflict with the corporate audit function; however, while it may give that appearance to some, it actually complements the audit department's function, as regards assets protection compliance. They are two separate and distinct organizations, each with a different statement of work but using similar processes and sharing overall objectives.

SCA provides a look at compliance from the perspective of those who have an expertise in security regulations, policy, procedures, processes and practices. It is always useful to have a second "set of eyes" looking at how a security operation works.

> The "corporate audit" function traditionally focuses on compliance while the SCA's main focus is on ensuring that assets are properly protected, regardless of compliance with the CAPP.

Internal corporate audit teams generally do not have security professionals as permanent members of their team. Thus, the SCA serves a worthwhile function in the goal of protection of corporate assets.

SCA ORGANIZATION

The SCA organization is an integral security function under the administrative security organization.

While the corporate audit department is responsible for determining compliance with all of the corporation's policies, procedures and contractual agreements, and external regulations and laws, the emphasis and focus of the SCA, as alluded to earlier, is limited in scope to the protection of the corporate assets.

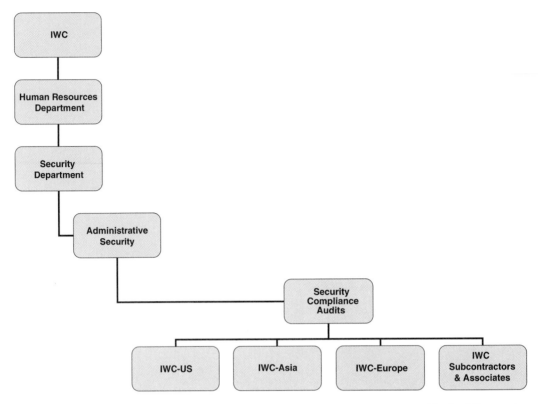

Figure 10-1   The organization chart of the administrative security organization with the SCA security function included. It provides a look at where this function may best fit within any security organization.

The SCA can be described as the security department's "internal audit" process. The SCA should focus on the following:

- Assessing whether or not assets protection regulations, policies and procedures are actually useful in supporting the protection of assets and, if so, are they not only effective but efficient
- Testing assets protection systems and processes to ensure they work as expected

Furthermore, the SCA process may be used to assess compliance of associated suppliers, subcontractors and partners that have access to sensitive proprietary assets of the corporation—in this case, those assets of the International Widget Corporation (IWC).

> *Like all other security functions, in order to begin an SMMP for this function, a list of drivers and the associated flowcharts must be developed.*

SCA DRIVERS AND FLOWCHARTS

The primary driver (see Figure 10-2) for this security function is the IWC corporate assets protection program (CAPP) itself. As we stated in earlier chapters, the CAPP is driven by the other security drivers, such as laws, regulations, IWC policies, procedures, contractual agreements, etc.

The CAPP drives the SCA function because the CAPP must be complied with by all IWC employees and associates according to their contracts. How does one know that each department and each employee in each department is complying with the CAPP and therefore fulfilling their obligation to protect IWC assets? The answer is that no one really knows unless someone checks to find out if everyone is complying with the CAPP; thus the need for the SCA function.

In addition, the SCA also tries to determine if the protections in place are actually protecting assets. For example, if the CAPP is being complied with, that does not necessarily mean that the assets are protected as they should be. There may be a flaw in the asset protection defenses. A proactive view—for example, testing attack methods against assets—is an SCA function to better determine the protection of assets regardless of policies, procedures and such in place.

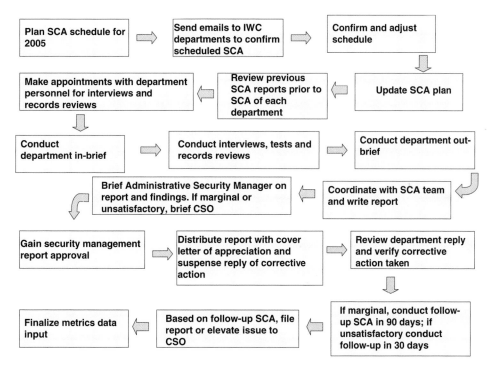

Figure 10-2 The workflow process of a portion of the SCA function, that of SCA inspection scheduling.

SCA METRICS

The SCA function, to be effectively and efficiently managed, requires that there be metrics in place to track performance. Measures such as the number and scope of security audits, project costs, resources used, and to the extent possible, benefits derived. Benefits derived are the positive attributes of the effort. For example, if during the SCA process it is determined that a portion of the CAPP is out of compliance with recent regulations, or operating ineffectively, there is value in discovering this condition and correcting it before there is a system failure or before an external agency discovers the problem or problems. Perhaps penalties can be averted by discovering and correcting problems before they reach a more severe level.

One of the SCA goals is to develop and maintain an annual schedule of all required security audits, tests and evaluations. This schedule should be published and distributed to affected parties. Moreover, it should be developed with input from all affected organizations. The goal is by the end of the year to successfully complete 100% of all scheduled SCAs. Another and maybe most inportant goal is to have IWC and all departments operating at a satisfactory level of compliance. This effort should prepare IWC for all external audits and help achieve a 100% satisfactory compliance condition. Operating out of compliance is a high-risk condition and the SCA process helps the CSO, and thus IWC, avoid that condition.

> *The primary effectiveness measure of the SCA's program occurs when all external auditing or inspecting agencies, after conducting an audit or inspection of IWC, and possibly the security department, at any or all locations, conclude the operations to be compliant. The achieved condition of compliance, along with measurable reductions in loss (or damage) of IWC assets are the real metrics on the effectiveness of the SCA.*

Of course, in terms of the SCA process itself and ensuring its effectiveness and efficiency, it is necessary to measure it. All SCA processes and products (security auditing processes, checklists, tests and evaluations, and reports) should be analyzed for efficiencies.

Using process flowcharts to understand how each works, tracking costs and use of resources will enable the CSO to better understand what it costs to manage and maintain an effective SCA. Moreover, measuring SCA performance allows the CSO to ask the questions, the answers to which will lead to a more effective performance. For example:

- Is there really a benefit to IWC in providing SCA tests and evaluations? In other words, are fewer assets vulnerable to theft or unauthorized destruction due to the process?
- Does the SCA produce value greater than it costs to maintain?
- Does the use of the SCA processes and products lead employees to better protect the IWC assets?
- If not, what other purposes do they serve?
- Are they (SCAs) a "nice-to-have" (producing little or negligible results) item with no visible return on investments?

An SMMP will help answer the above but also assist the CSO in making better management decisions. In times of corporate frugality, such a function may seem somewhat redundant when one considers the CAPP is subject to other audits—internal (corporate audit) and external (outside agencies such as those with regulatory authority over business and industry and those specifically engaged in a contractual relationship with IWC). However, if measurable results demonstrate the success of the SCA as a value-added security function, it will be harder to make a case that the SCA function should be eliminated.

Without measurable results, a great deal of pressure may be placed on the CSO to eliminate the SCA function because of using finite resources for an undefined or ill-defined result. That may also be used as the rationale by IWC executive management or others for eliminating the security function when the real reason is that the SCA reports have made them look bad due to their noncompliance with some portions of the CAPP as required.

Regardless, if the SCA is being done, it must be done as cost-effectively as possible. There may be other methods of implementing a SCA and therefore the following questions should be asked:

- Can such a function be done more efficiently by having each IWC department conduct a self-audit once a year?
- If so, what are the cost-benefits?
- Can they be done as effectively or is there a risk of the "fox watching the hen house"?

> *One key factor to always remember: when approaching such matters, the CSO should look at them with a holistic, or IWC-wide, approach. In this case, are costs in terms of resources used or productivity losses actually being reduced, or is there just a transfer of costs from one function or department to another?*

Whether a security audit is being accomplished by another internal department employee or an IWC security specialist, if the hours spent are roughly the same, then from an IWC viewpoint, the costs may be transferred from the security department to the other IWC department. However, although the costs in time and effort are the same, due to differing levels of expertise, there may be hidden costs buried in the quality of the effort. Someone with specific security expertise is more likely to understand the nuances of the security function and may be better able to identify problems than someone with little or no security (assets protection) experience.

SCA METRICS CHARTS—A SAMPLING

The following are examples of some of the macro-level security metrics, graphically depicted in charts that can be used to begin an evaluation of not only CAPP compliance but also the relative importance of the SCA function in terms of costs versus benefits.

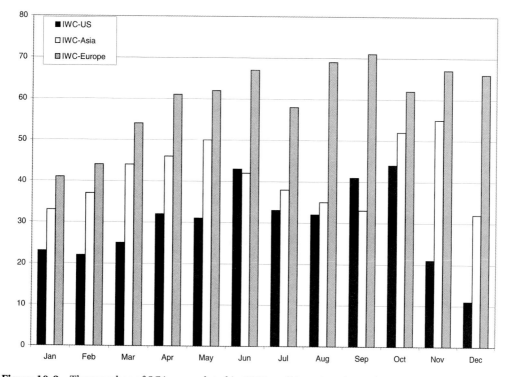

Figure 10-3   The number of SCAs completed in 2005 at all locations by region.

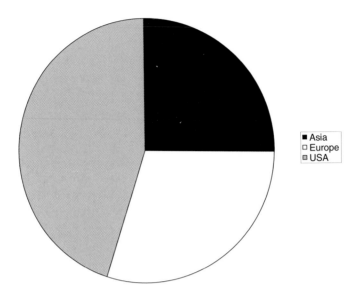

Figure 10-4   A pie chart indicating the ratio of the world-wide SCAs by region.

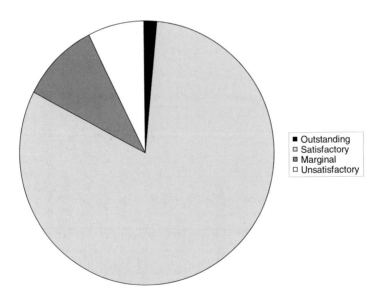

Figure 10-5   The SCA ratings over a year period.

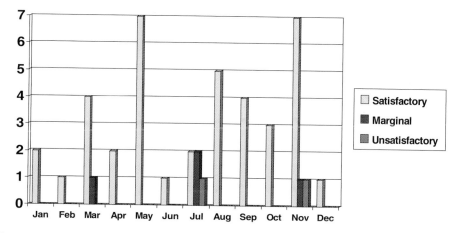

Figure 10-6   The SCA results ratings during 2005.

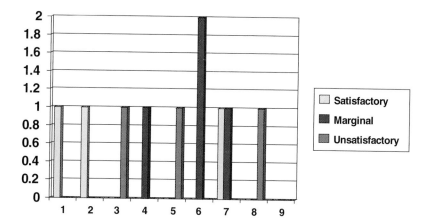

Figure 10-7   SCA findings by individual IWC departments.

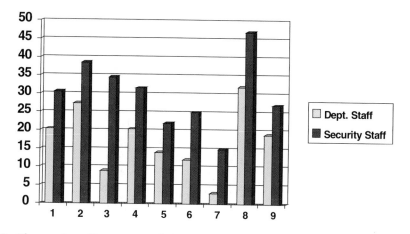

Figure 10-8   The number of hours expended in each department for the SCAs.

THE WHO, HOW, WHERE, WHEN, WHY AND WHAT OF SCA METRICS TRACKING

As with all other security functions, where security metrics management techniques are applied, the CSO must determine who performs what data collection and tracking task. What is tracked, and who tracks it, along with the when, where, how, why, etc.

Who should track the functional metrics input data? As with all security functions, the tracking of the data and data collection should be done by the person at the lowest level who is responsible for the day-to-day SCA activity.

What to track? To begin with, all major tasks should be tracked and gradually, data collected in more detail as one moves through the work-breakdown structure of the SCA. To start with, the tracking and data collection should focus on basic data. That includes the number of security audits conducted, the security audit results, and their impact on assets protection and of course their associated costs.

Why track it? Because the SCA is an important security function, expending much employee time and resources, so it must be efficiently managed. All subprocesses (e.g., employee time worked, travel time and other expenses, report writing, production and distribution of reports) must be identified and measured. Once these factors can be quantified and qualified, then the process of analysis can begin to determine more cost-effective and efficient ways of providing the SCA service and support to the CAPP and thus IWC.

How to track it? To begin with, the tracking of data collection costs and lost productivity of workers can be accomplished by tracking the time spent by security specialists in doing the security audit preparation work and actually conducting the security audit along with the time spent by employees within a targeted department preparing for and interacting with security audit team members during the security audit. How much time each involved employee spends, the resources they use, and the amount of time not spent doing their normally assigned tasks are all part of the cost of the SCA.

Once the SCA is completed, then the time involved in each step of the process (using a detailed flowchart of that process as a guide) can be entered into a spreadsheet and the total time spent conducting the SCA can be calculated, as well as the average time spent by each employee. This can later be compared with the SCA results over time, as well as whether or not assets subsequently are found to be vulnerable or lost.

Such losses, for example, can then be used not only as part of the SEATP as previously stated in Chapter 9, but also as part of an SCA evaluation. In other words:

- What happened after the SCA was conducted in the department that contributed to or failed to prevent the loss of an important asset?
- Could it be the SCA was not done as effectively as possible?
- Was something missed?
- If so, that would require correction and changes in SCA procedures, and related processes.

As you can see, the process of measurement leads to continuously looking at data in an attempt to discover areas for process improvement.

When to track it? Various aspects of the SCA should be tracked by updating all related spreadsheets and databases as each SCA is completed. Maintaining accurate and current records is critical. Trying to reconstruct data at a later date usually ends up with an inaccurate depiction.

Where to track it in the functional process? Each SCA's data would be collected as each stage of each of the SCAs progressed. The collection points should at a minimum be at all of the primary transaction or action points noted in the process flowcharts for the SCAs primary and subprocesses.

Once data collection is complete, the data must be depicted in a useful form—refer to Figures 10-3 through 10-8 for samples of data depiction. In analyzing the data depicted in graphic format, the CSO can begin to understand just how the process is really working. Trends and anomalies in performance, costs and use of resources can be examined. Positive and negative assessments can then be made, followed by decisions to implement process changes as appropriate. Costs in terms of hours expended and materiel costs can be shown on spreadsheets and charts for analysis.

Changes to the SCA process can be implemented on a trial basis based on the suggestions by the department personnel and security specialists to determine if the changes would result in a more cost-effective SCA program. However, changes made based on data analysis almost always produce better results. This is particularly true when attempting to improve productivity—real data is necessary as a point of comparison. Anecdotal data (we think we are doing a better job) is interesting, sometimes informative, but not useful for real analysis.

Note also that SEATP, SCA, and investigative metrics can be compared to determine effectiveness of SCA, SEATP and the CAPP. For example: stronger emphasis on SEATP and a good CAPP leading to less SCA findings and fewer investigations? After all, isn't that the goal—to protect assets?

SCA CASE STUDY

The CSO was asked by the boss, "What is this security compliance audit function and what is it used for?" As a CSO, how would you answer? The IWC CSO thought about it and told the boss:

The SCA function complements all other assets protection functions. It provides a second look at how the CAPP, its assets protection policies, procedures, projects and processes are working. Moreover, it is a mechanism that can be used to determine how the entire company is fulfilling its responsibility to protect the corporate assets.

The SCA process is best conducted by the security organization, but it could be accomplished at the department level. Let's assume that a self-audit (that is each individual department) program was implemented and the SCA function discontinued. The work would still be accomplished but would it be of the quality needed to ensure the CAPP is effective and efficient?

Are nonsecurity "auditors" as effective as security professionals in conducting security audits of the IWC assets protection processes? They do provide that "outside" perspective, but their lack of security and of assets protection knowledge may lead to flawed or less than optimal audits. In addition, if one is doing a security audit of their own department, can they be objective to the point of issuing a marginal or unsatisfactory rating if that was the result of the security audit?

Each approach brings its own advantages and disadvantages. Only after careful analysis can the CSO make a determination as to which approach is the most effective and efficient. However, other mitigating factors may drive the decision one way or the other. If there are resource issues challenging IWC, there may not be sufficient security professionals to do this work. It may be necessary for the functional departments to conduct their own assessments, or not do them at all. Further, the amount of resources dedicated to the SCA process may be a factor in how much risk IWC executive management is willing to take. If external oversight agencies are not that demanding, greater risk acceptance may be an option ("Hey, they aren't closely watching us so we can let things slide a little."). However, that is not viewing the matter from an assets protection viewpoint, is it?

In any event, the CSO should drive decisions regarding the SCA based on data collected and analyzed to better assess performance. This is the only logical departure point.

The IWC CSO then went on to show the boss the SMMP data collected and their supporting charts to further explain the SCA function.

SCA SUMMARY

The SCA function is an integral part of the administrative security organization. It is more than security auditing for CAPP compliance as it is driven by the goal of ensuring all defenses are in place and compliance is achieved in accordance with the security drivers—that is, external regulations and laws, as well as internal policies, procedures, projects, plans and processes. The ultimate goal is the efficient and effective protection of corporate assets—essentially, achieving an effective CAPP.

The SCA process can be a very costly function in terms of resources used by the SCA team and time spent by IWC department employees who would take time out from their normal jobs to support the security audit.

Identifying the costs and benefits to IWC requires measurement. Measurement must be conducted in an organized and comprehensive way. Data has to be collected, depicted in a meaningful and understandable form and analyzed. The analysis provides the CSO with sufficient information to cause process changes as needed. Changes that are made must drive improvements in terms of effectiveness and efficiency.

Collecting data and depicting it graphically is not a difficult task. As shown in this chapter, the basic charts to use for simple graphic depiction include the organizational chart, process flowcharts, and security metrics management charts such as those showing the number of security audits conducted, their results, and the correlation of those results with the noncompliance incidents and investigations related to the loss of IWC assets, as well as incorporating the time being spent by all involved in the SCAs.

Chapter 11

Surveys and Risk Management

This chapter will address the use and measurements related to the conducting of security surveys. Furthermore, the use of risk management metrics methodologies and their associated specific metrics will be discussed.

INTRODUCTION

The term "surveys" as used here basically refers to a combination of risk management methodologies combined with targeted, proactive evaluations of various groups of valuable assets to determine how well they are protected, what the threats are against them, their specific vulnerabilities, any risks to them, the protection measures in place, and their costs, as well as identifying more cost-effective methods for the assets' protection.

The security surveys are an exclusive security function to be performed only by the administrative security organization's (see Figure 11-1) security professionals. As needed, support will be drawn from other security functions or external experts. Within the International Widget Corporation (IWC), these security surveys are best performed within the administrative security organization.

The risk management security function is an integral part of the security survey process. However, the CSO has mandated that the risk management philosophy and related methodologies be part of the decision-making process of the entire security department's staff.

After reading Chapter 10, you may wonder what the difference is between conducting security surveys and security compliance audits. They are alike in some ways. Where they differ is the following[1]:

- Compliance security audits focus on assessing internal compliance with existing company policies and procedures along with external laws and regulations and validity of CAPP.
- Security surveys focus on assessing risks by identifying the threats and vulnerabilities to company assets.

---

[1] They are both represented in this book to offer some different ways of looking at the protection of assets: Are the protection mechanisms working? What are the risks to the corporate assets? You may want to combine the SCA and SRM into one function depending on your assets protection approach and environment.

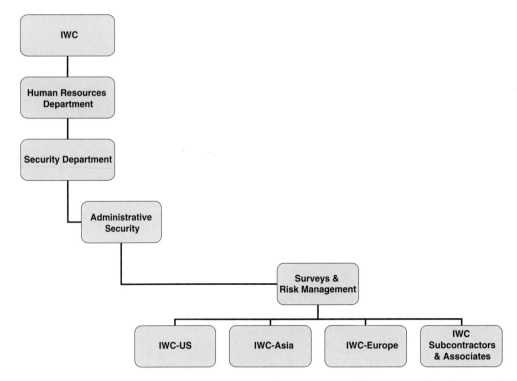

Figure 11-1 The relationship of the surveys and risk management functions in the administrative security organization.

Security surveys are often used to target certain assets for evaluation, with emphasis not on compliance with the corporate assets protection program (CAPP) but from the viewpoint of risk reduction. Essentially the survey helps the CSO better protect an asset from threats while recognizing and considering its vulnerabilities.

For example, a security survey may look at the threat agent potential to dial-up computer systems within IWC. That may include using a software program to dial all the telephone numbers used by IWC and document those that acknowledge with a modem tone. Penetration attempts would be made against those systems using common hacker tools. The findings would be documented and reported to IWC management along with recommendations for protection changes, revision of the CAPP and other applicable changes.

Another security survey may be to use social engineering techniques to try to gain information from employees and possibly gain physical access to facilities.

> *Social engineering is a process whereby an outsider attempts to contact a company insider (employee, in-house contractor, supplier, etc.) and, under false pretences gain access to assets.*

Security surveys are a more proactive way of determining if assets are properly protected, as the security professional conducting the security surveys uses common threat agents' techniques to try to obtain access to valuable assets.

The risk management methodologies are then applied as part of that approach. Risk management is an often misused term and is a philosophy and methodology that is sometimes incorrectly applied.

> *As part of any executive management briefing, the CSO must provide information as to the overall risk management strategy that is to be integrated into the security department staff's assets protection decision-making process and the reason for that approach.*

When it comes to risk assessments, risk analyses and risk management, there are those who argue quantitative versus qualitative. Regardless of your preference, risk assessments are still only best guesses—ideally, a best educated guess.

SRM DRIVERS AND FLOWCHARTS

As with all security functions, the security surveys security metrics management system requires that we begin with the drivers and the flow process that follows (see Figure 11-2 and Figure 11-3).

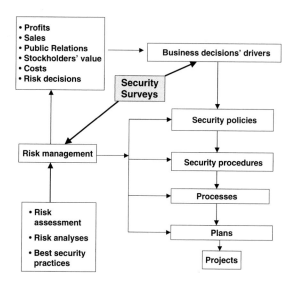

Figure 11-2   The security drivers related to the security survey function.

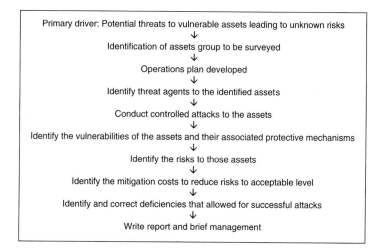

Figure 11-3   The flow process related to the security survey function.

SAMPLE SRM METRICS CHARTS

The following are some of the higher level security metrics charts that can be used to conduct and monitor security surveys and their related costs versus benefits.

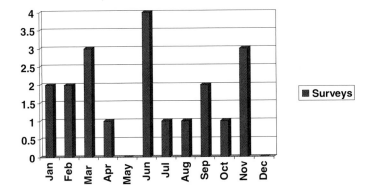

Figure 11-4   The number of surveys completed in 2005 at all locations.

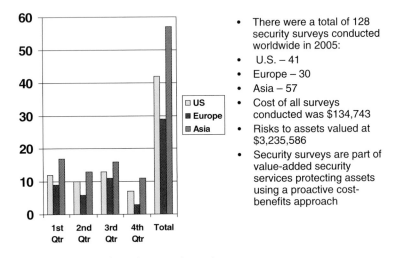

- There were a total of 128 security surveys conducted worldwide in 2005:
- U.S. – 41
- Europe – 30
- Asia – 57
- Cost of all surveys conducted was $134,743
- Risks to assets valued at $3,235,586
- Security surveys are part of value-added security services protecting assets using a proactive cost-benefits approach

Figure 11-5   Security survey conducted in 2005 by region.

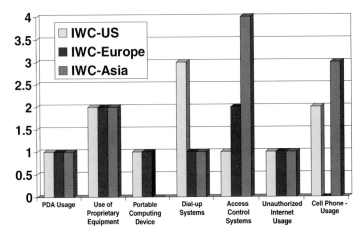

Figure 11-6   Types of assets surveyed by region in 2005.

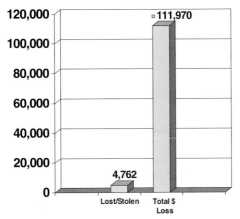

- 4,762 PDAs lost-stolen: in all cases due to carelessness.
- No employee reimbursement requirement in place.
- Loss of $111,970 in purchase value of PDAs.
- Potential compromise of lost, sensitive information maintained on the PDAs is in the millions of dollars, e.g., IWC Customer's Lists, Executive Management home phone numbers.

Figure 11-7 The total number of IWC PDAs, number lost/stolen and costs of the losses/thefts.

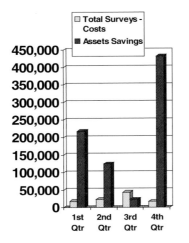

- The costs of the security surveys are actual costs of labor and resources for all regions by quarter.
- The total assets savings was calculated by identifying the assets' value that were demonstrated to be highly vulnerable to loss (destruction or theft).
- Proven highly vulnerable through use of known threat agents' techniques.
- Average ROI was $217,489 per survey.

Figure 11-8 2005 costs of security surveys versus savings to IWC.

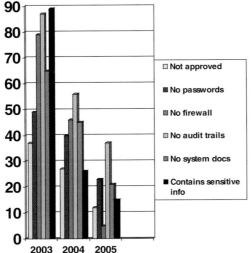

- A 2003 security survey found this is a major problem since annual surveys began
- The deficiencies noted included recurring problems
- Systems were vulnerable to external threat agents' attacks
- Numerous systems contained sensitive information that on at least two occasions were hacked and not reported

Figure 11-9 The results of a security survey dealing with dial-up IWC systems.

THE WHO, HOW, WHERE, WHEN, WHY AND WHAT OF SRM METRICS TRACKING

As we have previously stated in other chapters, the first step in data analysis and measurement is data collection. With each security function and its processes, the person(s) responsible for tracking and collection must be identified. Moreover, what, when, who, where, why and how of data collection, measurement, analysis and depiction must also be identified.

Who should track the functional metrics input data? As with all security functions, the tracking of the data and data collection should be done by the person at the lowest level who is responsible for the day-to-day leadership role for the security surveys.

What to track? To begin with, all major tasks should be tracked and, gradually, data collected in more detail as one moves through the work breakdown structure of the security survey function. For this function, the tracking and data collection should be that of the number of surveys conducted, their location, any departments who are found to be deficient, the survey results, their impact on assets protection and, of course, all of their associated costs; the type and frequency of all resources involved; and in particular, the costs of meeting the drivers' requirements, in this case the primary driver, which is the potential threats, vulnerabilities and risks to the specific assets being surveyed.

Why track it? This function should be tracked because it is a function that is vulnerable to elimination when cost-cutting time comes around. This is a valuable function but, unlike most of the others, this one could be eliminated or integrated into various other security functions as part of the other functions' processes. Security surveys have little to do with accomplishing the routine tasks a security organization faces each day. They have much to do with assessing how well processes are working. During periods of high budgetary pressure, processes that don't directly contribute to the day-to-day security operation are often eliminated or deferred. Therefore, it is important to continually identify the cost-benefits of this function and its associated return on investments.

How to track it? It should be tracked through each step and as part of a subprocess in the individual security survey's operations plan.

When to track it? The tracking of various aspects of the security surveys should be done by updating all related spreadsheets and databases as each security survey is completed.

Where to track it in the functional process? Each survey's data would be collected as each step in the operations plan was completed. The collection point would be at all the primary points noted in the process flowcharts for the security surveys, as well as during each contact with an employee and its duration with a member of any department being impacted by the security survey.

As with the security compliance audits and other security functions, analyzing the security survey metrics charts, the CSO can begin to understand the costs and impact, both positive and negative, of the security surveys.

The charts also can be used to look at the costs in lost productivity as would be done with all the other security functional metrics management systems.

CASE STUDY

With the increased threats to IWC assets throughout the world as IWC expanded on a worldwide basis, IWC executives wanted to know what the IWC CSO is doing to understand and mitigate today's threats to corporate assets and, in particular, the potential threats of terrorism.

The CSO thought that the best way to provide that information was with a basic briefing addressing the potential threats related to IWC worldwide, how those threats were viewed by the security staff, and what was being done to mitigate the threats.

The CSO viewed this matter as too important to be glossed over lightly and decided an introductory briefing was best suited for executive management, with follow-on briefings to be scheduled as the executives deemed appropriate.

The CSO provided the following information to the IWC executive management in the form of an executive management briefing and discussion.[2]

Introduction

- This briefing will discuss the general characteristics of threat agents that can be identified and measured as an integral part of a security survey incorporating risk management techniques with emphasis on cost-benefits and return on investments
- The method has been tested against historical data (in this case with open source information) to establish the validity of the metrics that have been developed
- Other characteristics of threats are outside the scope of this presentation

Why Develop a Threat Method?

- The measures that are presently used to protect corporate assets need to be cost-effective
- Returns on investments must be identified
- Current risk assessments rely on knowledge of the probable threat(s)
- The need to develop a system that allows scenarios to be modeled
- Need to produce a threat assessment that can be understood and used by management in their decision-making processes

The Threat Problem

- Current practice for the production of threat assessments is the use of "experts" who have considerable experience preparing assessments from all sources of intelligence
- The whole process is currently subjective and cannot be accurately modeled.
- The production of a threat assessment cannot be easily repeated at short notice (scarce resources, tasking of intelligence assets, time taken to produce assessment)

---

[2] This "case study" will be more of a discussion of the one individual's viewpoint (the CSO) with a metrics management slant to risk management: "A Method for the Calculation of Threat in an Information Environment" developed by Dr. Andy Jones, PhD, Group Leader, British Telecom, United Kingdom. We thank Dr. Andy Jones for providing this information which is further developed in his new book, *Risk Management for Computer Security: Protecting Your Network & Information Assets,* published by Butterworth Heinemann, March 2005. This case study is being offered to provide the reader not only subject matter of high visibility today, but also one that can be tied into a SRM security function.

- The logic and the factors that were used in developing the assessment cannot be easily tested
- The resources best used to produce threat assessments are not normally available for business and industry and are not in sufficient detail to meet the needs of organizations comprising the Critical National Infrastructure
- Most of the available "experts" have little or no knowledge of the information environment—their expertise was gained in the physical and personnel areas
- At IWC, understanding the information environment is crucial due to IWC's reliance on high technology as the underpinning of our competitive edge
- Based on these issues, surveys with integrated risk management techniques are used here at IWC

Some Risk Definitions

- **Risk**: One current accepted definition of risk is: Risk is the result of a threat agent exploiting a vulnerability to which they can gain access in order to produce an unacceptable impact on the target system or organization
- **Threat**: A threat is a natural disaster, an unintentional act by an individual that causes harm or, a malicious act by an individual or a group of individuals, such as terrorists. In order for a malicious individual or group to be an effective threat, it is necessary that they have intention (motivation) and capability

Preliminary Research

- Before work started on developing a method for Threat Assessment, the following areas were examined for any relevant concepts or methods:
  - Risk assessment methods
  - Insurance underwriting
  - Gambling (horse and dog racing)
  - Government methods (The FBI Computer Crime Adversarial Matrix)
  - Construction industry
  - Airline industry
- This was done in order to adopt and adapt validated methodologies already in place

The CSO went on to explain the various aspects of the threat assessment philosophy as part of the SRM using the following charts:

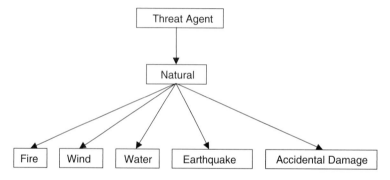

Figure 11-10   Diagram of the natural threat agents.

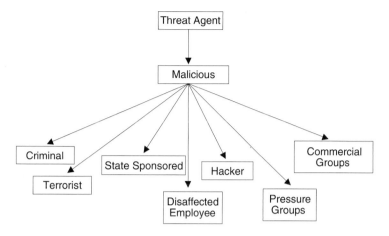

Figure 11-11   Diagram of the malicious threat agents.[3]

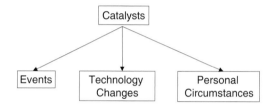

Figure 11-12   Diagram with malicious threats agents' catalysts.

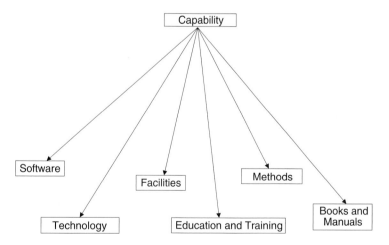

Figure 11-13   Threat agents' capabilities.

---

[3]   These figures deal primarily with the capability and motivation of a malicious threat agent.

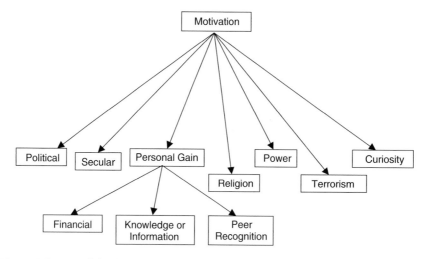

Figure 11-14   Diagram of the threat agents' motivations.

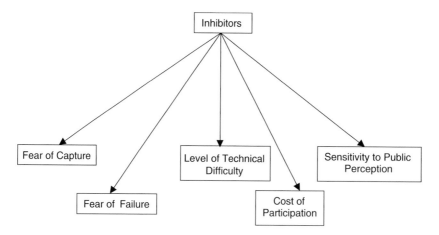

Figure 11-15   The threat agents' inhibitors.

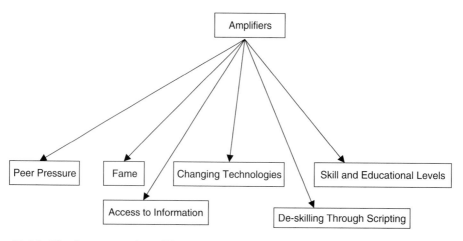

Figure 11-16   The threat agents' amplifiers.

Factors	Afghanistan	Argentina	Australia
Adult Population	14.7 Million[2]	23.5 Million[2] 23.3 Million[8] 23.5 Million[9]	12.9 Million[2] 12.9 Million[9]
Gross Domestic Product (per capita)	800 US$[2]	7500 US$[8] 7700 US$[9]	22200 US$[2] 23200 US$[8]
Level of Literacy	34.4%[2]	96.2%[2] 96.2%[8]	100%[2]
Cultural Factors	Sunni Muslim – 84%[2]		
Other Factors	Major Drug production area Support of islamic militants worldwide	Dispute with UK over Malvinas Money Laundering Drug transshipment	
Government	Currrent coalition government after period under the Taliban, a self-proclaimed fundamentalist government (dictatorship?)	Democracy	Democracy
Power Consumption per capita	15.7 KWH[2]	2081 KWH[2]	9904 KWH[2]
Telecomms Infrastructure	2900 Fixed[2] 0 Cellular[2]	7.5 Million Fixed[2] 3 Million Cellular[2]	9.58 Million Fixed[2] 6.4 Million Cellular[2]
Internet Access	(1 ISP)[2]	900000[2]	7.77 Million[2]
Technological Developmer Level	Low (Industry 15%, Services 15% of labour force)		High (Industry 22%, Services 73% of labour force)
Technical Expertise	Very Limited	Adequate	High Level
Allied Nations Capability	Limited	High	Very High
Known Indigenous IW Capability	None	None	Some

Figure 11-17   Examples of the threat agents' capabilities: nation-states.

Factor	Weighting Value				
	1	**2**	**3**	**4**	**5**
Adult Population (P)	< 1,000,000	1,000,001 – 10,000,000	10,000,001 – 50,000,000	50,000,001 – 100,000,000	>100,000,001
Literacy Level (L)	< 50%	51–65%	66–80%	80–90%	> 90%
Internet Access (I)	Very Low	Low	Medium	High	Very High
History of relevant Activity (H)	None	Intermittent	Occasional	Regular	Regular and Widespread
Technical Expertise (T)	None	Very Limited	Limited	Adequate	High Level
Gross Domestic Product per capita (G)	< $ 1000	$1,001 – $5,000	$5,001– $10,000	$10,001 – $20,000	> $20,000
Allied Nation Capability (N)	None	Limited	Medium	High	Very High
Indigenous IW Capability (AA)	None	Limited	Medium	High	Very High
Other Factors (AB)					Religious Fundamentalism /Support of International Terrorism (*)

(*) This value is assessed to be of high weighting for this type of threat agent. This is not considered to be a value that would have a lesser importance expression.

Figure 11-18   The threat agents' capabilities: Nation-States: Afghanistan.

Factors	Environment	Threat agent	Target
Peer Pressure		X	
Fame		X	X
Access to Information		X	
Changing Technologies	X		X
Skills and Education Levels		X	
De-Skilling through Scripting		X	
Law Enforcement Activity (LE)	X	X	X
Target Vulnerability (TV)			X
Target Profile (TP)		X	X
Public Perception (PuP)	X	X	X
Peer Perception (PP)		X	

Figure 11-19   The threat agents' amplifiers.

Factors	State Sponsored	Terrorist	Criminal	Pressure Group	Commercial	Hacker	Disaffected Staff
Personal Gain:							
Revenge			X		X	X	X
Power						X	X
Curiosity						X	
Financial			X	X	X	X	X
Peer Recognition						X	
Knowledge or Information			X	X	X	X	X
Competitive Advantage			X		X		
Crime		X	X				X
Secular Influence		X		X		X	X
National Political/ Military Objectives	X	X		X			
Religious Influence	X	X		X		X	
Pressure Group Action		X		X			

Figure 11-20   The threat agent motivation—general.

Factor	Weighting Value				
	0	**12**	**25**	**37**	**50**
Crime	No criminal influence	Occasional criminal involvement	Regular criminal involvement	Strong criminal connections	Criminal backing or reliance on funds from criminal activity
Secular Influence	No secular influence	Slight secular influence	Moderate secular influence	Strong secular influence	Overriding secular influence
National Political/ Military objectives	No political or military objectives	Limited political objectives	Moderate political objectives	Political or limited military objectives	Military or strong political objectives
Religious Influence	No religious influence	Slight religious influence	Moderate religious influence	Strong religious influence	Overriding religious influence
Pressure Group Action	No pressure group connection	Slight pressure group connections	Moderate pressure group connections	Strong pressure group relationship	Overriding pressure group relationship

Figure 11-21   The threat agent motivation (Terrorist—Al Qaeda).

Factor	Weighting Value				
	0	**4**	**8**	**11**	**15**
Access to Information	Not interested in gaining information	Information is only of peripheral interest	Information is a secondary benefit	Information is seen to be of significant interest	Primary reason for attack is to gain information
Changing Technologies	Not providing any new opportunity	Potential new opportunities	Limited new opportunities	Providing significant new opportunities	Providing major new opportunities
Law Enforcement Activity (LE)	Strong and active law enforcement activity in target or base country	Laws in place and enforced with reasonable success in target or base country	Laws in place and enforced with limited success in target or base country	Laws in place but not actively enforced in target or base country	No effective law enforcement activity in target or base country
Target Vulnerability (TV)	Target not perceived to be accessible	Target accessible with considerable effort and/or resources	Target accessible with reasonable effort and/or resources	Target accessible with limited effort and/or resources	Target is extremely vulnerable
Target Profile (TP)	Does not match group requirement	Slightly matches group requirement	Partially matches group requirement	Mostly matches group requirement	Fully matches group requirement
Fame	Group actively does not wish to be attributed with activity	Group prefers not to be attributed with activity	Group is indifferent to being attributed with the activity	Group is content to be attributed with the activity	Group actively seeks to be attributed with the activity
Public Perception (PuP)	Strong negative effect	Negative effect	Neutral effect	Beneficial effect	Strong beneficial effect

Figure 11-22   The threat agents' amplifiers.

Factors	Environment	Threat agent	Target
Fear of capture		X	
Fear of failure		X	
Level of technical difficulty	X		X
Cost of participating		X	
Sensitivity to public opinion		X	
Law enforcement activity	X	X	
Security of target			X
Public perception		X	X
Security of system		X	X

Figure 11-23   The threat agents' inhibitors.

Factor	Weighting Value				
	0	**4**	**8**	**12**	**16**
Fear of capture	Relishes capture – martyrdom?	Seeks capture	Indifferent to capture	Avoids capture	Capture not an option
Fear of failure	Failure would not have any effect	Failure would have a minimal effect	Failure would have an impact but can be accepted	Failure would have a negative impact on the group	Failure would severely damage image or capability
Level of technical difficulty	Easy to obtain success	Success achievable with limited effort and/or resources	Success achievable with reasonable effort and/or resources	Success achievable with significant effort and/or resources	Extremely difficult to achieve success
Sensitivity to public perception	Strong beneficial effect	Beneficial effect	Neutral effect	Negative effect	Strong negative effect
Law enforcement activity	No effective law enforcement activity in target or base country	Laws in pace but not actively enforced in target or base country	Laws in place and enforced with limited success in target or base country	Laws in place and enforced with reasonable success in target or base country	Strong and active law enforcement activity in target or base country
Security of target	Target unprotected	Poor security	Reasonable security	Good security	Target extremely secure

Figure 11-24   The threat agents'-terrorists' inhibitors.

Factors	
Change of Personal Circumstances	X
War or Political Conflict	X
Significant Events	X
Significant Anniversaries	X

Figure 11-25   The threat agents' catalysts.

Factor	Weighting Value				
	0	**8**	**16**	**24**	**32**
War or Political Conflict	No current political or military hostilities	Low level of hostile political activity	Medium level of hostile political activity	High level of political activity and potential for military action	Currently directly involved in a war that is taking place
Significant Events	No significant events	Awareness of event of limited peripheral significance	Awareness of event of minor significance	Awareness of event of significance	Awareness of event of major significance
Significant Anniversaries	No anniversary of significance to either the threat agent or the target	Anniversary of limited relevance to the threat agent or the target	Anniversary of relevance to the threat agent or the target	Anniversary of some significance to the threat agent or the target	Anniversary of high significance to the threat agent or the target

Figure 11-26   The threat agents'-terrorists' catalysts.

	Capability	Motivation	Access	Inhibitors	Amplifiers	Catalysts
Nation State (Afghanistan)	24	62	45	40	50	92
Terrorism (Al Qa'eda)	47	62	42	34	50	67
Crime (Cali Cartel)	77	45	54	59	47	25
Pressure Group (ALF)	82	39	38	57	64	78
Hackers (Silver Lords)	85	37	53	42	83	83

Figure 11-27   The threat agents—where does this all lead?

Using this information, the CSO went on to explain that a values matrix can be developed and some calculations made that can be used to quantify the risks of today's threat agents to IWC assets.

The CSO told the group that once values have been established for each of the threat elements, it is possible to establish an overall value for the threat. This is not an absolute and will currently only give a relative value. It will allow for the threat from various agents to be compared and it will allow a range of scenarios to be modeled and compared.

When conducting any type of SRM relative to potential terrorist threats to IWC, the CSO's SRM team also considers other issues such as:

- Likelihood of an attack
- Likelihood of a successful attack
- Value of lost revenue
- Cost of system repair
- Cost of reputation damage
- Third-party damages
- Cost of loss of confidence

The CSO continued to explain that there are current and foreseeable threat scenarios not only from terrorists but also:

- Pressure groups
- Collateral damage from other events
- Organized crime
- Nation-state government threats where IWC has offices

Using a security survey approach, the IWC CSO explained that the security department will maintain current information relative to terrorists and other miscreant's attack techniques and test them (obviously in a simulated or controlled manner) on a periodic basis.

A security metrics management process will be put in place to collect data for risk analyzed by the security survey personnel. The data would be compiled into charts for the CSO's monitoring of the threat-related risk management issues. They would also be used to support periodic reports and briefings to the IWC executive management.

The data collection would include:

- number of security surveys conducted relative to terrorism,
- the targeted areas,
- the results,
- the costs of the surveys,
- the value of the assets currently and adequately protected and at what costs relative exclusively to the terrorists threats
- the protection deficiencies identified through the surveys,
- the risks to those assets,
- the cost of mitigating the risks, and
- status of implementation of additional protective measures.

SUMMARY

Conducting security surveys with an integrated risk management approach, when done in a proactive way, can help provide more cost-effective and successful assets protection programs.

The metrics that are to be used in this process should include data collection of the time spent conducting the surveys and their results in terms of acceptable levels of risks regarding assets protection.

Of particular interest are the threats posed by terrorist groups that may target IWC due to the location of its international offices (Asia, Africa, Middle East) and also since it is a U.S.-based corporation.

Chapter 12

Corporate Assets Protection Program

The corporate assets protection program (CAPP)[1] is the primary reason why security exists. The role of security is a protective role. Protection of people, information and physical assets is the leadership purview of the security professional and the security organization.

Historically, security has been viewed as a necessary support function. In many corporations and certainly in government this is changing. More often we are seeing security characterized as a mission-essential function and not just a support function. Considering the scope of the CAPP (from protection of information to contingency planning) and its impact on the company, this is as it should be.

INTRODUCTION

How and why a corporation protects its assets are institutionalized in a CAPP. The CAPP can be viewed and managed as the overall continuous plan to protect corporate assets or it can be viewed as a program. The choice is based on the corporate culture or how the Chief Security Officer (CSO) decides it is best to manage the effort. Within IWC, the CAPP is a program and also a macro security plan for protecting corporate assets. Approaching the CAPP as a plan offers the advantage of dividing that plan into subplans or logical (separations) sections that deal with the different aspects of the assets protection effort.

The method used may or may not have a bearing on how security metrics is used to manage the assets protection efforts. In any case, the CSO must first identify exactly what is needed as far as data to manage the entire program.

As a CSO, what data do you think you need? For example:

- To be able to manage the assets protection program?
- What data will assist you in managing the program effectively?
- Should it include all the metrics for all the security functions identified in this book?

---

[1] You may wonder why we are presenting this chapter now instead of at the beginning of this book, since we often mention the CAPP in previous chapters. The logic used was that this is a plan and falls under the administrative security organization. Furthermore, we wanted to expose you to the philosophy and examples of the SMMP before getting into the CAPP in any detail.

The answer is not the same for all corporations or security departments. Each corporation is different and operates in an environment unique to them. Furthermore, what is most important to one CSO may not be as important to another. With that in mind, each CSO must develop and use data and security metrics measurements that work best in their own environment.

As a new IWC CSO, one would first want a macro view of the organization before examining the more micro processes. In reality, that will occur soon enough as the CSO is presented with the daily problems of any security operation. So, what are some of the more important security metrics management program (SMMP) data that would be needed?

Let's start with the CAPP's basic objective or goal: the CAPP is a tool to protect corporate assets and mitigate risks to the corporation. Ideally, the goal is to accomplish this objective in as effective and efficient a manner as possible. Therefore, any data collection through security metrics management charting and oversight should be focused on those goals:

- Is the CAPP working as planned?
- Is it effective?
- How much does it cost?
- How can it be done better?
- How can it be done cheaper?

A CSO would want to have an overall depiction to begin with of the security functional charts used in earlier chapters, on which the security drivers are identified. This will help refresh the CSO and others as to what drives the need for a CAPP. There are various ways to view these drivers and to flowchart them (see Figure 12-1, 12-2 and 12-3 for examples).

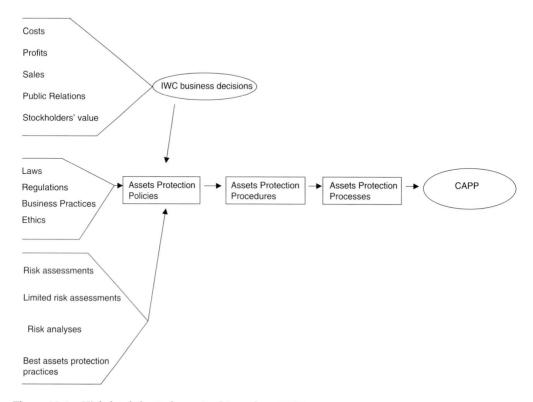

Figure 12-1   High-level chart of security drivers for a CAPP.

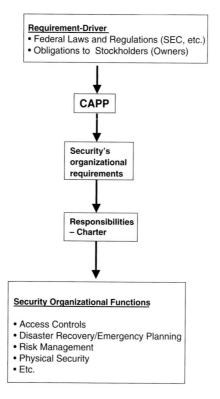

Figure 12-2   High-level chart of security drivers from a single (example) driver down through related security functions.

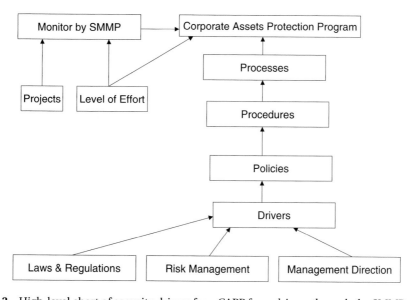

Figure 12-3   High-level chart of security drivers for a CAPP from drivers through the SMMP.

THE CAPP AND OTHER DRIVERS, PLANS AND THEIR FLOWCHARTS

The CAPP must be (or at least should be) integrated, to include incorporating the other security plans such as the annual, tactical (short-term) and strategic (long-term) plans. These plans in turn must be integrated into the overall corporate plans. After all, the security department is a service and support organization that does perform mission-critical tasks. Security plans should be integrated into and support corporate business plans (see Figures 12-4 and Figure 12-5).

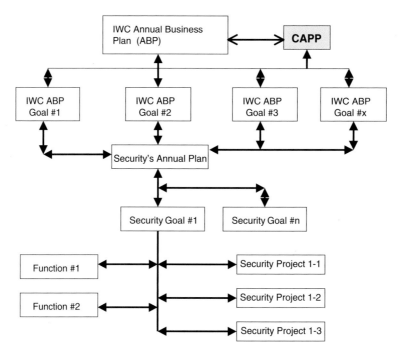

Figure 12-4 High-level view of how security department functions and goals connect or feed into the corporation's annual business plans.

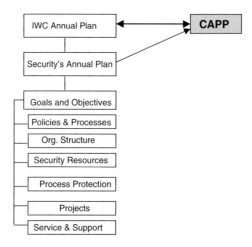

Figure 12-5 Depiction of how security functions fit or flow into the security organization's annual plan and then into the corporate plan.

As a CSO, you should develop such flowcharts, of course in more detail, that demonstrate how security goals and objectives (and other security activities) flow into the corporate business plans. A graphic depiction of how security processes integrate into corporate business plans is a useful tool when demonstrating the value security brings to the corporation. After all, if you are not supporting the corporate plans, you are marching to the wrong drummer.

CAPP DATA COLLECTION AND SECURITY METRICS MANAGEMENT

As shown in the figures above, as a CSO, you want to be able to pictorially show the relationship between the security department's goals, objectives, projects, functions, plans, policies, procedures, processes and how they relate to providing service and support to the corporation. In today's corporate world, you must look and act as a "team player." Such flowcharts and security metrics charts assist in that portrayal.

Once you have developed such flowcharts, "connecting the dots," you must decide on what security metrics you want to collect, analyze and use as part of your SMMP, overall CAPP and security department management functions.

Earlier in this chapter, we discussed key questions that you as the CSO must be able to answer and explain to the corporation's senior management, since they need and want the answers too. If you recall, these questions are the following:

- Is the CAPP working as planned?
- Is it effective?
- How much does it cost?
- How can it be done better?
- How can it be done cheaper?

Let's discuss these one at a time from the SMMP perspective.

IS THE CAPP WORKING AS PLANNED?

The goal of the CAPP is the protection of information, people and physical assets. It is a plan that is documented and contains goals and objectives, as well as the details of the assets protection program. It must be documented to ensure its availability to those who need it and to use as a baseline for measuring against performance.

In order to determine if the CAPP is working, many measurements will be needed. Ideally, the fewer measures the better, particularly when attempting to depict success or failure to senior management. One of the ideal depictions would show the relationship of the value of corporate assets to the actual losses experienced over a defined period of time.

The overall chart would show the amount of corporate assets in one form or another, broken down into values for people, information and physical (facilities and equipment) assets. However, when it comes to the value of some of these assets, that may be difficult to assess (for example, what is the cost of each piece of information? what is the value to the company of an employee's life?).

That would not be an easy task or maybe not even practical. However, we can collect data from the investigative organization as to the losses of or damage to assets. Also, we can collect information from other IWC organizations, such as health and safety personnel or property management. What we can more readily collect is information showing where the CAPP is not working from the standpoint of protecting corporate assets.

In addition to the overall data collection and their related metrics charts, other data should be collected and their related "backup" metrics charts would be developed based on data collected showing (see Figure 12-6 and Figure 12-7):

- Categories of asset losses
- Their value (in current terms of the cost of replacement)
- Time-productivity lost
- Vulnerability that allowed the loss or damage to occur
- Consequences of that loss or damage
- Corrective action to be taken
- Cost of the corrective action versus the cost of the assets (e.g., if the corrective action costs more than the estimated losses or damages over a period of time, say five years, then maybe it is not worth correcting the vulnerability). After all, it is a matter of costs-benefits.
- If corrective action is deemed appropriate, a project plan for that action

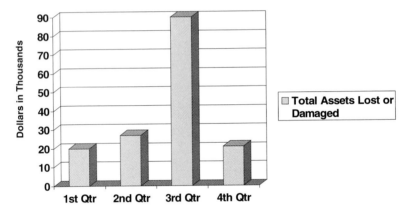

Figures 12-6   The consolidated number (rather than another chart showing the type of assets) of corporate assets lost over the past year.

NOTE: Of course this can also be depicted by year or even over a five-year period, as trend charts are valuable charts to manage assets protection. If the trend is positive (downward loss trend) then as a CSO, you should find out why and praise/reward those responsible. After all, they certainly catch hell when something goes wrong! So, why not also recognize them when something goes right? If the trend is negative, identify the reasons and establish projects to correct the problems.

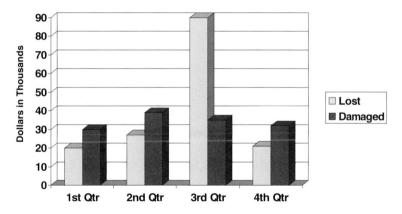

Figure 12-7 The loss of versus damage to corporate assets in total in a year.

IS IT EFFECTIVE?

As a CSO, how will you determine if the CAPP is effective? In other words, are all the parts that make up the IWC CAPP designed and integrated to such an extent that the entire IWC assets protection effort is effectively working?

As the CSO, you can get a sense of whether or not it is effective by looking at the trend charts of damages and losses of assets over time. If they are low or the trend is neutral or indicates less damages or losses, then it is effective. Figures similar to Figures 12-6 and 12-7 will show that over a longer period of time—for example, five-plus years' trend charts.

By the way, when discussing losses, we mean all losses that include loss due to theft, damage, misappropriation, and "I don't know what happened to it but it must be here somewhere—I think." (Assuming it can't be found in a reasonable amount of time.)

One of the important data points that ought to be depicted in one of your "subcharts" is one showing recoveries and the value of the recovered assets with and without the cost of recovery.

> *Based on the results of the data collected and the trend charts supported by the data, as a CSO, you would implement projects to identify and mitigate losses using a risk management approach.*

HOW MUCH DOES IT COST?

The costs of the CAPP would be measured by the total costs of the security department—that is, the security department's total budget, as well as factoring in the sum total of all costs as collected through each security function where the productivity impact to non-security personnel has been calculated—and that should be identified by each security function (see Figure 12-8).

> *The process for data collection for this metric would be through identifying the cost data for each security function summed plus the security department's budget, excluding any redundancies, of course.*

Remember, if assets didn't need protecting, there would be no need for a security department. Therefore, the security department's budget as a minimum must be included in your cost calculations. It is the easiest data to obtain—assuming you as the CSO have a total security budget. If not, well, that scary thought is beyond addressing here. However, one "war story" may be worthy of telling here:

One of us had once worked in a very large international corporate division. When hired and asked about the organizational budget, the boss, a senior executive and vice president, said that there wasn't a budget but we were all expected to spend only the funds necessary to meet the needs of the organization and successfully accomplish our objectives. Well, you can guess the results. Sure enough, there were cost overruns on some contracts and most of the business unit's managers were spending as if they were multibillionaires without a money care in the world—clearly a poor planning process that ended up being very costly to the corporation.

This author took it seriously and, as usually happens, when the budget crash hit, we were all affected. So, while others already had many of their desired wish list items, we in security went wanting and also unrewarded for our conservative and ethical efforts. So, one word of advice (and as a security professional, one should never expect rewards anyway), let your ethical conscience be your guide if you are ever placed in that position!

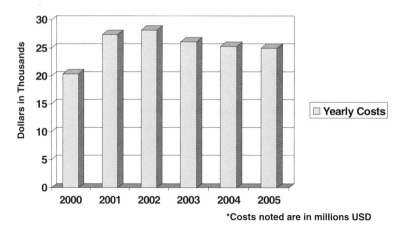

Figure 12-8   The total costs of the CAPP per year over a six-year period.

As you view Figure 12-8, think about what back-up, detailed information (in data collection and metrics charts form) should be available to help you answer some obvious questions. For example, why the increase or decrease in specific years? If you were using an SMMP to manage the CAPP over the years, you would know that answer.

As a CSO, you may want to change the metrics chart and use a different one which explains why the upward or downward trend has occurred (see Figure 12-9). It also may be a good idea to do an annual average chart over the six-year period to show the long-term trend. In other words, develop your data collection and subsequent metrics charts for analysis, decision-making and briefings using a work-breakdown process.

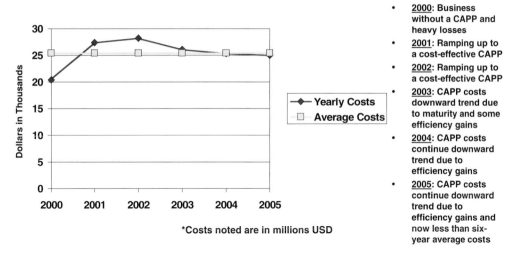

Figure 12-9   The total costs of the CAPP per year over a six-year period, with explanation and average costs.

HOW CAN IT BE DONE BETTER?

Doing it better—more effectively—is a product of taking what was learned from the data collection and metrics charting of an SMMP and using that information to improve related security processes. Tracking that performance can be accomplished by comparing the year-to-year trends in losses as a percent of asset value. Ultimately, changes should be made to the point where there are diminishing returns. That is to say, it costs more in security expenses than in value of losses prevented.

HOW CAN IT BE DONE CHEAPER?

Doing it cheaper—more efficiently—usually involves activities such as process analysis (including time-motion studies where appropriate), process modifications, continuous process improvement (CPI) and total quality management (TQM) techniques. (There are many others but those stated tend to fit well with the analysis of security processes and functions.)

   These management tools actually do work when properly applied but often get a "bum rap" by those who fight change or don't know how to properly apply these types of tools. All too often they are not properly used, or employees are not properly trained as to how to use these tools, which in turn causes the employees to discredit the processes.

   One often hears the employees' cries, "Why can't we just do it like we've always done it?" What would be your reply? Obviously, as the CSO and in a leadership role, you should explain the corporate and business environment, the global marketplace issues, competitive advantage philosophy, and the goal of making each security function and its related process as effective and efficient as possible.

   The security staff should also be told that this is not a way to downsize the security staff (although it certainly may cause that to happen—one never knows at the outset what the results will be). As is usually the case, one can always find work for the security staff and one approach may be to only eliminate positions when required to do so by upper management.

CASE STUDY

The IWC CEO is concerned about the cost of the CAPP and wants to know what exactly is involved in protecting the IWC assets. As the CSO, how would you respond?

Since the CEO's time is limited, the CSO decided to provide a 10-minute briefing using no more than five charts with each chart to be briefed for no longer than two minutes. 10 minutes are also set aside for comments and questions, for a total of 20 minutes.

Which type of metric, in what type of graphic depiction, if any in this chapter, would you choose to use?

- Those which show assets expenditures, losses and damages with their associated costs
- Ratio of costs to damages and losses
- Those showing efficiency gains over the last six years or whatever years are available
- Any data and related metrics charts showing a favorable return on investments

The data and metrics charts used may of course be different depending on the CSO, the CSO's SMMP, CEO's request, and the CEO's preference for briefings, as well as the corporate culture and environment.

SUMMARY

The CAPP is a program consisting of the following:

- List of corporate assets protection drivers (reasons for security and protection)
- Policies, procedures, processes and plans used to define protection parameters, requirements, projects and objectives.
- It is institutionalized in document form and available for all who support the CAPP for review and consultation.

The security metrics management data collection and graphics depictions are tools used by the CSO to help manage the CAPP. Data is generally collected, analyzed and depicted by function and as a total organization.

The key to the security metrics of the CAPP from a management standpoint is the ability to answer, through data and supporting metrics charts, the following questions:

- Is the CAPP working as planned?
- Is it effective?
- How much does it cost?
- How can it be done better?
- How can it be done cheaper?

Chapter 13

Contingency Planning

The fundamental elements of each contingency planning component and the process of using security metrics to measure and manage its cost, benefits, successes and failures will be discussed in this chapter.

INTRODUCTION

Within corporations, security is often the organization responsible for contingency planning. This responsibility is usually attained as a default action. Since the security organization is the organization serving as the primary first responder to an incident or emergency, the transition to assuming the lead responsibility for contingency planning is a logical one. It is the experience as a first responder that leads to an expansion of that role and into the role of the contingency planner.

Since the World Trade Center attacks, corporations and government agencies have become more sensitive to the need to plan and prepare for an emergency or crisis. To that end, security professionals in the United States and some other countries have expanded their contingency-planning capabilities beyond their traditional responsibilities for emergency response and crisis management to focus on the effort to recover from such an event. It is becoming quite common to see security professionals responsible for the entire spectrum of contingency planning. This includes the following elements:

- Emergency Response
- Crisis Management
- Business Continuity—consisting of the following subelements:
  - Business Recovery
  - Business Resumption

> *Contingency planning has always been an important part of assets protection—today, more so than ever. To be done effectively and efficiently, it must be measured.*

It is critical that security professionals learn from actual events and planned exercises (drills) and apply that learning to improve future actions. Contingency planning is and must be a dynamic process where systems are tested and regularly revised. The security professional cannot afford the all-too-common situation of developing comprehensive plans but never testing them or never changing them as they learn from actual events. In simpler words, contingency plans do not belong on shelves collecting dust. They must be read, revised, tested and shared to be as effective as possible. Keep in mind that perhaps more important than the planning documentation itself is the process of learning what occurs by everyone who participates in the planning, testing and implementation of such plans.

A Chief Security Officer (CSO), such as the IWC CSO, who is responsible for contingency planning, must have a clear understanding of what this all means. After all, much rests on the CSO's ability to do this well.

Since contingency planning is as much a learning process as it is a planning process, it is a good idea to start with a basic foundation. The most important part of that foundation is establishing a common language. Many terms are used in the process of contingency planning. It is critical that all parties have, and understand, a common set of definitions. Below are samples of definitions for some key terms used in the contingency planning process.

If these definitions do not fit well within your organization, change them. What is critical about these definitions is not that they be standard throughout all of business and industry but that, when they are used, they have a common meaning understood by everyone within the organization using them. They can be tailored uniquely to your own organization's needs.

- *Business Continuity*: Minimizing business interruption or disruption caused by different contingencies. Keeping the business going. Business continuity plans encompass actions related to how one prepares for, manages, recovers, and ultimately resumes business after a disruption.
- *Business Recovery*: Refers to the short-term (generally less than 60 days) restoration activities that return the business or government agency to a minimum acceptable level of operation or production following a work disruption. Used interchangeably with the term *disaster recovery*.
- *Business Resumption*: The long-term (generally more than 60 days) process of restoration activities after an emergency or disaster that return the business to its pre-event condition. (Keep in mind that restoration to the exact pre-event condition may not be necessary or even desirable. However, making this determination may not be possible without proper planning or going through the actual resumption process.)
- *Contingency*: An event that is a possible but uncertain occurrence or is likely to happen as an adjunct to other events.
- *Contingency Planning*: The process of planning for response, recovery and resumption activities for the infrastructure, critical processes and other elements of IWC based upon encountering different contingencies.
- *Crisis Management*: The process of managing the events of a crisis to a condition of stability. This task is best accomplished by one of the businesses' integrated process teams (IPT) made up of members from different disciplines throughout the company. This IPT serves as the site or business deliberative body for emergency response and crisis management planning and implementation.
- *Critical Processes*: Activities performed by departments which, if significantly disrupted, due to a major emergency or disaster, would have an adverse impact on the business operations, revenue generation, customer schedules, contractual commitments or legal obligations.

- *Emergency Response*: The act of reporting and responding to any emergency or major disruption of a business.

The process of contingency planning at IWC is focused to achieve the following:

- *Secure and protect people*—in the event of a crisis, people must be protected
- *Secure the continuity of the core elements of the business*—the infrastructure and critical processes—minimize disruptions to the business
- *Secure all information systems*—that includes or affects suppliers' connections and customer relationships.

CONTINGENCY PLANNING ORGANIZATION

At IWC, the contingency planning function falls under the administrative security organization (see Figure 13-1).

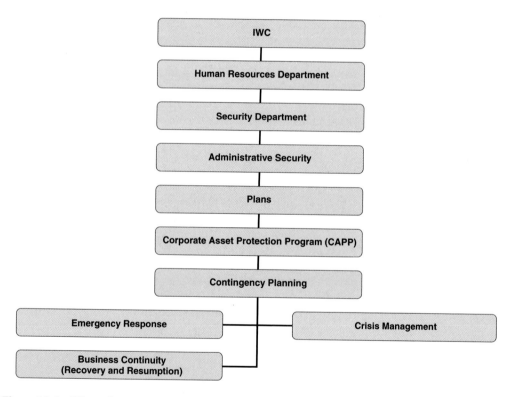

Figure 13-1   Where the contingency planning function fits in the IWC security organization.

CONTINGENCY PLANNING DRIVERS AND FLOWCHARTS

The main driver for contingency planning is of course the need to protect corporate assets and that need derived from the other drivers stated earlier, such as laws and regulations. That need must include the ability to rapidly get back to normal business in the event of an emergency, disaster or other significant business disruption.

Contingency plans formally establish the processes and procedures to protect employees, core business elements, information systems and the environment in the event of an emergency, business disruption or disaster. These IWC plans, also incorporated into the IWC corporate assets protection program (CAPP), discuss specific types of emergencies and disasters and address the mitigation, preparedness, and response actions to be taken by IWC employees, management and the organizations charged with specific response and recovery tasks.

These plans contain basic guidance, direction, responsibilities, and administrative information. At IWC, the CSO recognized the criticality of regularly evaluating and improving company contingency plans. To that end, the CSO formed a project team to evaluate the entire IWC contingency program. Furthermore, it was decided that effective measures must be put in place to assist in managing the successes, failures, and costs of the program. The IWC CSO needed to develop a metrics management program. Before developing this program, the IWC CSO needed to further define the parameters of the company contingency planning program. The following section addresses those parameters.

The project team decided that to develop contingency plans, the preparedness process must include the following considerations and elements and be supported by an SMMP:

- *Assumptions*: Basic assumptions need to be developed in order to establish contingency planning ground rules. It is best to use as a baseline for planning, several possible "worst case" scenarios relative to time of event, type of event, available resources, building occupancy, evacuation of personnel, personnel stranded on site, and environmental factors such as weather conditions and temperature. Furthermore, consideration should be given to establishing response parameters for emergency events. Define what constitutes a minor emergency, a major emergency and a disaster.
- *Risk assessment and vulnerability analysis*: An IWC crisis management team was recommended by the project team and subsequently formed, with the responsibility to identify known and apparent vulnerabilities and risks associated with the type of business and geographic location of the enterprise. An assessment of risk and vulnerabilities will be made prior to upgrading contingency plans. All planning will be accomplished in accordance with a thorough understanding of actual and potential risks and vulnerabilities. The project team's risk assessment and vulnerability analysis also included an assessment of the policies and practices of IWC's critical relationships. That meant involving suppliers and customers in the contingency planning process. Regardless of how prepared IWC may be, if a critical supplier or many key suppliers are not also prepared for various potential contingencies, their inability to recover will adversely impact IWC. Therefore, critical suppliers will be integrated into the contingency planning process.
- *Types of hazards*: Planning for each and every type of hazard is not practical nor desirable. Grouping hazards into similar or like categories will allow for planning to address categories of hazards. Since many hazards have similar consequences and result in like damages, it is best to plan for them in categories. The following is a list of common hazards IWC may face:

  - Medical Emergencies;
  - Fires;
  - Bomb Threats;
  - High Winds;
  - Power Interruptions;
  - Floods;

- Hurricanes/Typhoons;
- Snow/Ice Storms/Blizzards;
- Hazard Materials Issues;
- Aircraft Crashes;
- Civil Disorders;
- Earthquakes;
- Terrorist Threats/Activities;
- Workplace Violence;
- Explosions; and
- Tornados.

- *Critical process identification*: The project team also decided that all critical processes must be identified. These processes must be ranked in accordance of criticality and importance to the productivity and survivability of the enterprise. The process of recovery will be focused on those critical processes that, when resumed, will restore operations to a minimal acceptable level. In essence, these processes are identified to be the first processes restored in the event of a major interruption to business operations. Failure to restore them presents the greatest possibility of damage or loss, including possible loss of IWC's competitive edge and market share.
- *Business impact analysis*: A business impact analysis must be accomplished to accurately determine the financial and operational impact that could result from an interruption to the IWC business processes. Moreover, all critical interdependencies, those processes or activities which critical processes are dependent upon, must be assessed to determine the extent they must be part of the contingency planning process.
- *Emergency response*: Establishing precisely who will respond to emergencies and what response capabilities are needed was considered by the project team to be essential. All participants in the emergency response process must understand what is expected of them. These expectations must be well defined and documented. Guidance for all employees on how to react in the event of an emergency and what their individual and collective responsibilities are must be documented and distributed. Organizational responsibilities must also be established to include the development of department-level emergency plans. Events such as building evacuation and role-call assembly need to be well defined so in the event of an actual emergency, there is no confusion or uncertainty as to what must be accomplished.
- *Incident management and crisis management*: The project team determined that as an incident escalates, the crisis management team should assume the responsibility of managing the crisis. How this process works and who has what responsibilities must be clearly stated in the contingency plans. In the event of an actual emergency, there will be people who will attempt to manage the incident or participate in crisis management; however, they should not have a role whatsoever in this process unless they were previously identified and trained as part of the crisis management team. Without established and well-defined incident management protocols and procedures, chaos is likely to occur.
- *Incident/event analysis*: When an emergency incident or event occurs interrupting or disrupting the IWC business process, the IWC security department personnel will be charged with responding to and managing the scene. They will also be responsible for conducting an incident/event analysis. This analysis will be conducted to determine the immediate extent of damage and the potential for subsequent additional damage. The appropriate resources must be notified and activated to assist in damage mitigation.

- *Business resumption planning*: The project team decided that the process of planning to facilitate the recovery of designated critical processes and the resumption of business in the event of an interruption to the business process must be performed in two parts. The first part focuses on business recovery in the short term while the other part focuses on business restoration in the long term. This process will also include establishment of priorities for restoration of critical processes, infrastructure and information systems.
- *Post event evaluation*: An assessment of preceding events to determine what went well, what went worse than planned, and what improvements to existing plans should be made is also part of the process. Learning from real events is an unfortunate opportunity. There is no better way to learn how to handle an emergency than to actually handle one. Unfortunately, experiencing an emergency may cause damage to IWC.

Now that you are familiar with the SMMP methodology, identify the various data, its purposes, and describe charts that would be used by an SMMP to support this effort.

As part of the contingency planning effort, the CSO wanted to develop a graphic depiction of the contingency planning function that shows how the business continuity planning program should be structured to include depicting the major elements of that structure. This tool could be used to help the CSO and corporate management focus on identifying areas where process measurements could provide a valuable insight into the effectiveness or efficiency of critical components of the contingency planning program. Additionally, the graphic depiction could be used as a training tool with executive management and all participants in this vital function. The IWC CSO's project team developed the chart shown in Figure 13-2.

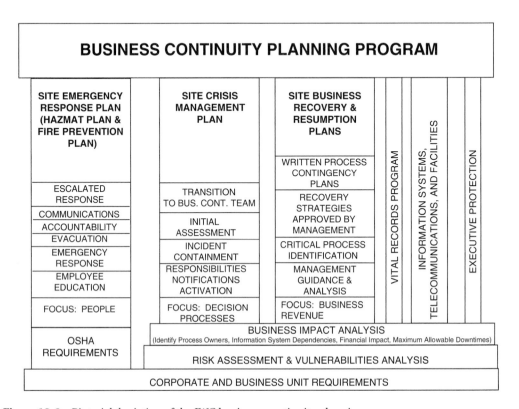

Figure 13-2   Pictorial depiction of the IWC business continuity planning program.

Another tool the IWC CSO decided would be useful would be a graphic depiction showing the relationship between IWC's crisis management team and business continuity team. The IWC CSO's project team developed the chart shown in Figure 13-3 to illustrate that relationship. As with the previous chart, the CSO will use this chart as a tool to assist in identifying potential metrics points and for briefing and educating executive management.

In addition, The IWC CSO wanted a simple chart to show the relationship between IWC departments and functions. Based on that need, the project team developed the chart shown in Figure 13-4.

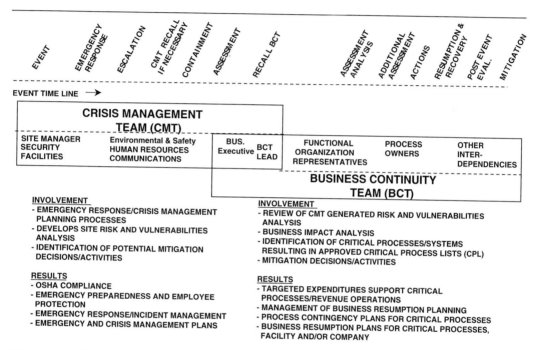

Figure 13-3 Pictorial depiction of the relationship between the IWC crisis management team and the IWC business continuity team.

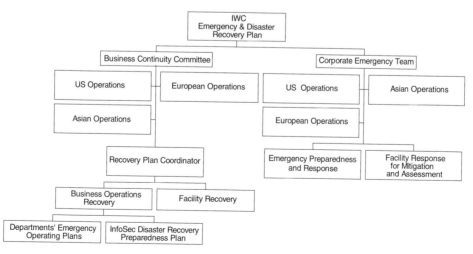

Figure 13-4 Pictorial depiction of the "organizational" relationship and structure of the emergency and disaster recovery plan.

At IWC, the information technology (IT) department and the information systems security (InfoSec) function were very closely related. In addition, the widget manufacturing was based entirely on computer systems and their associated networks. Therefore, the IWC CSO wanted a flowchart developed that would show the relationship between the general security functions in the event of an emergency and the InfoSec function led by the information systems security officer (ISSO).

Working with the CSO-appointed contingency planning project team, the ISSO and team developed a flowchart that depicted how they were currently established to deal with an emergency (see Figure 13-5).

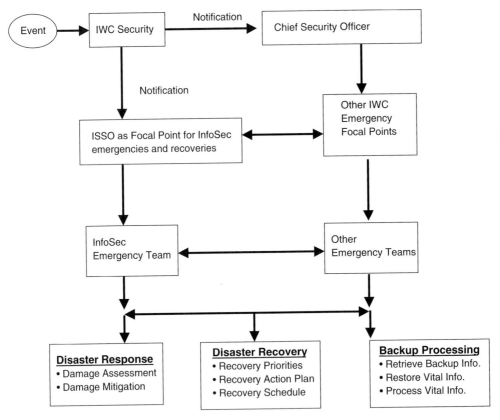

Figure 13-5   The communication and overview of the workflow between the CSO and the ISSO.

The CSO decided that this chart was sufficient as a tool to be used to demonstrate how communications and functional processes worked between contingency planning leader (CSO) and the information systems security lead (ISSO). It was also a tool that could be used to help identify critical areas in the process requiring regular measurement. Supporting this effort, process flowcharts could be developed to further break down the process activities.

In furtherance of understanding the contingency planning process, the IWC CSO determined it necessary to develop a threat matrix to link together the relationship between specific assets and infrastructure and related threats. The intent was to focus limited resources on planning for categories of scenarios that have a high likelihood of occurrence (see Figure 13-6).

The matrix chart[1] can be used as a tool not only to determine if the threats are mitigated through contingency planning policies, procedures and processes but also to test various aspects of the contingency plan by targeting potential threats to specific assets.

Threats	Data	Software	Hardware	Physical Facilities	Media & Supplies	Telecom	Employees	Other
Windstorm								
Snowstorm								
Earthquake								
Volcano								
Landslide								
Minor Fire								
Major Fire								
Catastrophic Fire								
Liquid leakage								
Environmental Problem								
Environmental Interruptions								
Telecom Interruptions								
Power Interruptions								
Power Fluctuations								
Human Errors								
System Errors								
Software Errors								
Data Errors								
Unauthorized Use of Assets								
Fraud								
Sabotage								
Unauthorized Disclosure								
Theft								
Denial of Service								
Others								

Assets

Figure 13-6   Matrix that can be used to link various threats to assets.

EXAMPLES OF CONTINGENCY PLANNING METRICS' MEASUREMENT TOOLS

One of the crucial elements of preparing for and especially reacting to emergencies is time. How quickly can an emergency response team, crisis management team, or business recovery team, react to any crisis? Since the precise time and location of a crisis or disaster cannot easily be predicted, preparation is difficult at best. For example, the CSO can anticipate a natural disaster will occur at his site in Florida during the hurricane season when a hurricane is identified as bearing down at the IWC location there. However, the CSO does not know if or when a large earthquake would occur in California. The best way to ensure contingency planning is effective is to test the plans before having to implement them during a real event. Ideally, the CSO and corporation will learn through testing and not the real event.

Much can be learned through testing (conducting drills). Gaps in the plans can be identified, team members will learn and become better prepared to react through practice, supporting resources can be identified and reaction times can be simulated. Does the CSO have any idea as to how long it will take to respond to a disaster and implement the appropriate contingency plan? The testing process will help the CSO learn and improve.

---

[1]   This matrix chart is one which has been in the authors "toolkit" for years. It is presented here as a basic method of identifying threats to assets as an initial step in addressing assets protection under contingency planning function.

Reaction and implementation time, along with other related contingency planning questions must be asked and answered through the testing process. The answers will help the CSO better frame the overall plan in a manner that considers the areas of highest risks and greatest vulnerability. With limited resources available, directing them at the most critical of processes is essential.

To address the reaction time problem, the IWC CSO directed that under the SMMP time and motion studies would be conducted to test each element of the contingency planning program to ensure that the processes implemented are effective and efficient. By that, we mean all planned actions are taken that would be necessary to maximize the mitigation of the threat.

The CSO's contingency planning project team developed a "Time-Motion Study Collection Data Sheet" (see Figure 13-7) to be used when testing various aspects of the contingency plan. Again, testing such a large-scale plan cannot be done at once, as this would neither be an effective nor efficient way to measure the results. As the saying goes, "How do you eat an elephant? A bite at a time!"

All components and processes of the contingency plan can eventually be documented and captured in a database as part of an information processing system for analyses. The value of resources necessary to prepare and implement contingency plans can be established and compared with the potential losses to IWC should a disaster strike. Furthermore, through drilling, redundant or unnecessary actions can be eliminated, thereby streamlining the process better and enabling the team to react and implement more efficiently. All these changes should be documented to include time variances between the old process and the new process, as well as materials used that can be translated into costs and incorporated into the SMMP.

Responding to an emergency requires skilled and trained persons working to a "practiced" plan. Recovering from a disaster quickly so as to minimize losses incurred with the operation shut-down, requires meticulous planning, preparation and testing.

As a CSO, are you prepared to handle a crisis as effectively and efficiently as possible? What actions can you take to help you get there if you are not? You can start by identifying in detail the contingency planning function and its components. How do the many processes work? Once that is established, test each process. In some case only a "table top" test will be necessary or practical (such as preparing to obtain additional monetary assets from a lender to assist with a situation). In other cases, an actual test will work (such as testing how long it takes to get a response team from one point to another). Through process analysis, time/motion studies and conducting test/drills, much can be learned to "perfect" the process. Document the results into the SMMP.

Keep in mind, in each phase of analysis, study and testing, data is collected and measurements are made. From this point, efficiency and effectiveness gains can be identified through additional data collection tools with the goal to continue to gain efficiencies while increasing effectiveness (see Figures 13-7 through 13-10 for examples of some of the basic security metrics measurement data collection charts that can be developed by following the data collection methods explained in previous chapters).

Time-Motion Study Collection Sheet

This sheet is to be used to record the individual units of a particular measured task.
It is to be used to track the time it takes to perform contingency planning functions that are part of your responsibilities under the contingency planning function.
A task identifier code will be used that coincides with the numbered task of the contingency planning detailed flowchart.
Cost at $15USD per hour based on average IWC salary and benefits costs.

Task Identifier		Start Time		End Time		Total Time		Cost (USD)

Figure 13-7   Example of a simplified form for collecting time and motion data.

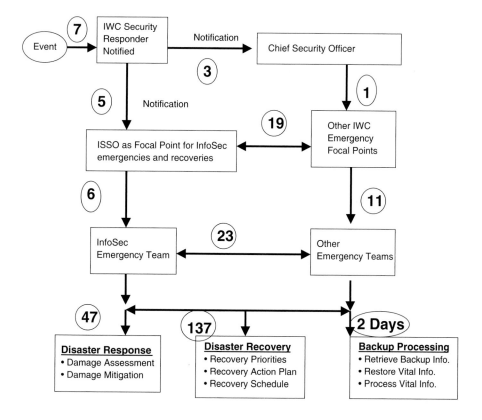

NOTE: All numbers are times in minutes, except where otherwise noted..

Figure 13-8   Example of a flowchart matched to the data collected through a time-motion study.

Once this portion was tested over time, an average response and recovery time can be established for each tested threat matched to each asset. This will take time to accomplish but, in both the short-term and the long-term, the CSO can begin to more effectively and efficiently manage this function.

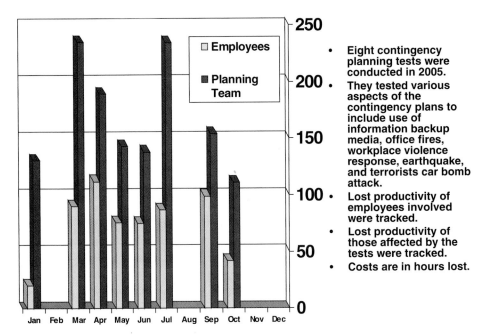

Figure 13-9   Example of a metrics chart based on data collected during contingency planning exercises which show the average lost productivity and other costs of contingency planning testing.

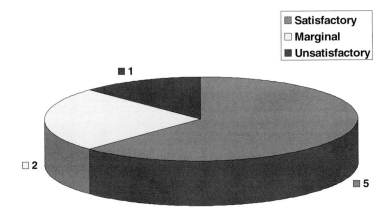

Figure 13-10   Example of a metrics chart showing the results of contingency planning test during a one year period.

CONTINGENCY PLANNING CASE STUDY

The CEO was concerned about IWC being prepared for any emergencies and disasters. The CSO was asked to provide a briefing to the executive management to inform them as to how well IWC was prepared to handle such incidents. As the CSO, what information would you provide the executive management using what metrics-related charts?

Much of what you brief and how you communicate it will be based on the culture and working environment at your corporation or government agency. At IWC, the CSO provided the following metrics-related briefing charts:

- Contingency planning internal and external (government regulations) drivers
- How the contingency plan was integrated into the total IWC CAPP
- How IWC was structured to react in the event of an emergency or disaster
- An example of the process flow if an emergency was declared
- An example of the process flow if a disaster was declared
- An example of how recovery would take place
- What IWC personnel were doing to prepare for emergencies and disasters
- The costs of preparation
- Examples of estimated costs of recovery using several emergency and disaster preparedness charts
- Results of the tests conducted year-to-date broken down from a summary chart to various types of tests conducted within what departments, etc.
- An overall summary chart

SUMMARY

Contingency planning may not be a traditional security process but, in today's global business environment, corporate security is assuming a much greater role and responsibility for its implementation. Even prior to the events of September 11, 2001, many organizations were becoming more conscious of the need to have contingency plans. September 11th accelerated the process for many, including IWC. A complete contingency planning program has three major elements:

1. Emergency Response
2. Crisis Management
3. Business Continuity: Business Recovery and Business Resumption

Contingency planning-related functions require complex preparation, documentation and testing. Such a critical business process—the contingency planning process—must be made as effective and efficient as possible. Measuring that process through process analysis and testing using metric tools designed to meet your organization's needs will ensure the overall process is as effective as it can be. Security metrics management can help manage this important function in a cost-effective way.

Section III

Physical Security Metrics

…Nestle Metrics Emphasize Prevention and Protection…When there is a civil war where your people are working, one physical security metric rises above all others: Keeping all of your employees alive… John Hedley, head of group security for Nestle in Vevy, Switzerland…[1]

This section incorporates Chapters 14–19 and includes the security functions that fall under the umbrella of what we choose to call "physical security." The security functions or subfunctions include:

- Chapter 14: Guard Force
- Chapter 15: Technical Security Systems
- Chapter 16: Locks and Keys
- Chapter 17: Fire Protection
- Chapter 18: Executive Protection
- Chapter 19: Event Security

Physical security has been around longer than any other security function and is the heart of any assets protection program. It is the most visible of the assets protection defenses and it is also often the most costly category of assets protection or security functions. Therefore, particular attention should be paid to cost-benefits.

An overview of the physical security drivers, concepts, organizational structure and basic flowchart used at IWC is presented in the following charts.

---

[1] Quoted from CSOONLINE.COM, "Where the Metrics Are" article, February 2005 issue.

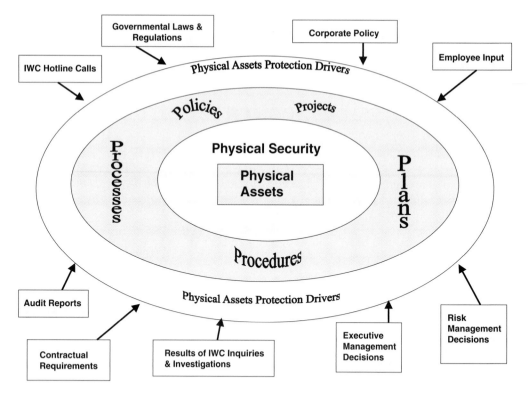

Figure Section III -1   The physical security drivers.

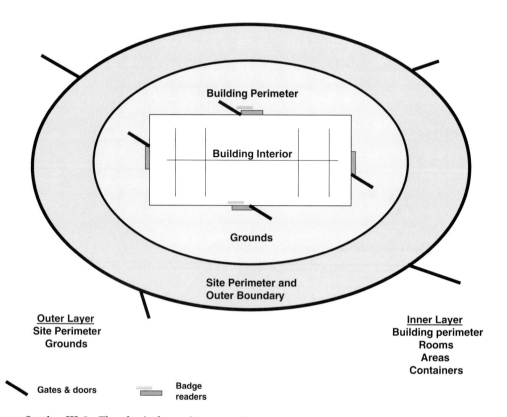

Figure Section III-2   The physical security concept.

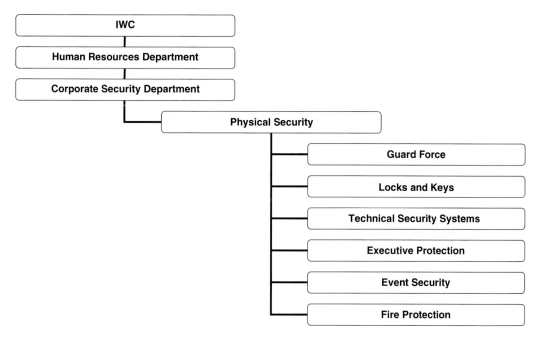

Figure Section III-3   The physical security IWC organizational structure.

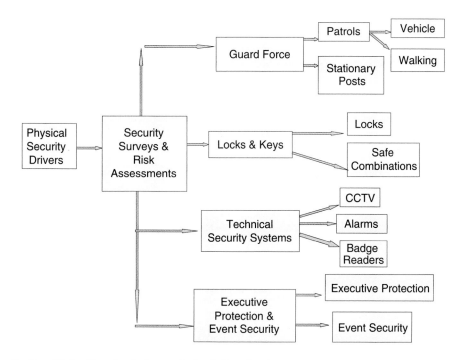

Figure Section III-4   The physical security basic flowchart.

Chapter 14

The Guard Force

This chapter will address the use of security metrics as a tool for managing a security guard force, which is one of the most costly, labor-intensive aspects of any corporate assets protection program (CAPP).

INTRODUCTION

Physical security is the first line of defense in the protection of corporate assets. Physical security has been a part of assets protection longer than any other security function and it is also often the most expensive. Security guards, the "human part" of the physical security functions, have probably been around the longest. Ever since there was something of value that owners wanted protected but could not do the job themselves, security guards have been employed to protect those owners' assets, as well as the owners themselves.

Security guard forces are either proprietary—in other words, they are directly employed by the company or government agency they support—or they are outsourced and belong to a security services provider. Proprietary security guards are employees of the company. Outsourced security guards are employees of a different company—one that sells security services. Which is best for a company or government agency and how to make that determination will be addressed in Chapter 24, Outsourcing.

Security guards serve many roles as part of the physical layer of protection provided for a company. Those roles include:

- Controlling the physical access of personnel to the sites, facilities or areas they protect.
- Controlling internal access to sensitive areas inside the buildings of the facilities they protect.
- External roving patrols on the corporate property, where they serve as observers and deterrents.
- Internal roving patrols inside the corporation's property as both observers and deterrents. They may have many additional tasks assigned to them in this role but observation and deterrence are usually the primary ones.
- Control Center operators, which usually includes alarm monitoring and closed circuit television (CCTV) monitoring.

- First responders to incidents and emergencies.
- Support the emergency response and crisis management process.

As part of the "front line" of protection and first responders, security guards are often the first on the scene to provide aid to the sick or injured and are therefore almost always trained in basic first aid. They also are usually the first organization representative a nonemployee sees when visiting a corporate office. In this capacity they serve as one of the corporation's unofficial public relations personnel. They are the initial image of the corporation. Because they make regular contact with most if not all corporate employees, they also become somewhat of an informal information officer.

> *One should always be cautious about the nontraditional use of security guards, as any duties that are not directly related to protecting assets detracts from their ability to protect those assets. Furthermore, as the CSO, that "nonprotection of assets" work is coming out of your budget!*

A good use of a security metrics program will include data collection relative to all the work the security guard force performs. That, coupled with some time and motion studies, will help determine if the security guards' time is being used cost-effectively in the protection of the corporate assets.

For example, more than once a roving security guard walking the inner areas of a company has been asked by someone who is "very busy" to do them a favor. When the guard passes by the company cafeteria, could the guard please bring back a sandwich for the "too busy" employee? The guard, wanting to be nice, obliges and soon it becomes more of a habit than a one-time favor. As a Chief Security Officer (CSO), you are paying for this "room service."

One of the difficult decisions that must be made is whether or not to arm security guards. Of course, the main consideration with this decision is one of corporate liabilities. Is risk to corporate assets at such a high level that it warrants the use of armed security guards? Clearly in many instances it is and also in many instances, it is not so clear. However, with the ever-increasing threats of terrorist attacks against corporations, especially at corporations operating in hostile locations throughout the world, the need to arm security guards should be first and foremost based on the perceived risks to assets, as well as the value of those assets. There may also be liability issues for not adequately protecting assets—keep in mind that includes employees—when dangers are known or when risks are high. One must also consider whether the local government allows the arming of corporate security guards.

As today's and tomorrow's advanced-technology physical security-based protection devices continue to become more capable and less costly, functions traditionally performed by security guards are gradually being performed with high technology—or at least the support of high technology.

From CCTV cameras with smart software capable of recognizing unusual behavior or situations, to the use of biometrics and other sophisticated sensors, technology in many cases can do much more than a human. However, as long as assets require physical security protection, there will always be a need for a human to respond to the scene of alarms and emergencies, at least until the day arrives when sophisticated robots can take their place. Furthermore, there are situations where human judgment is needed and that has yet to be effectively replicated through the use of high technology.

GUARD FORCE SECURITY ORGANIZATION

As a CSO, one must be sure that the security guard force is logically located in the proper organizational structure. At IWC, (see Figure 14-1) it falls within the physical security organization.

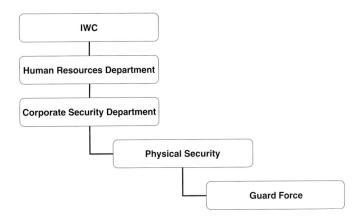

Figure 14-1   The security guard force's location within the IWC organization.

GUARD FORCE SECURITY DRIVERS AND FLOWCHARTS

As with all security functions that are related to assets protection, there are certain drivers that cause the need for security guards:

- Laws and regulations
- Corporate policies
- Risk management decisions
- Executive management decisions
- Contractual requirements that impact physical assets protection
- Input of employees relative to physical assets protection
- Situational events and emergency situations

These all drive the need for physical security. A major portion of most physical security protective measures includes the use of security guards. Understanding how effective they are as part of the protective profile and the CAPP is the job of the CSO.

As with all security functions, an analysis of the function should be made and graphic depictions developed of how the processes work (see Figure 14-2). That includes detailed flowcharts relative to the security guard function, procedures, and processes.

The guard force flowchart shows the basic process used for IWC's proprietary guards. This chart is then the basis for more detailed flowcharts. However, even from this initial flowchart, one can see an area where the security metrics management process might help reduce costs. Can you identify that particular part of the flowchart? (See the case study below.) Often, the easiest way to begin the security metrics management program is to begin with the first step of a security function as shown in their flowchart. After that is in place, move on to the next step and the next, etc.

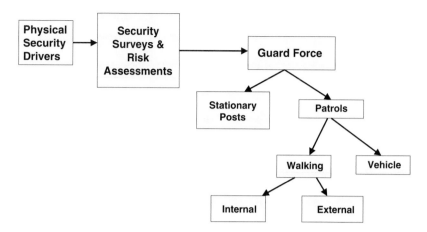

Figure 14-2 High-level flowchart for the guard force organization.

GUARD FORCE METRICS CHARTS EXAMPLES

As we stated earlier, security guard forces are probably a corporation's most expensive form of physical security. Therefore, it behooves the CSO to track the costs of the security guard force and a security metrics management program (SMMP) is one of the ways of doing so. It does not matter if the security guard force is proprietary or managed as an outsourced contract. It will still be expensive, and therefore the costs-benefits should be tracked and analyzed.

> *When trying to maximize assets protection functions with limited staff (and what CSO does not have staff limitations?), one should prioritize the projects to maximize cost-benefits of security functions by starting with the most costly first. In that case, the security guard force will probably be the number one target for security metrics management and cost-minimizing analyses.*

There are certain security processes that are not directly related to the protection of assets. These processes should be addressed first because, as a CSO, you are paying for security guards that are to protect assets; however, they are not always doing that. For example, consider the hours each guard spends in meetings and the total number of hours and costs of security guards spent in pre-position posting meetings (see Figure 14-3). Yes, providing information and communicating with the shift's guard force is necessary; however, there may be better ways to do it.

One obvious objective is to find ways to either reduce such meetings or some way to eliminate them altogether. Quite often, security guards are being paid overtime, which can be expensive (see Figure 14-4). One security metric would be to track the scheduled work hours against the overtime hours and then find the systemic cause of the overtime hours. The next step would be to try to eliminate or at least minimize the overtime hours. For example, some security guard forces are paid from the time they show up at work, punch-in, and then sit around awaiting roll-call. Obviously, this would be one area to try to eliminate. Although one must always be cautious—guards are people, too—in working these projects and reducing costs, while trying not to adversely impact guard force morale. That won't be easy, especially if you want to take away the overtime and impact their expected compensation.

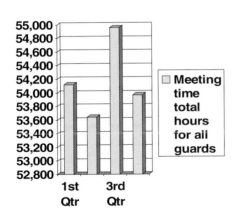

- Objective: Determine if there is a more efficient yet effective way to meet pre-posting meeting goals for the guard force.
- Method: Collect time guards spend in a pre-post meeting.
- Tool: Sign-in and out log: all guards will sign in and out of pre-posting meeting.
- Process: Each guard's time in meeting summed and totaled for each meeting. Then that total is entered into a spreadsheet and summed each quarter and mapped to a bar chart.

Figure 14-3   The number of hours the shift guard force spends in pre-posting meetings.

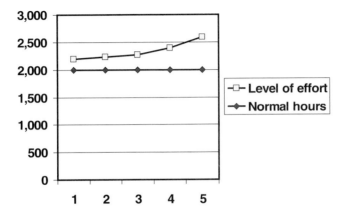

Figure 14-4   The number of hours that are budgeted for a guard versus the hours spent working. The difference is the overtime hours to be paid.

One last word of caution: some proprietary guard forces are unionized. That means that any changes must be negotiated with the union. Current contractual agreements may preclude immediate action; however, the issue must be considered when negotiating a new contract.

When dealing with a union guard force, the CSO must have a good understanding of the union contract and all related issues. Failing to do so may adversely impact the CSO's ability to find a way to achieve cost efficiencies. If a CSO does not understand the contract and how to go about using an SMMP with a unionized security guard force, the CSO does so at his/her peril. A CSO would be smart to work with the human relations specialists in this area along with the company legal staff and contract specialists in order to stay out of trouble, as security guard force processes and procedural changes are always a very sensitive issue.

186 Physical Security Metrics

GUARD FORCE CASE STUDY

The guard force at IWC is a proprietary guard force—all security guards are employees of the IWC. The guard force flowchart (Figure 14-2) depicts the various functions and processes at a high level. As you develop your security functional and process flowcharts, you would of course go into much greater detail. For example, you may drill down in to subprocesses, depicting such processes as the assignment of vehicles and the process for maintaining them.

However, even this high-level chart provides some points where metrics measurement can and should take place. For example, there is that pre-posting guard meeting. The guard force is made up of hourly employees. That means that they must attend the pre-post meeting. Since they are hourly employees, they must be paid for this time. The "problem" is that they are paid to be on duty protecting IWC assets. They are not doing that sitting in a meeting. Yes, the meeting is important, but what is the cost of that meeting? Is there a more efficient yet effective way to meet the objectives of that meeting? Looking at it from an SMMP perspective may provide some ideas once the data is collected.

Let's assume that at IWC the proprietary guard force is a nonunionized guard force. Therefore, there are fewer complications because there are no contract issues to deal with. Now, how would you begin to look at efficiency gains, thus making the guards more productive? This would include:

- Being on duty on time;
- Providing them the required information;
- Ensuring that they are presentable in appearance; and
- Save money by not having them attend the pre-posting meetings.

Of course, there are some things that quickly come to mind, such as having computers built-in to the patrol vehicles, LAN connections, or mainframe dumb terminal connections at each post. They would receive up-to-date information via their computer terminal and it would also allow them to sign-in for work by logging into the system. In addition, their assignments for the next day would be sent to them via email before the end of their shifts. That way they could just show up the next day at their posts for work.

As far as proper appearance, one must trust them to have sufficient pride in themselves that they would show up for work in proper appearance and in proper physical condition. In addition, the shift supervisor must make the post rounds and could determine if their appearance met IWC standards.

All of that sounds good on the surface, but what are those costs? So, you see, we are getting ahead of ourselves. First, we should look at this project by isolating the target to be the pre-post meeting. That being the case, what is the first question that must be asked?

Hopefully, you immediately know that answer: "What are the drivers that require that meeting to take place"? Yes, every stage of the process has drivers that drive the process to be performed the way it is being performed. However, who decided that was the most effective and efficient way of meeting the objectives that were to be met by the pre-post meeting? Was it decided after a thorough and detailed analysis? Probably not.

It was probably done that way because that is the way it was done in the military or law enforcement, and the person who was hired to manage the guard force may have been ex-military or ex-law enforcement—or maybe retired from one or the other. Also, there is the old fall-back reason: "We have always done it this way!" (Yes, that way since at least the last two millenniums!) The point being, you can pretty much assume very little formal analysis was done on which to base the decision to have a meeting.[1]

The objective of the metrics management approach to this project is to save time and therefore money by finding more efficient and yet at least as effective a process to meet the objective now being met by the pre-post meeting.

So, what are the steps, the tasks, to be completed for this effort? They should include:

- Identify the drivers that make the meeting necessary[2]
- Validate the drivers as actually being necessary
- Develop a *detailed*[3] process flowchart of the pre/post meeting process
- Analyze the process flowchart to identify centers of data collection
- Develop security metrics management spreadsheets and charts that are to be used to graphically and statistically display for analyses and briefing the results of the security metrics management process

The charts shown above are to be used by the IWC guard force manager and the CSO to support at least one of the project goals, and that is the goal of determining the true cost in terms of hours that can simply be converted to a monetary value. This is an efficiency gain goal and not a productivity enhancement goal since the guards are being paid to attend a meeting and not protect assets at the meeting.

Let's look at an example: if you have a 20-person-per-shift guard force and shifts rotate every eight hours, 24/7, and their pay and benefits is $12 per hour, then each shift costs IWC $240 per hour for pre-posting meetings or $720 each 24 hours. If one hour is spent in a pre-posting meeting per shift, that is costing the CSO's budget, thus IWC, $262,800 a year just to attend the pre-posting meetings!

As you can see, the numbers are substantial in both hours and dollars spent. When first looking at the process, one would never know that the costs would be so high. That is the advantage of using a process flow analysis coupled with an SMMP.

The next step of this process would be to brainstorm first with the manager and supervisors of the guard force and each of the supervisors with members of their guard force to look for alternatives to having these meetings and still be able to meet the goals of the meetings.

---

[1] This may seem like a very simple activity to be talking about in dealing with security metrics management; however, we are trying to show you some of the logic that goes into viewing security metrics management and showing you a technique. So, bear with us as we show you a process. Concentrate on the thinking that goes into the process as that process, that logic, can be applied throughout all the security functions and subfunctions.

[2] Don't forget that drivers are not the same as requirements. For example, requirements may be thought of as what is required to be done during the meeting and not what requires the meeting in the first place. By always starting with the drivers, one can be sure to maintain clarity when analyzing and also discussing this and related projects with others.

[3] A detailed flowchart is required so that every aspect of the process can be analyzed. You may be surprised at how many times some little aspect of the process is ignored as being too inconsequential, which ends up being one of the major factors in the process as other tasks are dependent on it. So, do not take anything for granted when developing a security functional process flowchart.

> *Not everyone affected by security metrics management will be supportive of it, even after they recognize the value of measuring performance and making changes.*

This all seems all well and good on paper and in theory. However, would it be prudent for the CSO to anticipate that effecting a change to this process may not be readily accepted by the guard force? Do you actually think that most of the guard force will enthusiastically support a project designed to drive change and ultimately reduce costs? Resistance can be expected even when the effort is well-communicated and participation and feedback from supervision and the guard force is sought. Change is not an easy thing for many to face. It is particularly difficult when it may adversely affect the paychecks of those being asked to make changes.

GUARD FORCE SUMMARY

The security guard force is often the most expensive component of the physical security function in any corporation, and therefore it should be a high priority for measuring processes through an SMMP.

As a CSO, you will probably find there are many ways to improve the performance, efficiency and effectiveness of your guard force. In this chapter we used the example of paying security guards for briefings that could be considered a very inefficient process, as in this process the guards experience a substantial amount of downtime and are being paid for that downtime. This inefficiency can lead to additional costs incurred, as it can lead to overtime expenses or even additional hiring. Remember, labor costs in physical security are generally the biggest portion of the security budget.

SMMP techniques can successfully be used to assist in the analysis of security guard force processes. Data collections, flowcharting, and process analyses are tools to better help the CSO understand how things are working and where efficiencies (cost savings) may be gained.

As a CSO, one must be cautious when dealing with collective bargaining units (unions) representing your guard force. Assistance from the legal staff, human relations and contract specialist is a must.

Chapter 15

Technical Security Systems

Technical security systems, when used properly, can efficiently and effectively support assets protection processes. How to measure those systems and benefits will be discussed in this chapter.

INTRODUCTION

When we discuss technical security systems we are referring to those systems that are used to support the physical security function. In particular, these systems are used to control and channel access to physical areas or other assets being protected. Generally, we are talking about intrusion detection systems (for our discussion we include fire alarm systems in this group; moreover, we will use the terms intrusion detection and alarm systems interchangeably in this chapter), access control systems and surveillance systems (primarily video).

The use of intrusion detection systems, access control systems and surveillance systems—the three primary security systems used and categorized as technical security systems (TSS)—are constantly evolving, becoming more capable, sophisticated and complex. With continued and rapid improvement of microprocessor technology, these systems are continuously improving.

The use of these systems, when effectively integrated into the entire physical security functional approach to assets protection, can provide reliable and cost-effective protection. One reason for this is that they can effectively supplement and in some cases replace the security guard force.

TECHNICAL SECURITY SYSTEMS ORGANIZATION

The technical security systems (TSS) organization is an integral part of the physical security organization of IWC (see Figure 15-1). TSS functions may also be outsourced where proven economical to do so. For example, having the capability to monitor intrusion detection systems (alarm monitoring) requires having a human in the loop 24 hours a day and seven days a week. This can be a costly proposition. Purchasing the service of alarm monitoring from a company that specializes in alarm-monitoring capabilities may be significantly less costly than performing that service internally, and it can be done remotely.

Using technical security systems does help reduce security costs—mostly the cost of human labor. However, for TSS to be effective, they do require human support. First of all, they are not maintenance free. For continued effectiveness, they should be periodically upgraded. One of the critical subprocesses of the TSS function is maintaining state-of-the-art systems to the extent that they are necessary. That requires the installation of system upgrades as they become available as well as ensuring maintenance agreements are kept current and maintenance is performed as required. TSS are often the first line of defense for a CAPP, e.g., surveillance systems—closed circuit television (CCTVs)—as they are used at the perimeter of a site, building, or area.

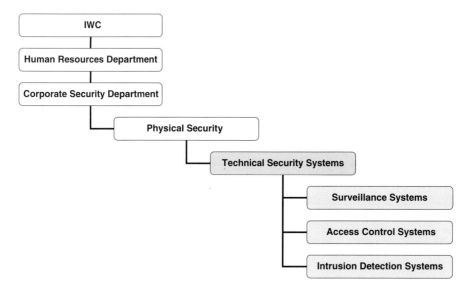

Figure 15-1   Where the TSS function and subfunctions fit into the physical security organization.

What drives the need for TSS? The same security-related drivers that drive the need for physical security drive all physical security subfunctions and subprocesses. Assets protection begins with physical security. Physical security is the foundation for all other aspects of security. Simply stated, without physical security measures, all other security measures are rendered less effective or ineffective.

TECHNICAL SECURITY SYSTEMS FLOWCHARTS

As we have stressed throughout all of the basic security functions' chapters, once the drivers have been identified and the security functions defined and integrated into a security organization, the next step is to analyze them to fully understand how they work. The analysis processes begin with developing process flowcharts, starting with a macro process view and progressing down to the micro view, (see Figure 15-2) then working into the more detailed flowcharts. As discussed in earlier chapters, creating process flowcharts allows for each step in a process to be identified and analyzed. The development of process flowcharts (diagrams) facilitates a better understanding of how the process really works and where areas for improvement may exist.

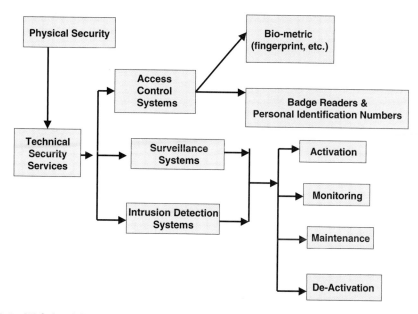

Figure 15-2 High-level flowchart for the Technical Security Systems organization.

As part of the TSS Organization flowcharts, let's look at a more detailed flowchart of a TSS subprocess. Let's look at the subprocess of issuing the new IWC employee a badge for access to IWC's "Proprietary Research Area" (see Figure 15-3).

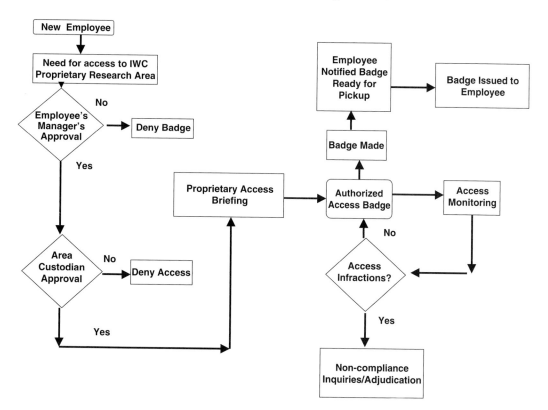

Figure 15-3 A more detailed portion of the TSS relating to issuance of an area access badge to a new employee.

Can you identify areas where security metrics will assist in determining the efficiency of this process? What methods are needed to analyze the function to identify more effective and efficient processing methodologies?

TECHNICAL SECURITY SYSTEMS METRICS

Intrusion Detection Systems (commonly referred to as alarm systems)

Intrusion detection systems are one of the different and sometimes many layers used in the protection of a facility. How they are used and to what extent should be determined in the planning process. The site physical security survey should identify vulnerabilities, current and potential, and the layers of protection in use. When assessed against known or suspected threats, the need for intrusion detection systems to augment physical protections should become apparent. Typically, intrusion detection systems are used at the perimeter of a building, facility or site. Moreover, alarms are used for highly sensitive internal areas requiring an extra degree or layer of protection.

Intrusion and fire detection systems generally save money by replacing people in many instances. In the long run, they are more cost-effective and efficient than just using guards alone. Before assuming additional risk, ensure that you consult with executive management and have them accept that additional level of risk. You can determine the cost-benefits and whether or not alarms will actually save you money by applying security metrics processes.

Alarm systems cost more to install than to maintain. The cost of alarm systems is greatest in the acquisition and installation phase. Once installed, maintenance and monitoring cost are generally much less than people cost. A return on investment can be calculated and used as a selling point on the value of alarm systems. Using alarm systems offsets the need for some guards. The savings in recurring guard costs can be compared to the cost for acquisition and installation of alarm systems. Remember, over several years, it is usually more cost-effective to use alarm systems to augment security than to rely on a larger guard force.

When seeking to use technical security measures to augment other physical security measures, it is important to develop a business case on the value of doing so. A key element in gaining budgetary approval for installing and maintaining a modern alarm system is through collecting relative data to demonstrate the cost-benefits (return on investment) and then develop an effective means of communicating that message. Essentially, tell the story using metrics graphically depicted. Some of the data collected and graphically depicted should include:

- Cost of current physical security—assets protection—processes (For example, security guard force posts)
- Cost of a replacement security system of alarms
- Recurring costs of the alarm system, e.g., maintenance, responding to false alarms

Let's take the recurring costs factor and, using a security metrics management process, look at what those incidents and costs would be over the first year after installation and reported over quarterly periods. (See Figures 15-4 and Figure 15-5.).

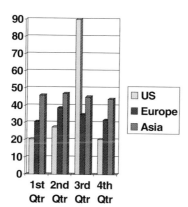

- IWC's alarm system was installed and maintained world-wide at all IWC facilities by XABY Global Alarms Company

- The high problem areas in the US corporate warehouse in the third quarter was due to numerous maintenance problems

Figure 15-4 The number of quarterly alarm problems over a year's period at all locations.

The issue of maintenance problems should be handled in conjunction with the corporate contract specialist to ensure that contractual specifications are met.

Why would one want to track such incidents and costs? Well, there is the obvious reason, which is that the data is needed to validate assumptions and to conduct a cost-benefit analysis.

Collecting this type of data may also be useful in other areas such as dealing with the manufacturer or contractor if problems with maintenance and reliability occur. There's nothing like having real data to characterize a problem and help you state your case.

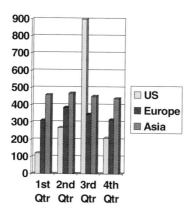

- IWC's alarm system was installed and maintained world-wide at all IWC facilities by XABY Global Alarms Company.

- The costs are the total costs of repair and maintenance at all locations converted into U.S. dollars (thousands).

- The costs include "alarm substitute costs" of using a security guard to replace the alarm system while it is under repair.

Figure 15-5 The number of quarterly alarm problems over a year's period at all locations.

What supplemental measures should be used with Figure 15-4's and Figure 15-5's to enhance the CSO understanding of related problems and help state "the case"? Actually, there are several, to include:

- How long the alarms were off-line on each occasion—total time.
- How long was each alarm off-line on each occasion—individual alarm total times.
- The number of times a security guard was required to supplement/replace the cumulative downtime of the alarm systems—total costs in time and money. You may find that some of your security guard overtime is due to such problems.

- The number of times a security guard was required to supplement/replace each downtime of each alarm system— total in time and money.
- The time from alarm malfunction to call to maintenance provider and their response time. That is to say from problem identification to problem fix. This would be very useful as the contract should call for the maintenance contractor to respond within a specific period of time and maybe after the response window has been exceeded, the contractor incurs all additional costs, for example, security guard expenses as substitute for the alarm system.

> *Automated Access Control Systems—Badges and biometric technology used as part of the system such as retina scanners and fingerprint identification processing.*

Today's technologically advanced access control systems offer several options, or combination of options, for controlling access through automated systems. The key is to provide a reliable, cost-effective, integrated system. How does one go about determining how to do that? The first step is to evaluate your specific needs. Before a CSO pursues the acquisition and installation of a new system he/she must understand what is needed and what is available to meet those needs. The focus of the analysis, once needs (based on identified drivers) have been established, should be to seek the best value. That system that provides the best return on investment and passes the cost versus benefit test should be selected.

Establishing the criterion for system requirements will be easier if the CSO has a metric management program in place. If the important measures are already in place, the CSO should have the necessary data to help make informed decisions. For example, if the CSO knows the systems currently in use have a 3% failure rate, which is unacceptable, then the CSO must seek out a system that provides a less frequent failure rate (something less than 3%). If the CSO has no real idea what the current system's failure rate is, it would be difficult to definitively declare what an acceptable failure rate for the new system must be.

As stated above, the use of metrics to help analyze an existing process or system and develop future requirements can help the CSO attain the best system possible to meet IWC assets protection needs. Keep in mind, the end result will only be as good as the analyses and the quality of the security metrics used in the analysis process. To that end, let's revisit Figure 15-3, which is a process flow diagram for the badge process and see what may be missing or how this diagram should drive additional questions to be considered as part of the analysis.

In this flowchart depicting the badge issuance process, you will note that the process seems to be logical from the standpoint of an employee gaining access to a restricted area where the employee will work. What is missing from this flowchart and what should be included are the"What ifs":

- What if the person doesn't show up to get the access badge?
- What happens if the paperwork (employee's manager and area custodian's justification and approval for access) is not received and the employee shows up for badge processing?

It is of course a wasted trip, resulting in loss of productivity on the part of the new employee, which always translates into a loss of money. When you, as a CSO, look at the flowchart (Figure 15-3), can you find other areas where there may be opportunities for potential changes that may decrease process and productivity costs? If so, what are they? One place to start is with a macro view.

From the first step to the completion of the last step:

- How long does it take, on average, to process one badge request?
- Is this reasonable?
- Is this desired?
- Could, or should, the process cycle time be faster?

These are some of the questions a CSO should be asking and thinking about as part of the process analysis.

Let's assume that the IWC Technical Security Systems Manager is directed by the CSO to determine just how effectively or efficiently the process to make a new badge is and to be prepared to depict that process in terms of cycle times. Now, why would the CSO direct that action? In this case, someone has complained that his or her employee has not received their badge, or did not receive it in a timely manner; thus, that employee's ability to perform their duties was adversely impacted. The CSO has heard this before and wants to get to the root of the problem and "fix it once and for all."

Once the cost in terms of time spent (which equates to productivity loss) is known, then one can further break down and analyze the process flow to determine potential areas for efficiency gains. Once discovered, a project plan could be developed to drive changes to the process. Moreover, security metrics should be developed to use in monitoring that process change to determine if it worked.

> *There is no use in making a change if you don't know what the current condition is and what you expect the future condition to be.*

When conducting the analysis of the badge issuance process, a review of existing process documentation for some specified period of time (a year would be good) showing all the dates of requests, approvals, and issuance of the badge should be part of the analysis. Essentially, first the CSO must understand how the current process performs. All captured information (security metrics data) should be placed into an automated database making it available for better analysis. For example, the data that should be considered for entrance into the database, making it available for analysis, is as follows:

- Date of request
- Employee's organization
- Manager's name
- Date of employee manager's approval
- Area custodian's name
- Date the custodian approved the access
- Date the request was received in the Badge Office
- Date the badge was made
- Date the employee was notified to come pick up the badge
- Date the employee signed for the badge

This information would allow the "badge process improvement project team" to not only identify the times that were spent in each step of the process but also who the people were in the process and their organizations. Why is this important information? Every step in the process must be examined to ensure the process analysis is complete. Failing to do so may cause an important step to be missed, thus resulting in a missed opportunity to improve the process. It is possible the apparent problem may not be with the badge-making process itself but with a related or supporting processes, such as delays in management approval of the badge requests.

Once the project is complete—that is, the process has been changed—improved—and effective measures are in place—the CSO and his staff need to monitor performance watching for changes and trends. Improvements are expected; however, if they are not achieved, the CSO should revisit the process analysis phase. Furthermore, with effective measures in place, the CSO can use graphic depictions of the metrics to demonstrate success to all interested parties, for instance to executive management to demonstrate improvements, cost savings or problem resolutions.

An important point to consider, as mentioned in an earlier paragraph, is the examination of related or supporting processes during the process analysis phase. The CSO may conclude after analyzing and measuring the badge-issuing process that the process itself works as designed and expected. The root cause of apparent process failures had more to do with supporting processes than the badge-issuing process itself. For example, if the badge-issuing process was actually performing better than expected but employees were failing to pick up their newly made badges in a timely fashion, then the delays or loss of productive time was actually caused by a supporting process. Process analysis will help the CSO uncover problems like this.

In the case of this project, the results of the study were depicted in graphic form and used as part of a presentation to management depicting the overall "State of Security." (See Figure 15-6 and 15-7.)

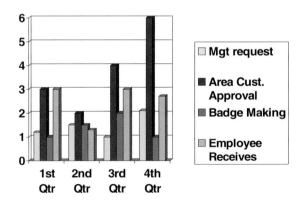

Figure 15-6   The average time it takes to process an employee's area access badge.

When you look at the chart, what stands out to you? It should be the length of time that it takes on average to process an area badge request starting with the longest amount of time, second longest and so on. It appears that the main problem here is the length of time it takes the area custodian to approve access to the area under the custodian's responsibility, followed by the length of time for the employee to pick up the badge. Therefore, this is an area which can be targeted for process improvement.

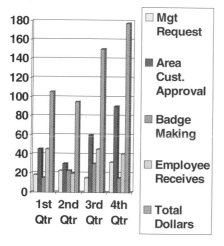

- The area access badge processing time is based on all badge processed on a quarterly basis during 2005.
- The average time was then converted to dollars using $15 per hour, that includes benefits' costs, as provided by the Human Resources staff.
- This is part of a project to identify the time and productivity losses associated with area access badge process and to analyze the data and find ways to improve the process in less time and productivity loss.
- During 2004: 1st Qtr: 27 badges; 2nd Qtr: 39 badges; 3rd Qtr: 15 badges; and 4th Qtr: 12 badges.

Figure 15-7   The area access badge processing—average time in dollars per badge processed.

When you analyze the chart, do you think anything is lacking on the chart or should be done differently? Generally speaking, no graphic depiction of metrics is perfect. In this case, it would be nice to have the actual numbers that are equated to the bars on the chart depicted on the chart under the bar chart itself. Some may consider it unnecessary or a "nice-to-have" item. The decision should be based on the:

- Point you are trying to make by briefing the charts and
- Preference of the audience

What is the audience seeing when presented with graphic depictions? What is meaningful to them? A critical point to remember when building and giving presentations is to know your audience. Different audiences are interested in different aspects of a problem or performance. What executive management wants or needs to see may differ significantly from what the process owner needs to see. Show the right data to the right audience.

When you are looking at Figure 15-7, what does it tell you? Does this chart really tell you how much it costs to produce badges? That may be one of the questions asked by one of the executives in your audience. Therefore, you should be prepared to show supplemental charts (see Figure 15-8), as one should always anticipate the attendees' questions ahead of time and how best to pictorially answer those questions.

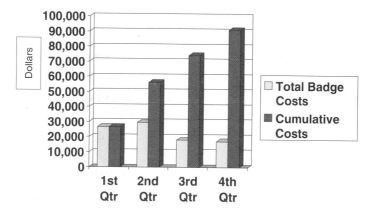

Figure 15-8   The total cost per quarter of processing all area access badge requests for a year.

Before you present the briefing using the charts we continue to discuss throughout this book, present the briefing to your managers, assuming you are a CSO with staff, and it probably would be a good idea to also present the briefing to your entire department. That way, they know what is going on, what it costs to do their job and to elicit their support in finding more efficient ways to do the security business.

As the charts depict, the costs to make badges for one area at IWC, where a special access badge is needed, is not small. Improving how badges are made and thereby reducing cost will produce a savings for security and IWC.

> *Efficiency, effectiveness, process improvement, increased productivity are areas all security professionals should be concerned with. They are as much about good security as are the security processes themselves.*

Surveillance Systems

Surveillance is an important tool for security in its effort to protect assets. Generally, surveillance is accomplished by using security guards or by using CCTV surveillance. Most frequently, a combination of both is used to achieve maximum observation and effectiveness for any facility.

As part of a site physical security survey, the need for surveillance should be identified. This need should then be assessed with the existing practice and capability. With this information, a plan for site or facility surveillance should be developed. The plan should consider the following:

* Purpose of surveillance: deterrence and/or observation
* Identify critical or high-risk areas
* Camera and guard mix
* Location of cameras
* Recording capability needed
* Need for hidden cameras
* Type of cameras needed: wide or narrow angle of view, low or high level of light; availability of solar-powered cameras should be considered.

Each has its strengths and each has its limitations. These limitations should be summarized in a chart that can be used as part of a security metrics management system (see Figure 15-9).

Such a chart can be made part of a cost-benefit analysis and report when deciding whether or not to install some surveillance systems in lieu of security guard forces. It can also be used as part of an executive management briefing when discussing security budgets and what you as the CSO have done to reduce costs while still maintaining the minimum CAPP required.

What security metrics data collection areas would you want to implement for the surveillance systems? Generally, they would be the same as used for the alarm systems.

	STRENGTHS	WEAKNESSES
CCTV Camera with recording capability	• Serves as a deterrent • Flexibility of recording • Permanent record • Reduce insurance rates • Deterrent for crime • Multiple angles of view • Night view—works in low light	• Cannot respond to incident • Cost of initial installation • Maintenance cost • Employee perception of being watched
Guards or Security Professionals	• Can act on observation • Deterrent • Mobility • Apply immediate judgment	• Can't watch everything • Human error • No permanent record of observation • Limited angle of observations

Figure 15-9   A table identifying the strengths and weaknesses of guards and CCTV.

TECHNICAL SECURITY SYSTEMS CASE STUDY

A CSO was faced with significant budget cuts. The largest area of security expense was with the guard force. As the CSO, what methods would you employ to determine current costs and ways to reduce costs?

Although each CSO has their own method, the following process is one that has been known to work for the authors:

- Identify current security guard force costs, to include benefits
- Identify the security driver for each guard post
- Identify the processes used by the security guard force
- Establish project plan(s) to look at security guard force efficiency possibilities in terms of hours and money saved.
- Analyze the possibilities of eliminating some security guard force posts
- Conduct feasibility studies to determine what technical security systems have the potential for replacing what security guard posts
- Conduct cost-benefit studies to determine if such security guard force "replacements" would be cost-effective in terms of start-up costs and recurring costs, e.g., upgrades and maintenance.
- Use an SMMP and develop security metrics charts along the way where one-time, short-term and long-term data collection and security metrics management processes would be beneficial.
- Make recommendations to management for a supplemental budget to implement projects for installing and maintaining technical security systems where they are shown to be cost-effective and also reduce costs of the security guard force.
- Implement and manage using the security metrics management system.

SUMMARY

TSS have become more reliable, sophisticated, cheaper, and useful in supplementing or replacing security guard forces. TSS's primary subsystems are the surveillance systems, access control systems and intrusion detection systems (to include fire alarm systems).

A security metrics management process can help determine the cost-benefits of replacing security guards with TSS subsystems; as well as manage the cost-benefits of such systems on a recurring basis.

Chapter 16

Locks and Keys

The locks and keys function is generally a very human-intensive process for security and affected employees. Measuring the cost of lost productivity due to this function will be discussed, as well as how to find more cost-efficient processes to achieve objectives of this function.

INTRODUCTION

Remember that a security department is an overhead function, albeit essential in supporting the mission, but nevertheless a security function that is supposed to provide services and support to the other departments. That means that the CSO should always strive to make the department as effective and efficient as possible. This of course means that the physical security subfunction of locks and keys must also be included in that philosophy. Locks and keys are the nonautomated part of the access control process, unlike electronic access control systems.

Locks and safes are common means used for protecting areas, electronic media, and documents. They can be used in different layers of the security profile or be a layer in themselves. Used inside a locked building or office, they are a layer of their own. Used on a perimeter gate or door they are part of that layer.

An axiom of locks is "the more secure the lock and the more reliable the lock, the more expensive it is." The type of lock used should be consistent with what the lock is being used to protect. For example, when protecting the contents of a desk drawer, a simple desk drawer lock should be used. When protecting sensitive trade secrets, a high-security locking device as part of a high-security safe or area ought to be used. Getting this equation right will ensure monies are properly spent. The locks, regardless of their type, whether key or combination, should be purchased where volume discounts are available and periodic-purchase contracts can be put in place.

A risk management philosophy should be used, which includes a cost-benefit part, to set the criteria for what type of lock or safe should be used to protect what types of assets. In some cases, it may be more cost-beneficial to install an automated access control system, such as for a room or storage closet where the telecommunications systems are installed.

LOCKS AND KEYS ORGANIZATION

The locks and keys function of course is a physical security function and, at IWC, it reports to the manager of the physical security organization (see Figure 16-1).

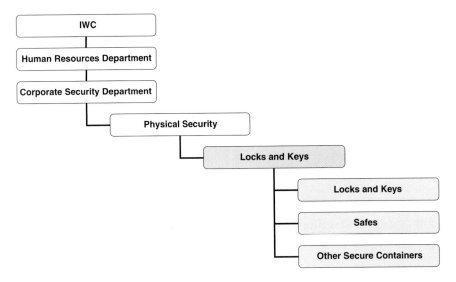

Figure 16-1 Where the locks and keys security function reports in the IWC security department.

LOCKS AND KEYS DRIVERS AND FLOWCHARTS

To maintain the integrity of this type of access control system, the issuance of locks, keys, combinations, safes, and security cabinets should be a centralized security function and not delegated to each IWC department. If so delegated, what happens when a person leaves and takes the lock or combination with them? How would the CSO know if a safe, security combination, lock or key met the risk management criteria for adequate assets protection?

In a centralized process, the lock and key function will, like many security functions, cause some productivity delays: container and lock request process, or picking up the combination or key for a container. For a lock combination, where the combination is always maintained by the security staff assigned to the lock and key function, no lock-picking expertise would be needed—a cost savings in time, training, equipment and/or outsourcing.

> *One word of advice: if at all possible, do not use keys unless the keys are used and maintained by the security staff. All too often, an employee will terminate employment and take the key when he or she leaves.*

With the locks and keys security functional drivers, like all the other security functions related to assets protection, there are certain drivers that apply to all and they are:

- Laws and regulations
- Risk management factors
- Executive management decisions
- Corporate policies and procedures

- Audit reports or security surveys showing deficiencies related to assets protection
- Contractual requirements which impact assets and their protection
- Input of employees relative to assets protection

These also drive the need for physical security and one way of meeting the need to comply with the security driver's requirements is the locks and keys subfunction.

When you look at the locks and keys security functional process flowchart (see Figure 16-2), even though it lacks a great deal of detail, it does show some possibilities for efficiency gains.

The locks and keys manager or supervisor and CSO should be able to quantify some savings in time and thus productivity.

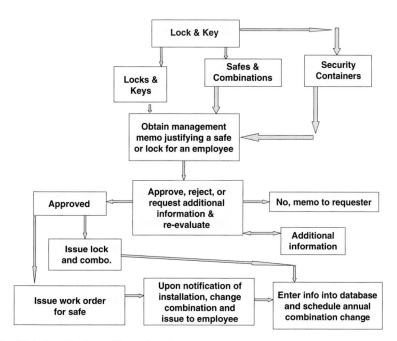

Figure 16-2   High-level locks and keys flowchart steps.

Once the locks and keys security drivers are identified and an evaluation conducted to determine the need for physical security to have a subfunction of locks and keys, then the next step would be to conduct an evaluation to determine if a separate organization is needed. In the case of IWC, a separate organization was deemed necessary. That being the case, the next step would be to document the locks and keys work processes beginning at a high level and then in subsequent lower levels.

The high-level flowchart (see Figure 16-2) shows the subfunctions and the basic flow of those processes. Then, based on that high-level flowchart, subfunctional flowcharts can be developed.

LOCKS AND KEYS EXAMPLES OF SECURITY METRICS

The Locks and Key security metrics management process would be based on the steps shown in its flowchart (Figure 16-2) and its more detailed flowcharts.

Think about what data collection points you would want to have based on the overall locks and keys high-level process flowchart. Then establish the data collection processes, to include data collection tools (see Figure 16-3).

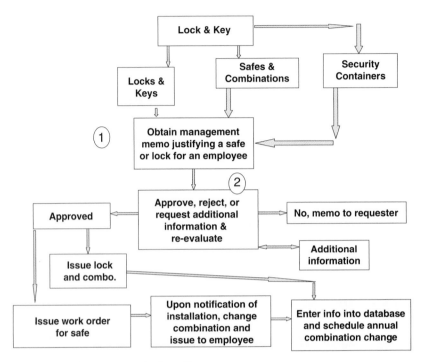

Figure 16-3   The #1 and #2 steps in a lock and key process.

A data collection tool for the #1 to #2 cycle process time (time motion study) items shown in Figure 16-3 could be a simple log or spreadsheet. A spreadsheet, of course, gives one the advantage of having automatic sorting, by person, department and by calculations, such as average time from request to lock issuance.

If one does not have an online system available for locks and keys personnel, then a paper log could be used and the data input later into an automated spreadsheet.

An ideal data collection system, if the CSO wants to know how long it takes to provide locks and keys service to employees, is to have a locks and keys office badge reader on both sides of the office door and have each employee do a "badge swipe" when they enter and when they exit the office. That way, the statistics could be efficiently collected assuming that all employees badge in and out of the office and not just hold the door open for other employees to enter or exit without swiping their badges through the badge readers. It also assumes that the system would be cost-effective.

Assuming a manual or automated spreadsheet would be the most efficient data collection method to track efficiency of locks and keys service to their internal customers, it could look like that shown in Figure 16-4. Figure 16-4 is only shown here as an example of the locks and keys security specialists' input spreadsheet that could be used as an on-line versus a manual data collection form.

Data Collection Log — Times Between Requests and Deliveries — Lock & Key										
Date	Time In	Time Out	Total Time	Name	Organization	Purpose of Visit	Lock	Key	Secure Cabinet	Safe
TOTALS	Sorted by Hour	Sorted by Hour	Avg. Time	Sorted by Name	Sorted by Org.	Sorted by Purpose				
NOTE: Items can be sorted, totaled, sub-totaled as shown by non-white cells										

Figure 16-4   A lock and key data collection tool.

One may wonder "Why sort by the hour for time in and time out?" The primary reason is to see when the busiest times of the days are. That way, the CSO can ensure that during those peak busy times, sufficient staff will be available. For example, perhaps most of the customers come in conjunction with their lunch time. The CSO should arrange for the security staff to take their lunch breaks during the non-peak service hours.

> *Remember, security is a service and support function and therefore must be available to meet the needs of their IWC customers in an efficient and effective manner.*

Sorting by organization and personnel will show which organizations have the most requests and therefore the most needs for assets protection safes, containers and similar equipment.

The items requested can be used as part of the locks and keys inventory systems (how many items, and of what type, are out) and then compare with those in stock. This helps with the ordering needs.

The ordering and delivery of these items should also be part of security metrics management process for locks and keys. This is especially true to document the delivery times so that one not only knows how far in advance to order new items but also to track contract compliance for delivery of items within certain time constraints.

LOCK AND KEY CASE STUDY

A CSO was hearing complaints from IWC managers that their requests for combination locks were not being met in a reasonable period of time. The CSO discussed the matter with the locks and keys supervisor. The supervisor advised that the combination locks were ordered in a timely manner; however, their delivery was sporadic and sometimes there were long delays in deliveries.

The CSO was shown the spreadsheet tracking (as shown in Figure 16-4), their inventory levels and ordering levels process charts.

If you were the CSO, how would you handle this matter? Some would be quick to say that they would order more combination locks at one time and order them based on maintaining a higher inventory level. Yes, that would easily solve the visible problem, at least temporarily—maybe. However, it would not solve the systemic problem, which is the lack of on-time deliveries to IWC by the supplier.

Actually, it has been shown that, with a cost-efficient system, a minimum inventory is maintained and uses a "just-in-time" approach. In other words, don't tie up budget in inventory but rely on the items being delivered on time, when needed.

Using the security metrics approach and documenting the average request-to-delivery time periods, one can see if it is more or less than the IWC customer average. You as the CSO or your locks and keys supervisor can discuss the contract with the IWC contracting specialists and determine what obligations and penalties the supplier must meet as far as contract specifications detailing delivery times and penalties.

In this case, the delivery time specifications from request to delivery was vague, within one week of request receipt. Furthermore, the contract did not address any penalties for not meeting contract requirements. As the CSO, what would you do to remedy the situation or would you do the "quick and dirty" fix and then move on to another complaint and crisis?

The CSO decided to put in place a total process using the security metrics management system as the tool to correct deficiencies in the process and monitor the lock and key operation. This includes the following:

As the CSO, you can build on the data collection tools in place and integrate them into a more "cradle-to-grave" approach which would include the information collected as shown in Figure 16-4 and the following extension of that spreadsheet to answer these questions and collect the identified data:

- What item was requested?
- When?
- From what supplier?
- Cost?
- Delivery date?
- Average delivery time (from request to on-dock)?
- Average delivery time from on-dock to placement in the locks and keys inventory?
- How long in inventory before issuance?
- Non-timely deliveries brought to contracting staff's attention
- Penalties incurred by supplier?
- If so, how much?
- If not, why not?

What data collection tools and charting formats would you use to track each of the above items? One type would be a timeline that would track individual and total average times from request, quantities to deliverance and sign-out to internal customers.

Another supplemental way to handle this is to contract to multiple suppliers. It is of course assumed that the bids for this work were and will be based on the lowest bidders who meets contractual specifications, in other words, the suppliers must be both responsive and responsible.

By using a security metrics management approach, not only will the process eventually be made more efficient, but the customers will hopefully be satisfied with the process time for their requests for services (lock or key) and IWC will in turn gain in productivity-efficiency of its employees since they will not be "wasting time" working on lengthy requests for services from the locks and keys function, getting their necessary security containers, locks and other equipment in a timely fashion. Also, suppliers who begin to incur penalties will be faced with the need to change their processes or you will go somewhere else for business.

SUMMARY

The locks and keys security function is a subfunction of the physical security organization and is a "key" (no pun intended—well, maybe) function to support the protection of corporate assets. The function is also time intensive and detracts from employees' productivity since they must spend valuable time processing a request for services and visit the locks and keys office to obtain their locks, keys and other related equipment.

Using a security metrics management approach, as with other security functions, the CSO can analyze the locks and keys function for areas to improve on. Basic cycle time and process data can be collected, analyzed and the changes made to the process to improve efficiency and effectiveness, thus contributing to the productivity of the security function and the productivity of the security department.

Chapter 17

Fire Protection

Many security organizations are also responsible for their corporation's fire protection program. Fire protection programs usually divide into two areas: fire prevention and fire suppression. This chapter will address the fundamental elements of a fire protection program and the process of fire protection security metrics management identification and establishment to determine costs, benefits, successes and failures.

INTRODUCTION

Many security organizations are also responsible for the fire protection program. Responsibilities for security and fire protection, when coupled, are generally a good fit as both are concerned with corporate assets protection. Although the disciplines of security and fire differ, there are significant points of intersection. Both organizations serve in a preventive and protection role and both are involved in the business of emergency response, and assets protection—especially the protection of people and property. Security, particularly the security guards' functions, fire prevention and suppression and to some extent, the safety function, all see their missions intersect in the areas of assets protection and emergency response. Furthermore, this intersection also continues into the area of contingency planning and employee asset protection awareness programs.

Under ideal conditions, fire prevention and suppression are best handled by a professional fire department. However, having a company fire department is often not an option. It costs money to maintain a fire department staffed with professional fire fighters. Small and medium-size organizations usually do not have large enough statements of work to warrant having a full-time fire department. Under these conditions, many companies rely on others to perform the duties of fire prevention and suppression.

> *Where there is no corporate fire department, fire prevention tasks are often performed by safety and/or security personnel. The task of fire suppression is left to immediate employees' response using fire extinguishers for small fires and a local fire department response to handle major fires.*

Fire protection programs usually separate into two areas: fire prevention and fire protection or suppression. Fire prevention refers to the effort to control the environment in order to reduce the possibility of fires from occurring. This includes good housekeeping practices, awareness training and fire safety inspections. Fire protection or fire suppression refers to the methods and equipment used to extinguish and suppress a fire.

Throughout this discussion, the terms *fire protection* and *fire suppression* will be used interchangeably. At IWC, the new CSO had inherited the IWC fire prevention and suppression program. Since this is the first time the CSO had this responsibility, the CSO researched the topic and then implemented a security metrics management program (SMMP) to provide an overview and management oversight process for the fire prevention and suppression program.

FIRE PROTECTION ORGANIZATION

Without a doubt, fire is one of the most damaging hazards any corporation can experience. Fire prevention and control is both critical and essential.

Fire prevention and suppression should be linked to the contingency planning program's three major processes:

*   Emergency response,
*   Crisis management and
*   Business continuity.

The CSO, in discussion with the IWC manager of the fire prevention and suppression organization, whose organization is part of the security department's physical security organization (see Figure 17-1), advised the CSO that IWC has a functioning and successful fire prevention and suppression program.

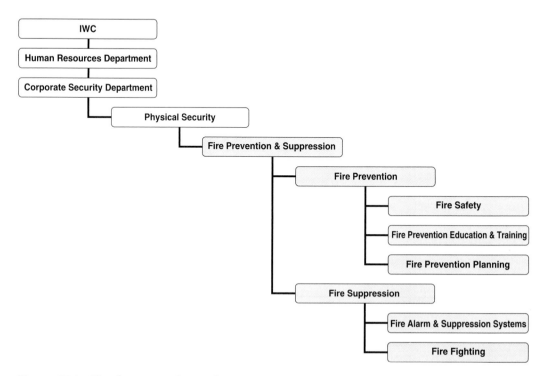

Figure 17-1 The fire prevention and protection organization as part of the physical security organization.

Since fire prevention was also a form of assets protection, much of the same philosophy could be used—fire prevention, like other assets protection programs, is the responsibility of all IWC employees. Fire safety is an integral part of the IWC fire prevention and suppression, as well as the IWC corporate assets protection program (CAPP), contingency plan, emergency response plan and other assets-related plans.

FIRE PROTECTION DRIVERS AND FLOWCHARTS

The United States' Occupational Safety & Health Administration (OSHA) requires employers to implement basic measures such as providing fire-fighting equipment and employee training in order to help prevent injuries and death from a fire. This requirement is one of the primary assets protection or security drivers for this function.

The IWC fire prevention and suppression (FP&S) processes had never before been analyzed to assess their effectiveness. To begin that process, the CSO planned to review all process flowcharts. Much to the CSO's dismay, none of the FP&S processes had ever been depicted in a process flow diagram or flowchart. Therefore, the CSO tasked the fire department chief to develop process flowcharts for all of his fire prevention and suppression processes, starting with the macro view of the processes of prevention and suppression and work down into micro views of all subprocesses. As part of this task, the CSO asked that all drivers for these processes be identified and documented. For operations within the United States, the primary driver was OSHA. International facilities identified their drivers to be the need to protect assets for the corporate owners, local laws and regulations, and the corporate policies and procedures for IWC.

The U.S. FP&S manager began with a high-level flowchart (see Figure 17-2) and subsequently added more detailed flowcharts (see Figure 17-3 as one example of a more detailed FP&S flowchart).

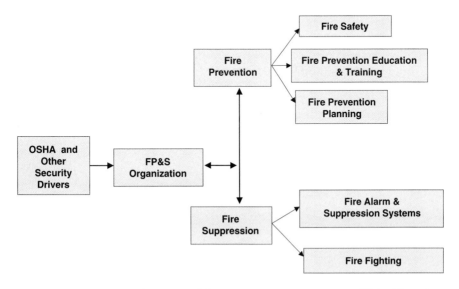

Figure 17-2 Process flowchart depiction of the FP&S macro processes established based on security drivers and the FP&S organization structure.

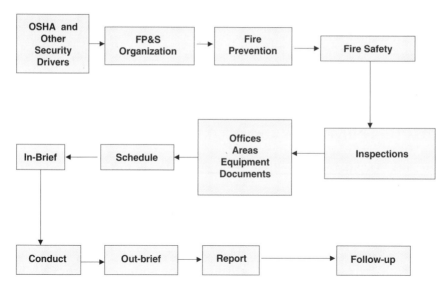

Figure 17-3   A more detailed depiction of the fire prevention process to include key subprocesses.

After completing these process flowcharts, the fire chief must then continue to refine them in more detail. For example, under "Preparation," the chief must provide further subprocess detail depicting the steps involved in preparing for an inspection, such as review last report, identify findings, identify inspected organization's response to findings, and prepare notes to validate inspected organization's reply to findings.

Under "Report," the detailed process of preparing the report, dispatching it to the inspected organization, establishing a response due date, and arranging follow-up inspections as necessary would be addressed, as well as of course input the data into the security metrics management program (SMMP).

Also under "Report," the IWC CSO directed that the FP&S chief initiate a project to analyze the reporting process. This includes report preparation, presentation and delivery.—how much time and resources are being used to prepare, present and distribute the inspection reports, and should report preparation and delivery be a web-based process, thus affording all participants to ability to contribute online in near real time?

Should the inspection process itself be changed to a random and unannounced process? This unknown factor should keep organizations prepared, as they will never really know when they can expect to be inspected. Another possibility is to rely on self-inspections with limited follow-up by FS&P personnel to ensure the self-inspections are conducted in accordance with IWC guidelines and maintain an appropriate level of integrity—or possibly convince the audit specialists to add this item to their auditing checklist when evaluating IWC departments' compliance with IWC policies and procedures. This approach would be a cost-effective way for the CSO to get the job done.

This is not to say that this is necessarily a good idea but simply one offering potential for possible savings—or is it? Remember that cost in terms of time and lost productivity, when transferred from one organization to another within IWC, is not really a savings. This is something to keep in mind when trying to save resources for IWC while meeting all security service and support requirements. Also, outsourcing this function should be considered.

FIRE PREVENTION AND SUPPRESSION METRICS EXAMPLES

If fire safety inspections are to be conducted regularly, their frequency will depend upon many factors to include the conditions and type of operating environment. At a minimum, inspections should have as their objective the following:

- Identify fire hazards, conditions, and housekeeping discrepancies
- Determine compliance with applicable laws and government agency requirements
- Identify contract provisions and insurance carrier requirements
- Ensure corporate and business area loss prevention programs are carried out as directed

The inspections should be conducted in the context of the following parameters:

- Establish and maintain inspection methods and intervals, consistent with corporate interpretations of federal, state, and local government codes, laws and standards applicable to fire prevention/suppression matters.
- Inspect work areas periodically to ensure compliance with fire regulations. Hazardous areas may require more frequent inspections as determined by fire professionals and regulation. Also, the following specific fire prevention and suppression areas should be inspected:
  - Fire pumps
  - Fire water supply
  - Main drain: residual and static flow tests
  - Sprinkler systems
  - Fire extinguishers and fire extinguisher records
  - Fire doors
  - Fire walls
  - Complete documentation (records) of fixed fire suppression equipment, including test and maintenance records, and fire insurance inspection reports need to be kept. They are important for the process of fire prevention planning and, in the event of a fire, will be subject to review.

The security metrics would be used not only to collect and track inspection data and results (satisfactory, marginal, unsatisfactory) but also by types of deficiencies. They could be correlated and if analyses indicated some areas where the majority of deficiencies were the same, such as outdated fire extinguishers, then a project could be implemented to look at the systemic problem which allowed this to occur.

In addition, other deficiencies within multiple IWC departments could be addressed through the security education and awareness program—emphasized in briefings, through awareness material, broadcast announcement via the IWC internal network, or other security awareness methods.

So, inspections are a candidate for data collection and process analyses as part of the SMMP. For example, overall inspection results could be tracked, as well as other data that would be useful in managing the FP&S program and depicted through the use of metrics (graphically depicted) to demonstrate to executive management and outside compliance agencies (i.e., OSHA) the effectiveness of the program. Even in areas where the program may be lacking or be ineffective, if an understanding of the problem along with a plan to take corrective action is shown to a compliance agency, chances are any penalty or fine would be mitigated.

Having a comprehensive SMMP in place will also be useful for IWC when dealing with insurance companies. A proactive program may help reduce insurance costs and thus show direct benefits. It also would be very useful in the event of a fire when executive management and the insurance provider demand to know the "who, how, where, when and what" of a fire, instead of you as the CSO saying, "It's not my fault! We did all we could to prevent the incident!" You can show a pattern of aggressive inspections, corrective actions, and so forth.

Fire alarm and suppression systems are a critical component of a fire prevention and protection system. Fire alarm systems detect fire and alert employees. They are similar to intrusion detection systems in that they, in and of themselves, do not prevent, but they only alert. Unless the alarm is false, when the fire alarm system alerts, it is due to fire or the elements of fire (smoke or heat). Like all equipment, automatic fire suppression systems require periodic maintenance to maintain serviceability and effectiveness. Maintenance must only be performed by qualified and certified personnel. When automatic fire systems are taken out of service, usually for maintenance, a fire watch should be instituted, using trusted employees, in order to be able to react in the event of fire.

False fire alarms (see Figure 17-4), fire alarms' periodic and troubleshooting maintenance (see Figure 17-5), and related costs (see Figure 17-6) are examples of fire protection-related topics where a CSO should apply security metrics management techniques.

By collecting data on problems, the CSO can use the information to better help understand overall performance and identify problems. Moreover, with data collected over time, trends will become apparent (both positive and negative), which the CSO can use as a tool to help drive process change and even changes to the specifications of the contracts with service providers. For example, if the alarm service contract specifies specific times for alarm response, maintenance call response, details on warranties, and costs, to include costs for repairing the same problem over a short and designated period of time—one month, for example—the CSO can use performance security metrics to drive the service provider to greater efficiencies and better performance.

False alarms are expensive. All false alarms require a response as they cannot be considered false alarms until an authorized responder makes that determination. This is a case where the life of employees or other building occupants are at risk. There is no margin for error here.

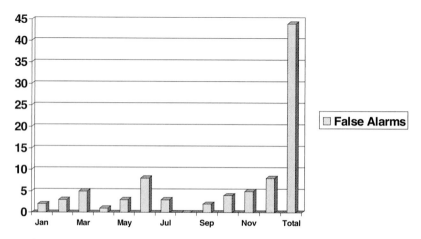

Figure 17-4   The number of false fire alarms during one year, shown in monthly increments.

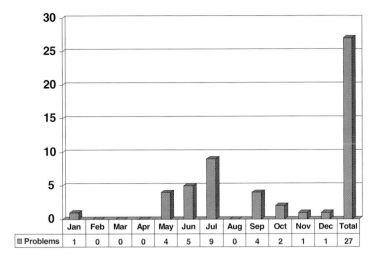

Figure 17-5 The number of problems with the alarm systems over a one-year period.

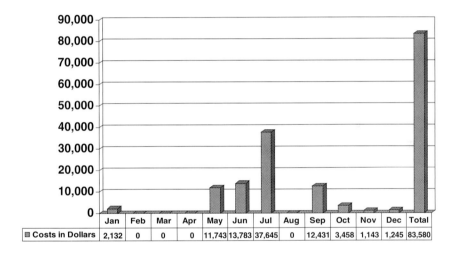

Figure 17-6 The costs of false alarms.

False alarms occur for a variety of reasons, including faulty equipment, environmental elements, and employee mistakes (accidentally activating an alarm). One way to help mitigate the negative impact of false alarms is to have in place a fire warden (employee designated for a specific area) program where trained employees respond first to determine if the alarm is false. The area that the fire warden covers, however, must be a small area so that the warden can respond to the area immediately. This again is a costly element of assets protection and this process should be incorporated into any SMMP for this security function. However, as in other instances, this too costs money. Do the benefits outweigh the costs? Use an SMMP coupled with its risk management aspects to find out.

Other data collection and charting processes should of course be set up for the other subfunctions of the FP&S organization. These would include:

- *Fire Prevention Education and Training*: The metrics processes used can be the same or at least similar to the security metrics management system used for the entire security education and awareness training program.

- *Department Evacuation Plans*: Plans must be tested. Security metrics can provide a database as to the number of tests conducted, the departments involved, number of personnel, costs, results and any follow-up action.

> *Again, the first step is to identify the drivers, identify the organization structure based on what will work in your environment based on those drivers, then develop detailed process flowcharts of macro and micro processes, determine what data should be collected for meeting what objectives, and then develop the data collection input documents, analysis processes, and finally then the charting and the management oversight and briefings can occur.*

CASE STUDY—OUTSOURCING FIRE PREVENTION AND/OR SUPPRESSION

The fire prevention and protection process is an outstanding candidate for outsourcing. Since IWC does not have as part of its core competencies professional fire prevention and protection capabilities, the CSO will be considering it for outsourcing. The CSO knows that the fire prevention program must be established and, to reduce the risk of fire, it must be effectively and efficiently established. However, it may be more cost-effective for someone else to do it.

Protecting IWC from damage and loss from fire cannot be ignored. However, the CSO reasoned that it can be done cost-effectively. Maintaining a capable staff to perform fire prevention and protection duties is costly. Skilled fire-protection professionals require regular training and certification. Finding capable outsource providers of fire protection services is not difficult. There are many capable companies, local and national, with resources and experience necessary to perform fire prevention services—which of course, includes the local city and county fire departments.

As the CSO wanting to determine if this function should be outsourced, what metrics would you use and how would you go about determining if outsourcing was a viable option?

Let's leave the details of security metrics management and outsourcing for later discussion (see Chapter 24). However, we do know that the security metrics such as the examples shown above are indispensable for analyzing the outsourcing possibilities of this function.

SUMMARY

Fire prevention and suppression programs are an important part of IWC's ability to conduct business. No one is immune to the threat or hazard of fire. Often the responsibility for administering fire prevention programs falls to the security department.

Although the discipline of security and fire prevention and suppression differ, there are a few common denominators. Both are in the business of assets protection and emergency response. Therefore, coupling security with the fire prevention and suppression process can be very effective in the overall assets protection program. It stands to reason then that the SMMP can also be useful in managing a fire prevention and suppression program.

Chapter 18

Executive Protection

This chapter will address the use of security metrics as a tool for managing an executive protection program. Although an executive protection program is a function requiring fewer resources than many other security functions, it is nevertheless a critical function. The focus of the executive protection program is the protection of the company CEO and other key senior executive leaders of the company. Executive protection is a high-profile function with little margin for error. Effectiveness of the program is critical. Security metrics can help the CSO assess effectiveness.

INTRODUCTION

Executive protection is the application of protective measures to reduce the risk to executives and mitigate threats. It is a proactive effort, not a reactive effort. Although there are reactive elements, pro-activity is the only way of effectively providing protection. Pro-activity calls for advance preparation, so in situations where reaction is necessary, it will be automatic. Part of establishing an executive protection program is to identify the executives requiring protection. How you do this depends on many factors, including the following:

- Culture of your corporation
- Threat to your corporation
- Negative profile of corporation (for example, some corporations have a negative profile attracting the attention of persons in opposition to their mission, an example being oil corporations as they are challenged by radical environmental organizations.)
- Habits of the CEO and other senior executives (for example, travel to high-risk areas)

At IWC, there are different levels of executives. Some are corporate executives and some are business unit executives. They hold different titles. Some hold the title of president, some vice president, while others are directors. Yet all are not deemed critical to the corporation. This is not to say they are not important to IWC. It is to say that only a critical few are so important as to warrant additional protection beyond what is afforded to other employees.

For executive protection to be effective, the protector (which may be an individual or a team) must know the following:

- Who is being protected?
- What are they being protected from?
- When are they to be protected?
- Where must they be protected?
- Why are they being protected?
- How must they be protected?

The executives at IWC who have been determined to require additional protection are the following: CEO, COO, CIO and CFO and the heads of each separate business unit. All other executives are protected in the same manner as any IWC employee is protected. How this determination was made focused totally on the criticality of each executive to the performance of their separate business units and to the success of the corporation. In other words, what would be the impact to the corporation if the executive was suddenly not available—permanently? Loss of expertise, continuity of leadership, and customer goodwill must be considered in the assessment. Moreover, the level of public exposure and international travel of each executive must be assessed to determine any operational risk.

In today's global business environment, there are many types of threats faced by corporations. All threats require some degree of attention and mitigation. The potential threat to business executives is no less of a threat to the total corporation than any other business threat and, in some circumstances, may be even more cause for concern.

High-profile executives leading corporations in controversial industries may find themselves potential targets since they are, or at least they represent, the leadership of that corporation. With some high-profile executives, they essentially become a personification of the corporation. This places them in a higher risk category as their visibility significantly increases.

The purpose of an executive protection program is to reduce the likelihood of an attack occurring against corporate executives, thus reducing the overall risk to IWC's business. This is a critical factor. Protecting high-profile or high-risk executives also protects the corporation. Furthermore, eliminating the potential for harassment or embarrassment to the executive is essential. Although embarrassment or harassment does not cause physical harm, these situations can impact the effectiveness of the executive, thus having a negative impact on the corporation. Eliminating risk is neither possible nor practical, but mitigating it is both.

An executive protection program should be designed to facilitate executives living and working safely and moving about efficiently. They can't be locked up. Their ability to move around and work freely is essential to their performance. Facilitating this mobility in a safe and secure manner is the objective of an effective executive protection program. In essence, the protected executive is being made into a hard target.

> *Some types of threats and risks include: harassment, kidnapping, street violence, attacks from disturbed people, or disgruntled employees, to include workplace violence, medical emergency and assassination.*

EXECUTIVE PROTECTION ORGANIZATION

Executive protection is primarily a physical security-related function. However, because of its importance, a CSO may elect to make this function one that falls directly under the purview of the CSO. In the case of the IWC CSO, the physical security organization was considered the best place to provide direct management oversight to this function (see Figure 18-1).

A CSO should stay close to the executive protection function as it is a critical and a high-profile function. However, the CSO ought to resist the desire to directly manage executive protection. Executive protection requires much time and attention and is best handled by someone who can devote the necessary time and attention and has the proper expertise to successfully manage the program.

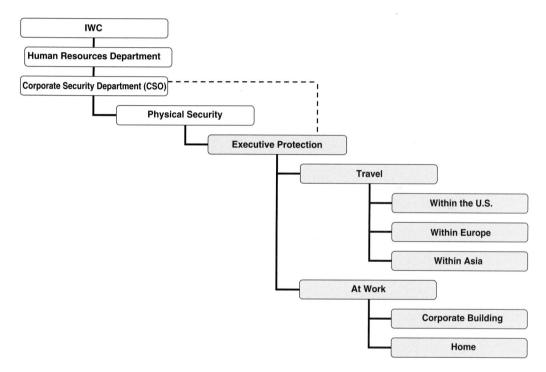

Figure 18-1 Where the executive protection is integrated into the security department. Note the hard line responsibility to the manager of physical security and the dotted line responsibility back to the CSO. An executive protection function should never be completely removed from contact with the CSO.

EXECUTIVE PROTECTION DRIVERS AND FLOWCHARTS

As usual, in developing a security metrics management program (SMMP) for this security function, a high-level flowchart is first developed and subsequently more detailed charts are developed, derived from their key functional process steps (see Figure 18-2). By now, you should have first been able to identify the drivers for this function before proceeding to the flowcharting. They are of course based on the drivers requiring the protection of assets and in this case the assets are people.

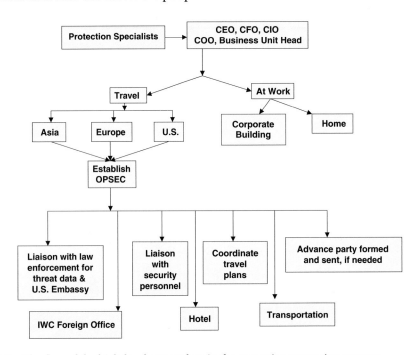

Figure 18-2   The flow of the high-level steps taken in the executive protection process.

> *It is very important that all process documentation and related information (flowcharts, metrics evaluations) be kept within the executive protection team (even from other security specialists who are not part of the executive team or team support functions) so as to prevent unintended release of operational procedures and plans. This is especially important in today's high-risk global environment.*

Terrorism, kidnapping, hostage situations, harassment or embarrassing situations are a greater threat to the corporate executive, particularly Western executives, than ever before. Therefore, discretion, privacy and good operational security (OPSEC) techniques are essential for success.

If the processes used to protect executives were made public, those miscreants wanting to harm or exploit a corporate executive could develop an advantage to their misdirected exploits.

Detailing the protection processes in flowchart form will better assist the executive protection specialists in preparing and understanding each process, as well as the time it takes on average and the associated costs of each step in the process. Moreover, the process diagrams are useful when establishing checklists for use by the executive protection specialists and the executive (and family where appropriate) being protected. It is also a method of looking for weaknesses in the process which could lead to previously unidentified risks to the protected executive.

EXECUTIVE PROTECTION EXAMPLES OF METRICS

As the IWC CSO, you must be intimately involved in executive protection even though it may be outsourced. When the executives are being protected, there must be constant communication and feedback between the CSO's office and those providing the protection. This would include preprotection meetings to review the itinerary of the executive and coordinate protective measures. Furthermore, the protective measures must include contingency or emergency procedures. Below is a checklist of things, which were developed from a detailed flowchart of the function, to consider and address as part of an advance assessment:

Getting there:
- Where is the venue?
- How will the executive get there (mode of travel and route)?
- What will they be doing while they are there?
- How many locations will they visit?
- Who will they be with?

Once they are there:
- Is anyone in the area considered a threat?
- Is there a threat to similar people (other business executives)?
- What type of information about the protectee is available and accessible?
- What is going on at the location, today and tomorrow?
- Who will be there? Any other high-profile persons?
- What type of assistance is available?

Conduct a site survey to identify issues, routes and layout of the following:
- Meeting location
- Hotels, resorts and restaurants
- Private residences
- Convention center
- Emergency facilities
- Airports

Identify all concerns and issues:
- Is there anything out of the ordinary to be concerned with?

Departure:
- What is the return route (direct and fast)?
- Establish alternate routes

Emergency Services:
- Where are the nearest medical facilities?
- Will medical personnel be available on site where the protectee will be visiting?

Once the advance effort is complete, review findings and share them only with those people who have a need-to-know. Also, be sure to brief the executive or executives involved so they are familiar with all plans and issues.

Once that checklist is established, details are added for each trip. After each trip, the time and costs needed should be collected and entered into a database or spreadsheet. This will be very useful when planning the time and costs of future executive protection budgets, trips and the like.

> *A separate budget should be used for executive protection and the CSO, staff and out-sourced assistance costs should be charged into that budget. However, as a CSO, you should consider requesting that the budget be placed under the executive management's overall budget so that your staff can charge into it. Your security budget should not incorporate those costs, which would make the security budget look much larger than it really is.*

Remember the checklist also has value beyond ensuring nothing is overlooked or forgotten. It can be used to help establish discrete and total cost of the protective measures or the operation. A cost can be associated with every protective practice. Cost and effectiveness can be evaluated post-event, allowing the protection specialists or the CSO to determine which protection measures are the most effective.

In the case of this security function, the CSO can consider additional security metrics and associated charts (see Figure 18-3 and Figure 18-4) as an example of tracking costs for this security function). The real determination of the success or failure of this security

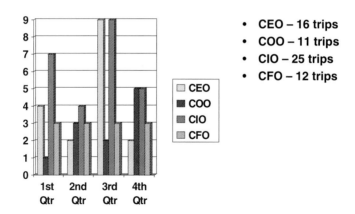

Figure 18-3   The number of trips taken in 2005 by quarter by IWC executives.

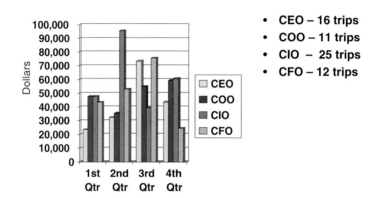

Figure 18-4   The number of trips taken by IWC executives and their associated costs per quarter.

function is whether or not the executive being protected has been harmed, harassed or his/her work disrupted. One does not need a chart or data collection for this; however, as with other functions, security metrics data collection on time and costs are always valuable, as it would not be unusual for an executive to want to know what all this protection is costing the corporation.

> *It is also important that on occasion the protectee be included in tests of the executive protection function so that he or she knows how the process works and what to do under hostile conditions.*

EXECUTIVE PROTECTION CASE STUDY

The IWC CSO was advised that one of the company executives identified as requiring protection by IWC executive management and the CSO has refused that protection, except when traveling internationally, and only to countries considered hostile to Western interests. As the CSO, what would you do?

The IWC CSO scheduled a briefing for all company executives identified as requiring some level of protection. During that briefing, the rationale for executive protection was briefed to include the threats, vulnerabilities and risks associated with executives in general and IWC executives specifically. All were briefed on the overall executive protection plan and how protective operations would be conducted. It was expected that all would agree to accept the protection as planned.

The CSO also anticipated that the executive refusing protection support would be swayed to accept that protection by his/her colleagues. If not, the CSO would prepare an "at-risk" memorandum to be signed by the executive refusing protection, sending a copy to the CEO. The CEO has the prerogative to waive the protection requirement or direct that the protection be provided as a benefit to IWC.

The same methodology would be used for those who wanted more protection, such as protection beyond what is normally provided to a senior executive of a global corporation. The perception of need for executive protection will vary from executive to executive. Most executives will readily accept (or expect) a reasonable level of protection appropriate to the threat or situation. In some cases, a few executives will expect much more, generally based on satisfying their ego as to their "importance" more so than knowledge of real and actual threats. The CSO must find a way to work with those executives and convince them to change their expectations. Ultimately, the CEO and/or board of directors make the final decision as to who is to be protected.

SUMMARY

Security metrics plays a limited role in supporting executive protection operations; nevertheless, it does have applicability and value. Executive protection is primarily a physical security function and therefore often led by the manager or supervisor of the physical security organization. Simplistically speaking, if the executive being protected is not harmed, embarrassed or harassed, then the operation was a success. If an adverse event did occur, then it was a failure.

Providing protection for key executives is both a good and essential business practice. Maintaining the leadership continuity of IWC ensures that IWC will be able to continue uninterrupted business operations. How protection is accomplished, who is protected, and to what degree they are protected must be based on a thorough threat and risk analysis conducted by the CSO or other qualified persons such as an executive protection specialists or consultant. The final decision as to who is protected is up to the CEO and/or the board of directors and not the CSO or the person to be protected.

Balancing threats, risks, vulnerabilities and costs will be necessary to effectively develop and implement any executive protection program. Security metrics can help track costs and analyses may find ways to provide for more effective and efficient protection; however, in this case, one must lean towards effective protection over efficient protection since people's lives are at stake.

Chapter 19

Event Security

Many corporations, in particular publicly held corporations, are involved in high-profile events, from annual shareholders' events to trade shows. Protection of personnel, facilities, and information can become very complicated during these events, particularly when they occur in a foreign environment. This chapter will address its supporting security metrics management processes.

INTRODUCTION

Conventions, trade shows, shareholders' meetings, ground-breaking ceremonies, new product introduction events and employee recognition activities are just some of the regular special events that IWC holds. Some of these events are held on IWC property, in IWC facilities and buildings. Many are not. Some are held in high-profile locations, such as trade shows held in major convention centers located in large cities, while others are held in international venues. Some of these locations are easy to secure while others are not. Generally these events involve large numbers of people converging on a single site. Often local and sometimes national media will be involved.

Special events are held for many reasons and in many locations. Regardless of where and when they occur, and even though the host facility, such as a convention center, may provide overall security, some form of security support for the corporation's specific location may be necessary. From access control to executive protection, security for special events can vary widely. Whatever the level of support required, the CSO or event security coordinator (ESC) will take the same approach for assessing the security needs and requirements for each event. For the IWC, the CSO will be serving as the ESC.

EVENT SECURITY ORGANIZATION

Although event security is a recurring function, such as for the annual stockholders meetings, it is not one that requires an actual organization like other security functions. In this case, the "organization" is formed using a team concept. It is formed prior to the event and is disbanded after the event's final report is distributed (see Figure 19-1).

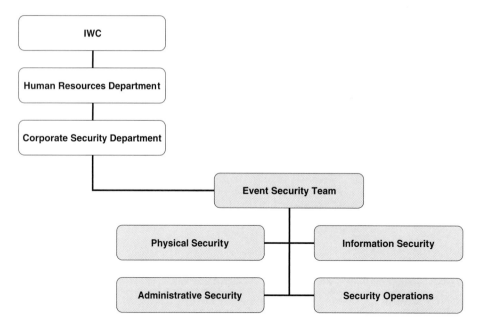

Figure 19-1   The event security team is led by the CSO.

EVENT SECURITY DRIVERS AND FLOWCHARTS

The event security driver is, as usual, the need to protect corporate assets. The specific assets protection techniques applied to events should be based on a risk management approach—threats, vulnerabilities, and risks considerations applied to the location of the event—and also the public relations considerations, such as stockholders in attendance going through metal detectors, being searched, etc.

Event security flowcharts are prepared like any other flowcharts. And as is the case with the Executive Protection flowcharts, these should only be distributed to those on the event security team and based on the "need-to-know" principle (see Figure 19-2).

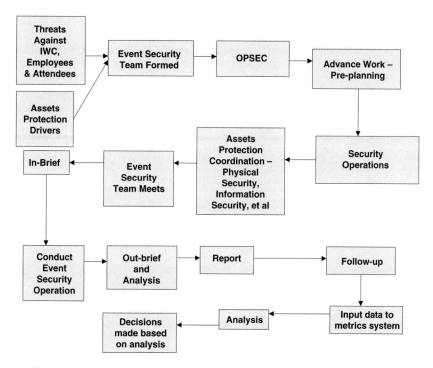

Figure 19-2   The event security project team flow of major event processes.

EVENT SECURITY METRICS

The objective of event security is obviously to protect the event—i.e., the people attending the event, facilities, other assets and any sensitive information not in the public domain. Much like executive protection, event security has obvious measures of success:

- Did something occur at the event to adversely affect that event?
- Did something go wrong?
- Was the event interrupted?
- Was harm caused to corporate property or personnel?

If the answer to all of these questions is no, generally the event can be considered a success.

It is possible for something to go wrong without notice. For example, the disclosure of sensitive information may not be discovered by the IWC CSO until a later date, if at all. A competitor (or adversary) could gain access to sensitive information, thus providing that competitor an advantage. That advantage may never be directly related to disclosure of information at the special event. (This situation is not the most likely, as most special events are not places where sensitive information is usually held.)

Special events tend to be structured in such a way as to control information so it is released only in the context of a controlled corporate communication. The corporate assets with the greatest vulnerability are people and property.

Like the Executive Protection function, event security metrics are generally limited to those related to successful planning and implementation of OPSEC, the security plan, budget versus actual costs.

As for applying security metrics management techniques related to OPSEC, one may have a difficult time since OPSEC is as much a process of planning as it is a process of action. Planning is a process that can be measured, but it is best measured in the context of comparison to prior plans and their success and failure:

- Were all relevant possibilities considered?
- Were all possible scenarios addressed?

The best measure of a new plan is to compare it with an earlier successful plan.

As for the event security budget, that is somewhat easier, as one can easily use a spreadsheet (see Figure 19-3) to:

- List budgeted line items
- Collect the actual costs for those line items
- Identify the variances
- Determine the reasons for the variances
- Re-adjust the event security budgetary process for future events.

EVENT SECURITY BUDGET ANALYSES

Event	2004	2005
Stockholders Meeting		
ID Threats		
ID Risks		
ID Assets Involved		
ID Team and their costs		
Implement OPSEC		
Set Up Security Ops Center		
Operate Security Ops Center		
In-Brief		
Operation		
Out-Brief		
Analyses		
Report Written		
Report Published		
Report Distributed		
Followup Work		
Total		
Variance		

NOTE: Costs include personnel, equipment, supplies, records checks, et al

Figure 19-3   A sample spreadsheet that can be used to track event security costs against budget.

Note that in your actual spreadsheet, every process step should be identified in an individual spreadsheet cell and its costs tracked. This can be done by using the process steps noted in a detailed event security flowchart—one that is obviously more detailed than that shown in Figure 19-2.

EVENT SECURITY CASE STUDY

Since the IWC is about to hold its annual shareholders meeting, the IWC CSO has begun preparing a security plan for the event. As a CSO responsible for such an event, how would you go about preparing a security plan and its budget for such an event?

The IWC CSO did the following, based on the detailed flowcharts and other SMMP-related documents:

- Reviewed the security plan and budget that was used for last year's shareholder meeting.
- Reviewed the following for applicability to this year's event and begin specific planning on a budget for each area:
    - Advance work—pre-event planning and analysis activities
    - Establishing a security operations center
    - Establishing physical security controls
    - Establishing information security controls
    - Identifying the need for personnel and executive protection
    - Preparing for likely contingencies
- Reviewed the variances between last year's event budget and the prior year's event budget (NOTE: determine why the variances occurred and take action accordingly. Cost overruns should be analyzed and, if needed, applied to the next event security budget. If due to poor planning, analyze the process and all costs involved.
- Developed a new budget based on the historical budget information, taking into consideration the variance in the event for this year and prior years, post-event security analyses, etc.

EVENT SECURITY SUMMARY

Providing security for a special event or offsite activity is part of the CSO's responsibility. These events are usually short in duration and occur with some degree of frequency and are important to executive management, stakeholders and IWC.

Working to ensure the event proceeds as planned without a security incident or an event disruption is essential. A single incident may damage or ruin the entire event, as well as the corporation's image and public relations. The IWC CSO must develop a security plan for all events that includes a separate budget.

Security metrics management techniques do not play a major role in such events, except that the success of an event means no adverse incidents took place. You don't need a security metrics management system to tell you that.

The primary areas where security metrics management plays a role are in the planning development and budgetary processes. Comparing new plans against old does provide a level of assurance all relevant issues are addressed—assuming it was done correctly the last time.

Measuring budget against actual costs not only helps you determine how well you planned for this event, but it also provides an overall evaluation of how you plan security budgets in general. The lessons learned from budget planning for events should also be incorporated into other budgetary planning processes.

Section IV

Security Operations Metrics

…Georgia power Metrics insight: Scorekeeping on government regulations compliance yields valuable performance measures…[1]

This section includes Chapters 20–24 and includes the security functions and projects that fall under the umbrella of what we choose to call "security operations." The security functions, subfunctions, processes and projects include:

- Chapter 20: Investigations and Noncompliance Inquiries
- Chapter 21: Government Security
- Chapter 22: Information Systems Security
- Chapter 23: Mergers, Acquisitions or Divestitures Security
- Chapter 24: Outsourcing

Security operations includes functions that are related to assets protection or are an integral part of assets protection but do not fit into what we have chosen to call administrative security or physical security. In addition, we have added the topics of mergers and acquisitions as well as outsourcing in this section. Although they are not recurring security functions, and are generally handled as projects, they are nonetheless an important part of today's security professional's duties and responsibilities and are considered "operations."

Some may argue with our categorization of security functions; however, that is not important. What is important is the information provided in each of these chapters. As a CSO, you are in a position to structure your organization in a way that meets your needs and the needs of your corporation or government agency. We have provided an example of a possible security structure.

An overview of the security operations, security functions and projects in the security organizational structure are shown in Figures Section IV-1 and Section IV-2.

---

[1] CSOONLINE.COM, "Where the Metrics are" article, February 2005 issue.

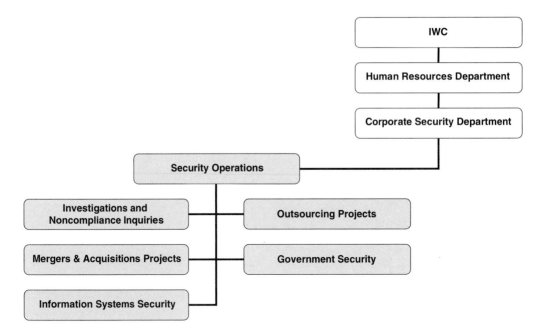

Figure Section IV-1   An example of a security operations organizational structure.

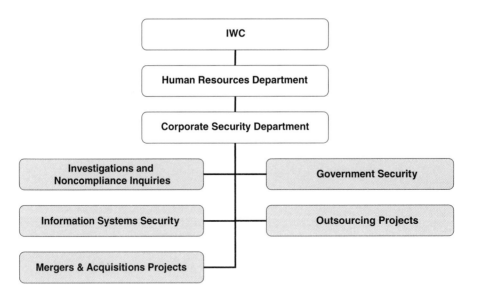

Figure Section IV-2   Another example of a security operations organizational structure.

Chapter 20

Investigations and Noncompliance Inquiries

This chapter will address the use of security metrics as a tool for managing the investigative and noncompliance inquiry (NCI) security functions. Process analysis will be discussed along with the use of metrics to assess the effectiveness, costs, benefits, success and failures.

INTRODUCTION

Investigations and NCI are security functions that, at some corporations, may be candidates for outsourcing. At this time, both are internal functions at IWC. At IWC, these two functions are much alike. However, the primary difference is scope and magnitude. That is to say, an NCI is used to describe an investigation which is conducted due to a violation of corporate policy or procedures where there has not been a violation of law. At IWC an investigation is generally a much more complex process associated with a more serious situation and may involve a violation of government law or regulation external to the corporation.

One primary reason for the differentiation is for public relations purposes. When one hears that an investigation is being conducted, it sounds more serious than if one hears an NCI is being conducted. In addition, an NCI may be used as a preliminary inquiry to assess if something is wrong and requires further investigation. An NCI may be conducted by almost any security professional or member of management. An investigation requires someone skilled in the techniques and processes of investigations and with a working relationship with different governmental investigative organizations (local, state and federal).

INVESTIGATIONS AND NCI ORGANIZATION

The investigation and NCI organization (see Figure 20-1) falls under the direct management of the CSO. It consists of not only the investigative function—noncompliance inquiries function—but also the function of risk assessments, liaison and awareness briefings. It is particularly important for the investigative element of this organization to report directly to the CSO. This function may handle some of the most sensitive issues within the company, sometimes involving the sensitive issue of employee misbehavior. Extra layers of oversight and management between the CSO and the investigations function are generally problematic.

Risk assessments are conducted in coordination with other applicable security functions and are conducted after an investigation or NCI indicates some corporate assets were determined to be vulnerable and at risk. This function is a proactive process used primarily to mitigate risks to assets and minimize the needs for an NCI or investigation.

The liaison function is carried out by both the CSO and investigations and NCI organization manager. Liaison is with the local, state, federal and foreign law enforcement, criminal justice and security officers; also with intelligence offers as appropriate. The awareness function is accomplished as a standalone process, used when management requires special information such as a "crime prevention" briefing. Other forms of investigations and NCI-related briefings are coordinated with the administrative security functional lead for security awareness briefings and training.

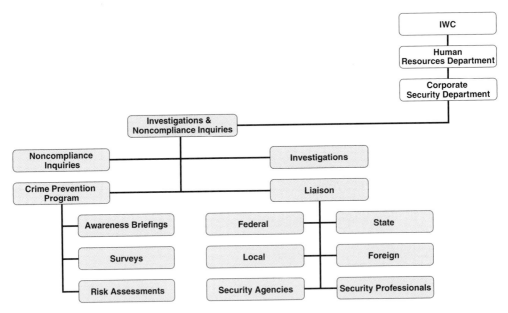

Figure 20-1   The organizational location of the investigations and NCI function.

INVESTIGATIONS AND NCI DRIVERS AND FLOWCHARTS

Of course, after the organizational structure of the investigations and NCI function is identified and charted, its primary drivers are identified and graphically depicted. In this case, the complaints and allegations from various sources are considered the security drivers. (See Figure 20-2 and Figure 20-3.)

Remember, one important driver for the investigations and NCI process is the total number of IWC employees: The more employees, statistically the larger number of employees who will violate IWC rules or government laws. Another is the number of requests for support from other organizations (such as the legal and ethics staffs and their need to have investigators support their processes). Remember that the investigations and NCI organization is also a service and support organization and as such must provide professional support to other IWC organizations when that service and support is requested, and determined to be warranted.

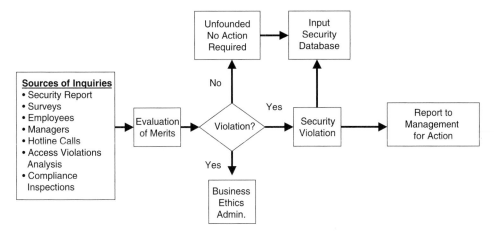

Figure 20-2   An overall flowchart of the drivers of investigations and noncompliance inquiries.

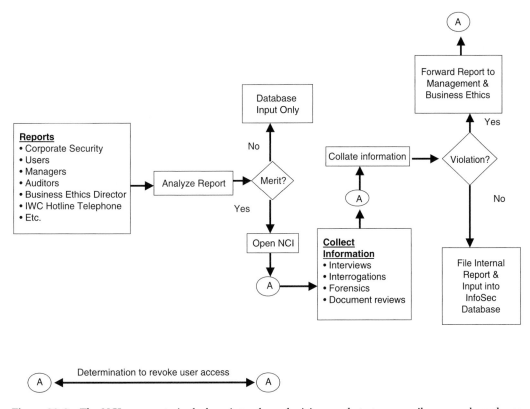

Figure 20-3   The NCI process to include points where decision made to temporarily suspend employee pending management action.

INVESTIGATIONS AND NCI EXAMPLES OF METRICS

There are many different security metrics that a CSO can use to help understand, assess and manage the investigations and NCI processes. A problem that may face the CSO, as with all other security metrics, is determining the most useful metrics. When in doubt as to the most valuable metrics, the CSO can start by identifying as many as possible and then sorting through them to determine which offer the most utility.

As previously stated in this book, the CSO may first want to develop a process flow diagram depicting the macro process and then develop flow diagrams for the investigative subprocesses or micro processes. Once accomplished, the CSO can begin to develop points for different processes measures. An example of such a data collection list for investigations may look like the following (one for the NCI function would be almost identical):

- Number of investigations opened per month
- Number of investigations closed per month
- Number of investigations pending per month
- Average time used to conduct an investigation
- Average cost in terms of investigator's time, IWC employees' time, administrative time, and cost of resources used
- Same information as above broken down by type of investigation
- Same information as above broken down by quarters, year and multiple years
- Identification of the IWC departments where the incident took place
- Identification of the IWC departments where the subject (employee) of the investigation was assigned
- Number of allegations proven correct
- Number of allegations proven wrong
- Subject employees of investigations position and job code
- Type of investigations broken down by departments
- Department information broken down monthly, quarterly, annually and multiple years
- Associate a cost chart with each of the above charts, where applicable

By using this approach, one can begin to get a sense of the type of information that offers potential for developing useful metrics. Furthermore, the CSO can relate the potential data points to what he/she needs to know. For example, if the CSO is attempting to determine the average time to conduct an investigation, tracking the time taken to complete all steps from the opening of an investigation to the closing of an investigation will provide that data. The CSO can further analyze that information by sorting investigations by type. An investigation into the theft of a physical asset, on average, may require less time than an investigation into misuse of information systems.

Metrics developed and used in the investigations and NCI process may provide value beyond the investigative processes itself. Trend data may be developed and used to drive changes in other routine security policies, procedures and processes. For example, if investigative trend data reveals thefts to be occurring during a specific time frame, additional protective measures could be implemented during that vulnerable period to either prevent the thefts or catch those committing the thefts.

The information gathered can be used proactively to reduce the number of incidents requiring investigations, thus reducing the overall workload for security investigators. Learning from security incidents helps prevent their occurrence in the future.

The following are just a few examples of graphically depicted security metrics charts that a CSO may find useful in the effort to assess effectiveness of the investigations and NCI process and better manage the organization.

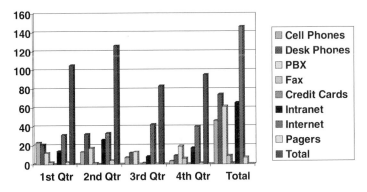

Figure 20-4   The number of technology-related NCIs conducted in 2005 broken down by type.

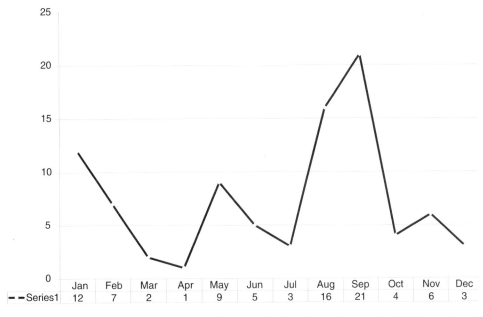

	Jan	Feb	Mar	Apr	May	Jun	Jul	Aug	Sep	Oct	Nov	Dec
— —Series1	12	7	2	1	9	5	3	16	21	4	6	3

Figure 20-5   The number of NCIs conducted in 2005 broken down by month. This is an important depiction to establish a trend.

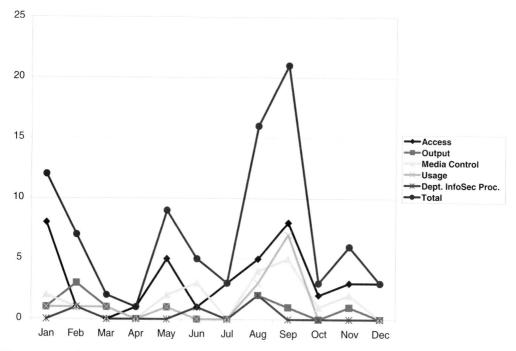

Figure 20-6   The number of information systems security (InfoSec) related NCIs in 2005 broken down by type per month.

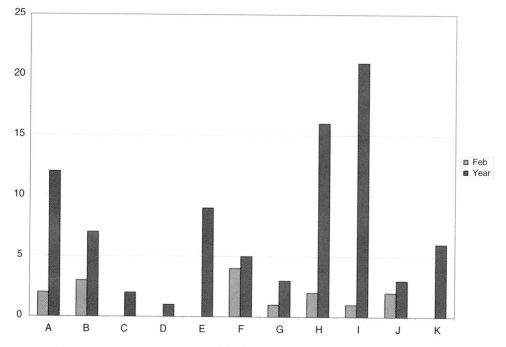

Figure 20-7   The number of NCIs conducted broken down by department, the past month and for the past year.

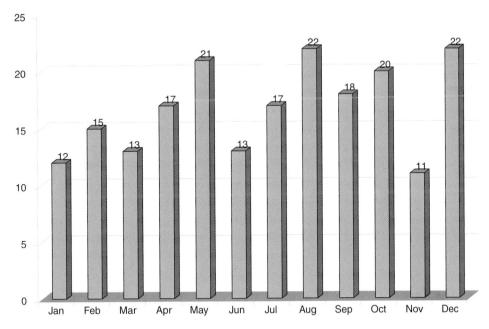

Figure 20-8   The number of investigations conducted per month for a one-year period for U.S.-only facilities.

- The number of IWC employees have increased based on IWC's need to rapidly build up the workforce to handle the new contract work.
- The number of noncompliance inquiries have increased during that same time period.
- The number of investigations have increased during that same period of time.
- This increased workload has caused some delays in completing the inquiries and investigations in the 30 day period that was set as the goal.
- The ratio of incidents compared to the total number of employees indicates:
  - Personnel may not be getting sufficient information during their new-hire briefings.
  - The personnel being hired may not be thoroughly screened prior to hiring.

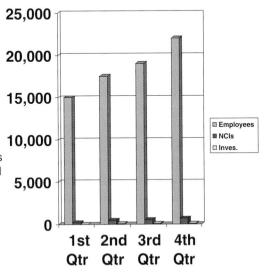

Figure 20-9   Different drivers of the investigations and NCI process.

Remember that as the employee population increases, generally so does the investigations and NCI activity. That in turn drives the need for additional supporting resources.

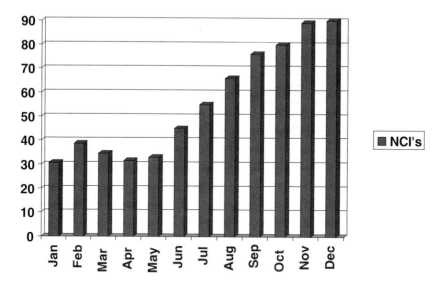

Figure 20-10   The total number of NCIs per month at all IWC locations.

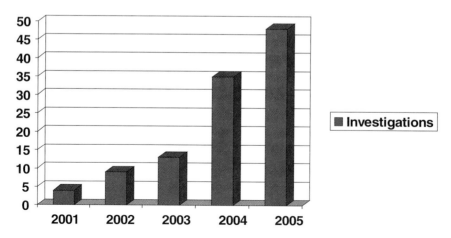

Figure 20-11   The total number of investigations at all locations from 2001–2005.

This is an important chart in that it depicts a trend. From this graphic depiction, the CSO can conclude a continuous yearly increase in the number of investigations. This trend should drive the CSO to analyze the investigative data to determine why. Action taken, or not taken, will be influenced by the results of the analysis.

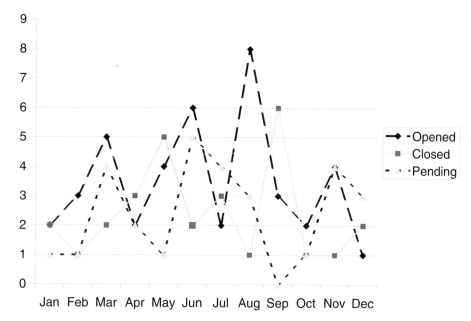

Figure 20-12   The percentage of NCIs opened, closed, and pending per month.

The figures in this chapter offer a few examples of the many security metrics a CSO may find useful in the effort to understand process performance and manage an investigations and NCI function.

Process measurements can tell much about a process. The type of measures used should correlate to what the CSO wants or needs to track and understand. For example, if it is important to the CSO to know what percent of cases are closed each month, then Figure 20-12 may be of value. The ultimate goal for the CSO should be to understand what is occurring that drives the need for investigations. Can those drivers be changed to such a degree as to eliminate or reduce the need for investigations? Measuring will also tell the CSO if the changes made had any effect on the process. Of course, cost issues must always be considered.

INVESTIGATIONS AND NCI CASE STUDY

As a CSO, you decided that it would be a good idea to use the security driver's metrics used for tracking the number of employees, the number of inquiries and the number of investigations conducted over time. You have gone through the analytical process to make that decision based on answering the how, what, why, when, who and where questions noted below.

- Why should this data be collected? To determine the ratio of employees to the workload; thus manpower requirements could be forecasted over time.
- What specific data will be collected?
  - Total number of IWC employees
  - Total number of noncompliance inquiries
  - Total number of investigations
- How will these data be collected?

- Total Employees: The collection will be accomplished by taking the total number of paid employees from the human resources department's master personnel database file.
  - Total Number of NCIs: This information will be gathered by the unit coordinator from the unit's NCI database file.
  - Total Number of Investigations: The unit coordinator will also gather this information from the unit's investigations database file.
- When will these data be collected? The data from each of the previous months will be compiled on the first business day of each of the following months and incorporated into the crime investigations drivers' graph, maintained on the investigations and NCI's administrative information system.
- Who will collect these data? The data will be collected, input and maintained by the unit's coordinator.
- Where (at what point in the function's process) will these data be collected? The collection of data will be based on the information available and on file in the investigations and NCI's database at close of business on the last business day of the month.

The CSO and organizational manager will analyze the NCI data, for example, to determine:

- The reason for each employee's noncompliance
- The position and organization of the employee
- Their seniority date
- Identification of the patterns
- Main offenses

That information would then be provided to the project team assigned to the goal of decreasing the need for NCIs and investigations. Based on that information, the briefings would be updated and more emphasis placed on those areas that caused the majority of problems.

Remember, there are numerous types of graphic depictions of data that can be a great tool for management. They include bar charts, pie charts, and line charts. The charts can be monthly, quarterly, weekly, or annually. The timeliness of the charts should be dependent on the manager's need for the information.

The key to the data collection and their related graphic depictions is to look more at trends than monthly numbers. The goal is to continue to maintain and improve on positive trends. Negative trends should be analyzed for systemic causes and project plans implemented to reverse the negative trends. The metrics could then be used to monitor the process and to determine if process changes actually cause the reversal of the negative trends. If not, then new analyses and rethinking of the problem are called for.

The organizational manager, in coordination with the CSO, began this process by of course identifying the drivers requiring the functions to be performed. Then the processes were flowcharted and a process analysis summary was developed to help provide a high-level view of the process.

That process summary included the following information:

- Security Department: Investigations and NCIs
- Process Definition: Provide professional investigative services in support of IWC and its customers.

- Subprocesses:
    - Conduct investigations
    - Conduct NCIs
    - Conduct crime prevention surveys
    - Conduct crime prevention special briefings
- Requirements and Directives that Govern the Process:
    - CAPP
    - Contractual security requirements
    - Position descriptions
    - Corporate policies
- Suppliers:
    - IWC Employees
    - Customers
        - IWC Management
        - IWC Customers
- Input:
    - Complaints
    - Allegations
    - Requests for Assistance
    - Security Requirements
- Output:
    - Investigative reports
    - NCI reports
    - Inspection reports
    - Security assessment reports
    - Briefings
    - Testimony
- Key Metrics:
    - Subprocess 1: Case totals year-to-date and five year trends, case aging charts
    - Subprocess 2: Crime Prevention Surveys completed; results; and cost-benefits charts
    - Subprocess 3: Number of NCIs completed each year; costs; and IWC departments where conducted
- Customer and Expectations:
    - IWC Management (Internal customers): Timely and complete investigative and NCI reports
    - IWC Customers: Timely and complete investigative and NCI reports as applicable to external customers

Using this identification process, the IWC CSO can view a summary of not only investigative and NCI organizational security metrics and process related information, but the CSO can establish a form or format for such summaries and require its use throughout the security department.

INVESTIGATIONS AND NCI SUMMARY

The investigations and NCI organization is a highly visible and important function within the IWC security department. Using a security metrics management program to assess effectiveness of the function is critical to a CSO. The information collected and analyzed can be used to improve the process and help mitigate risks, and thus better protect IWC assets.

Chapter 21

Government Security

This chapter addresses the fundamentals of a security program designed to support a corporation doing business with the U.S. government and in support of classified contracts. Useful security metrics will be identified that may assist a CSO in assessing the effectiveness of the corporate, or in this case government, security program.

INTRODUCTION

When one thinks of government security and government contractors, the image of corporations that build weapons systems for the federal or central government come to mind. However, there are many other types of services and products that a government contracts for. There are corporations who engage in contracts with the government for intellectual products (information), such as "think tanks" and universities. There are also government contracts for office supplies, janitorial services, equipment, bolts and nuts, and everything in between. The preponderance of work and activity is unclassified, although a large part involves classified work.

Classified work is work that falls under the realm of national security regulations and access to classified information, areas, products, and/or equipment that are based on a security clearance (stringent vetting process) and a need-to-know principle. That is, if you are needed to help support the contract, you have a need-to-know. Need-to-know, coupled with a government-issued security clearance, are required by any individual before being granted access to facilities, data, information or material classified under national security laws and regulations. If you are not involved in any aspects of the contract, then you do not have a need-to-know and access by you is denied.

Government contracts range widely in scope, product and services. There are government contracts in the United States, for example, at the local, county, state and federal level. They may be handled like any other contracts between a buyer and seller of products or services. However, at the federal level, there are also those contracts of a national security nature that are identified as "classified." That is because these contracts require access to or generation of classified material. The contracts are kept secure and access to classified material is based on two factors: 1) possession of a government security clearance and, 2) having a "need-to-know" (NTK) for related information as previously stated.

These contracts may be publicly known with portions of them requiring access to classified information and material. Some are also known as "special access programs" (SAP) or "sensitive compartmented information" (SCI) programs because of their extremely and highly important national security nature. These require even more stringent access requirements and security controls. Others may not be known and are referred to as unacknowledged programs because this existence is unknown to all but those few granted access.

Government contracts carry with them certain specifications that may be universal or common and can be found in most contractual agreements between two corporations, with one being the buyer and the other the seller. However, there are contract specifications that are unique to government contracts. This is especially true if the contract is classified requiring protections under national security regulations.

If a corporation has a government contract, the contracts will often have specifications dealing with the corporation's responsibilities to protect the government assets being used and under the care of the corporation. In addition, if the contract is a classified government contract, the CSO is also responsible not only for the protection of the government assets related to the contract, but also providing a special security umbrella due to the classified nature of the contract.

In order for a corporation to do classified work with the U.S. government, that corporation must enter into a security agreement with the government and will be bound by applicable government security regulation for protecting classified information and material. Failure to comply with security requirements could lead to contract default, termination and disbarment from doing future classified work with the U.S. government.

Some of the best assets protection practices that can help protect corporate assets can be found in the government contract environment. When you think of it, there is little difference between the two. Whether it is personnel, information or some form of physical assets, they all require protection. Furthermore, they all require protection in an efficient and effective way. Even the reasons for the assets protection are similar:

- The loss of sensitive, corporate information may adversely affect a company causing it to lose a competitive edge or market share. If that loss is large enough it could do serious harm to the company.
- The loss of assets by a government could have serious and dire consequences, such as the defeat of the nation-state in war.
- Both have at stake the potential for a major loss of assets, leading to their demise or at least weakening them.

In the United States, the National Security Industrial Program (NISP) is the program that establishes security requirements for industry when engaged in classified contracts with the U.S. government. The Defense Security Service (DSS) has security cognizance over all Department of Defense contractors. Other government agencies have security cognizance over their own security programs. (See the DSS web page at http://www.dss.gov for additional information.)

The United States President has established the Office of Homeland Security to be the focal point homeland protection. This relatively new agency works with industry to accomplish its objectives. One may wonder if that really has anything to do with protecting corporate assets. Keep in mind much of the nation's infrastructure is in the hands of or under the control of corporations and industry. For example, the commercial communications infrastructure within the U.S. is largely controlled by communication corporations. Homeland Security is charged with ensuring the protection of the nation's infrastructure and, in the example of the communications infrastructure, must work with the owners—corporations—in order to effectively provide protection.

Homeland Security engages with corporations in all sectors where corporations own or operates some or the entire infrastructure. This engagement includes providing threat information, conducting security assessments, offering guidance and any other protection action or measure that may be required or necessary. Furthermore, corporations work with Homeland Security in providing it products and services to support the homeland security mission. Much like the Department of Defense, Homeland Security relies on corporations to develop and produce the tools it needs to accomplish its mission.

Information and the nation's information infrastructure are also of paramount interest to the U.S. in terms of the necessity to protect. This is not unique to the U.S. Every nation-state has a need to protect its own infrastructure and acts to do so (see http://www.nipc.gov/about/about.htm).

CSOs whose corporations are considered vital to their nation-state's information infrastructures have a vital role to play in their protection by protecting the assets of their corporation and thus also the information infrastructure of their nation-state.

IWC'S GOVERNMENT SECURITY ORGANIZATION

If a corporation has classified contracts with a U.S. government agency and if those contracts are large, involving the generation or handling of large amounts of classified information and material, it may be necessary to establish a separate organization to handle all government security issues and activity. At IWC, this is the case. Therefore, the CSO formed an organization to meet security specifications of these contracts (see Figure 21-1).

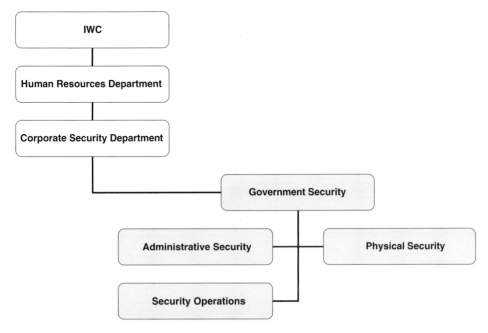

Figure 21-1   The IWC government security organization under the leadership of a manager reporting to the CSO.

At IWC, the government security organization, due to its numerous and large government contracts, is a "mini-IWC security" department by structure. However, for the most part, a matrix management system is used. That means for all but some primary, dedicated security personnel, the security functional expertise needed to meet the needs of the contract are drawn from outside the government security organization. For example, noncompliance inquiries (NCI) may be accomplished by those assigned to the IWC security department's operations organization (investigations and NCI organization).

This is a cost-savings approach because the NCI function may not require full-time support considering the level of activity. Moreover, this structure provides for the flexibility to allocate and assign security assets in areas where they are needed. It also makes for more efficient support of government contracts. Of course, these security personnel who are "matrixed" to the government security organization would have the security clearance and NTK for supporting the contractual work.

GOVERNMENT SECURITY DRIVERS AND FLOWCHARTS

The security drivers for any classified government contract are the contract security specifications contained within the contractual document and addresses specific protection and security requirements. Fulfilling the contractual security requirements is essential in order to avoid such actions as increasing the potential for compromise of classified information, defaulting on the contract, and other serious consequences.

As the CSO of IWC, the government security process is handled like all other security processes. It is important to graphically depict the macro process and related subprocesses. After all, any process analysis will begin here (see Figure 21-2). Once the government

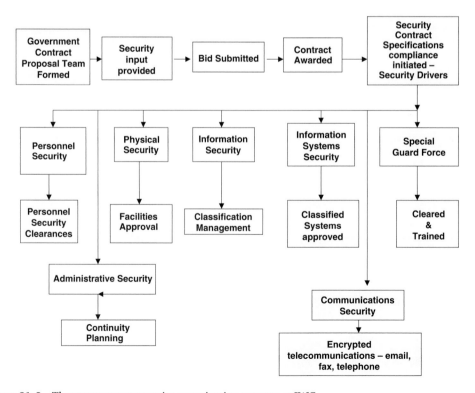

Figure 21-2   The government security organization process at IWC.

security process flowchart is developed, the CSO can draw from other security functional flowcharts and embed them in the government security charts as applicable. Where the security functional processes are different, those flowcharts can be modified. This is a simpler and a more efficient method than developing the flowcharts from the beginning.

The flowchart can also be used as part of a brief to government security personnel and others who will be inspecting and auditing the performance of IWC regarding meeting contractual specifications.

GOVERNMENT SECURITY EXAMPLES OF METRICS

Assessing and managing performance within the government security program is just as important (if not more important) as in other security processes. Generally, companies doing classified business with the government spend more on security than purely commercial companies, as the provision of the National Industrial Security Program (NISP) requires a higher degree of protection for national security (classified) material and information.

> *For some federal government classified contracts, national security information is to be protected from compromise that would allow an adversary to compete in building similar systems, developing countermeasures, or delaying operational use of the systems.*

What measures are used and how performance is assessed are influenced by the provisions of the NISP and organizational needs as determined by the CSO. The following (see Figures 21-3 through 21-7) are some examples of graphically depicted metrics. These charts, of course, are based on a formal data collection process as part of the IWC security metrics management program (SMMP). They are vital when briefing the status of security to the government customers.

These examples of security metrics can also be very useful for a CSO in the effort to understand the government security profile (size and shape of the effort) and better help in the effort to evaluate efficiency and effectiveness. Of course, all the related-security metrics data and their associated charts from the matrixed security functions would also be used as modified for use in analyses and briefings to include only specific contractual-related data and charts—e.g., personnel security: number of accessed IWC employees to each particular classified contract.

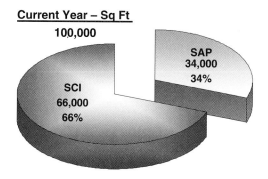

Figure 21-3   A facilities utilization profile for classified activities.

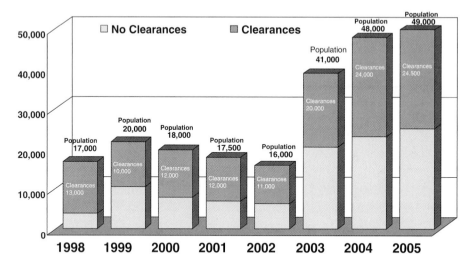

Figure 21-4   The IWC employee to security clearance ratio over an eight-year period.

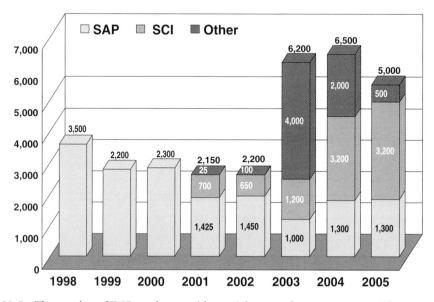

Figure 21-5   The number of IWC employees with special access clearance over an eight-year period.

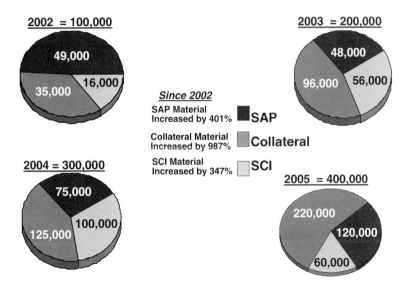

Figure 21-6 The various types and associated numbers of classified material over a four-year period.

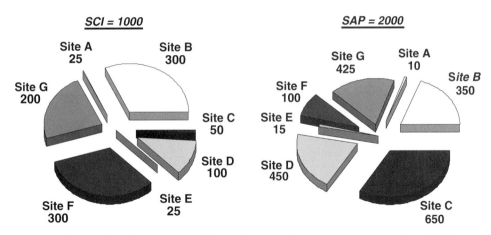

Figure 21-7 The number of employees with special access for one year segregated by IWC department sectors.

GOVERNMENT SECURITY CASE STUDY

As the IWC CSO, you have just been informed that the cognizant government security officer for one of IWC's classified contracts will be coming to the main IWC facility to conduct a security compliance inspection. What would you do to prepare for such a visit?

The IWC CSO immediately notified executive management and broadcasted an inspection notification to all managers and employees working on the contract. The CSO requested that they all conduct a self-inspection using one of the previously provided security compliance checklists for self-inspections. Furthermore, if they needed assistance or advice, they should contact the manager of the IWC government security organization. The CSO also had the security staff conduct a contractual compliance inspection of its own (security department) operations.

In addition, the CSO directed the manager of the government security organization to prepare a status briefing for the government security inspection team. That briefing would consist of the following:

- IWC's government security organizational chart and how that department is integrated into the IWC security department
- The government security macro process flowcharts along with key micro process functional flowcharts
- The specific security functions performed under the contract
- The number of dedicated (direct-charge personnel time and materials) security staff supporting the contract
- The number of indirect (overhead charges of personnel and materials) security staff supporting the contract—that is, the number of matrixed security staff supporting the contract
- The amount of classified material by category possessed for that contract and their locations
- The number of approved standalone and networked information systems used to process, store, display and transmit classified and unclassified information in support of the contract
- The location of offices and areas where contract unclassified and classified work was being conducted
- The number and types of security containers and areas being used to store classified materials

An example of a composite chart that can be used as part of the briefings is noted below (see Figure 21-8). The data collection and supporting charts can provide great "public relations" value to IWC and the government customers by showing how the government's interest is being safeguarded under each contract.

DSS / Customers Inspections = 50
    Satisfactory – 48
    Marginal – 1
    Unsatisfactory – 1
    Adverse Reports submitted to DSS - 30

Information Security
    Site classified LANs – 29
    Site classified WANs – 19
    Site classified stand-alones – 350

Pre-Employment Investigations
    PEIs Performed – 2500

Cases denoting derogatory information – 39
Total Cost All PEI's – Approx. $250,000

Workplace Violence (WPV)
Prevention Program
    Incidents – 12

Guard Service Outsourced		
	Use	Provider
Site A	Yes	Service provider A
Site B	Yes	Service provider A
Site C	Yes	Service provider A
Site D	No	Proprietary
Site E	Yes	Service provider A
Site F	Yes	Service provider A
Site G	Yes	Service provider A
Site H	No	Proprietary
Site I	Yes	Service provider A

Figure 21-8   An overview chart of IWC operations to include information relative to the security customer's classified contract.

GOVERNMENT SECURITY SUMMARY

Many corporations do business with governments. When doing business with the federal government, a corporation may be involved in classified work, which is work related to the national security and governed by legislation, regulation and related directives. Classified contracts with the government include specific security requirements often more stringent than corporations doing only commercial business typically encounter. Adherence to the security requirements of classified contracts is critical, and failure to do so may lead to contract default or termination.

Security metrics management techniques can be used as a tool to assist a CSO to better understand his/her organizational support to the government customers and the government contracts, and how all those support processes flow—their effectiveness and costs—as well as provide that visibility to the government customers.

Chapter 22

Information Systems Security

This chapter addresses the use of security metrics as a tool for managing the information systems security (InfoSec) function. It expands on information security as stated in Chapter 7 and offers another look at InfoSec in a corporation. Process analysis is discussed along with the use of metrics to assess effectiveness, costs, successes and failures.

INTRODUCTION

InfoSec has an interesting history as a security function. It was developed and shaped within the information technology (IT) community and not within the security community. This was due to the fact that only the IT community had sufficient expertise to understand the information technologies being used, their applications, and their vulnerabilities. In the emerging years of IT, security organizations were not equipped with sufficient technical expertise to provide appropriate protections (beyond physical security), so the responsibility for most of today's InfoSec has stayed within the IT community.

This condition has created problems which still plague us today. One way of looking at this condition is similar to "the fox guarding the henhouse." Perhaps the best way to understand the current condition is to recognize that the service provider is also responsible for protection. When conflicts arise, delivering services is usually a priority over protection. Therefore, security—that is, protection of these valuable corporate assets—takes a back seat. What that has led to is a history of security being an afterthought, leading to preventable but frequently occurring security problems with information systems and their other related assets. Compromise of information, corruption of data integrity, denial of services, and theft of the hardware are just a few of the continuous security problems plaguing information systems. Nonsecurity IT professionals have a very poor track record of protecting these most valuable of corporate assets.

In today's information-knowledge-based society, information and those systems and networks that support information generation, processing, dissemination and use, are essential to the success of corporations. In the business world, effective and efficient information systems support a corporations' ability to meet global customers' needs. After all, information is power, today more than ever, and that can equate to a competitive edge in the marketplace.

The security professional generally maintains responsibility for the physical protection of physical assets related to InfoSec (computers, servers and all other related hardware). Moreover, personnel security falls within the domain of the security professional. Furthermore, within the government security function, the security professional almost always has responsibility for leading InfoSec, particularly as it involves classified information. Since the security professional traditionally manages the government security function within corporations, they generally assume responsibility for all classified InfoSec.

INFOSEC ORGANIZATION

In today's corporate world, the protection of these assets is often under the authority of the "Chief Information Security Officer" (CISO). The CISO reports to the Chief Information Officer (CIO), who generally reports to the Chief Executive Officer (CEO). (See Figures 22-1, 22-2 and 22-3.)

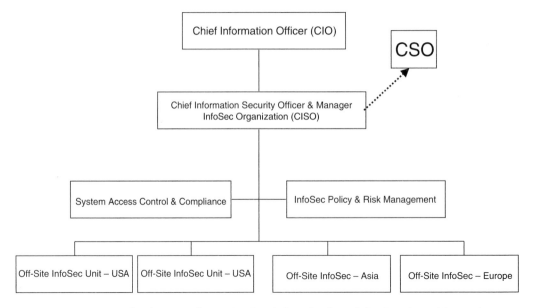

Figure 22-1   An example of an overall organizational chart for the InfoSec function with matrix reporting to the CSO.

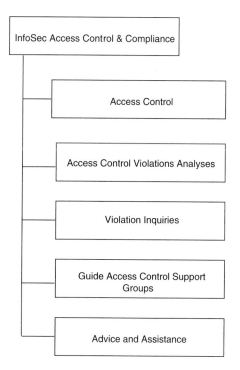

Figure 22-2   An example of a sub-organizational chart for the InfoSec function.

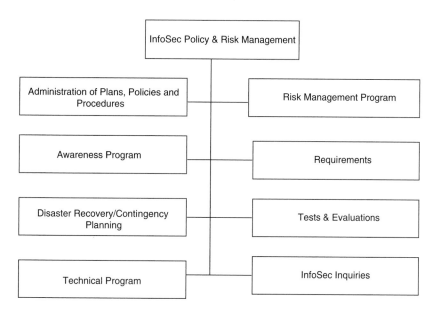

Figure 22-3   An example of another sub-organizational chart for the InfoSec function. Sometimes the functions of the CISO overlap with those of the CSO when it comes to protecting these valuable assets.

INFOSEC DRIVERS AND FLOWCHARTS

The InfoSec function derives its purpose from the security drivers as do the other security functions (see Figure 22-4).

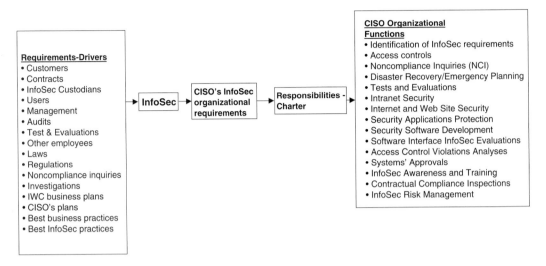

Figure 22-4   The security drivers of InfoSec functions.

One of the primary drivers for the InfoSec statement of work, or security workload, is the number of information systems users driving that workload (see Figures 22-5 and 22-12). As the number of users increases, the amount of associated security work also increases. The other primary workload driver of the InfoSec function is the number of information systems (see Figures 22-6 and 22-13). In today's modern corporation, information devices includes PDAs, notebooks, cell phones, and their associated functions of digital cameras, Internet access capabilities and so forth.

Since information systems and users are significant drivers, the IWC CISO, who is matrixed to the CSO, concluded it was essential to understand and document the macro process for user activity. From that, key subprocesses that drive additional security work could be identified.

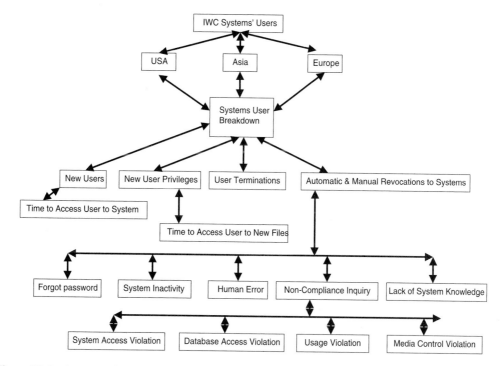

Figure 22-5 An example of a system user-process for the InfoSec function.

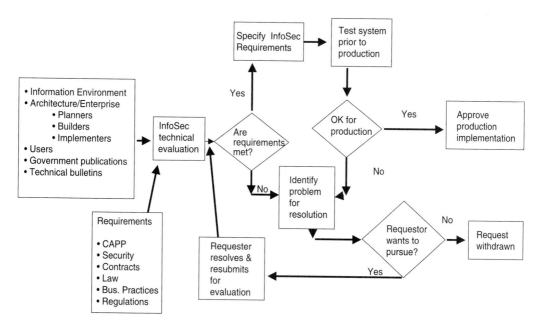

Figure 22-6 An example of a system approval process for the InfoSec function when sensitive IWC information will be displayed, stored, transmitted and processed by IWC systems.

The CISO, working with the CSO, developed additional InfoSec flowcharts for incorporation into both the CISO and CSO security metrics management programs (see Figures 22-7 through 22-11).

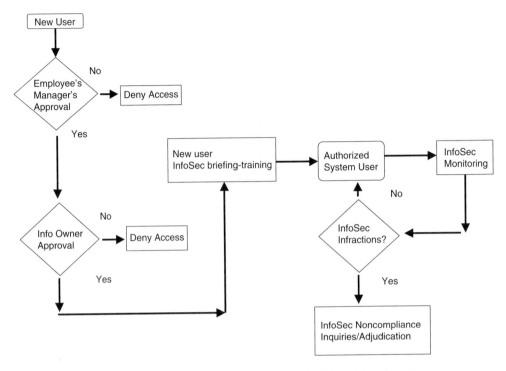

Figure 22-7   An example of adding a new systems user as part of the InfoSec function.

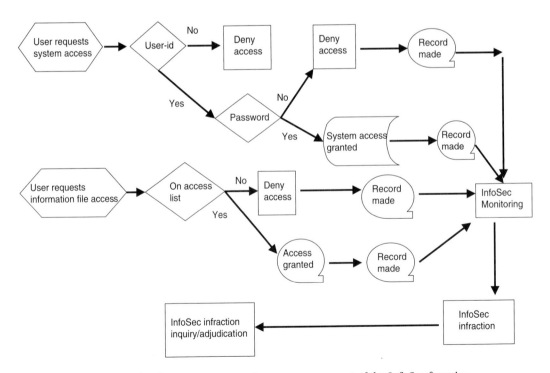

Figure 22-8   An example of a systems process for new users as part of the InfoSec function.

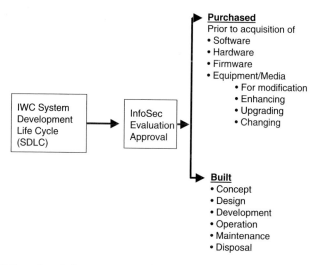

Figure 22-9 An InfoSec related chart to system development lifecycle.

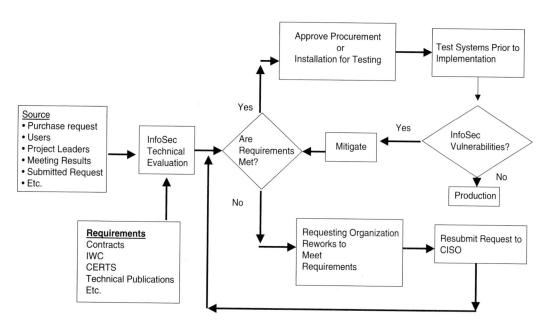

Figure 22-10 An example of a system technical evaluation for system purchase as part of the overall InfoSec function.

   The CISO also decided to provide the CSO with a flowchart that mapped InfoSec support to goals (see Figure 22-11).

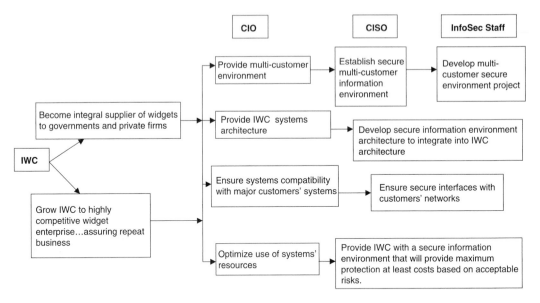

Figure 22-11   An example of a flowchart which mapped InfoSec support to goals.

INFOSEC EXAMPLES OF METRICS

The CISO, using the InfoSec metrics management system which is a subprogram of the CSO's security metrics management program, began collecting and graphically depicting data to support the CSO's analysis of information systems assets protection efforts (see Figures 22-12 and 22-13).

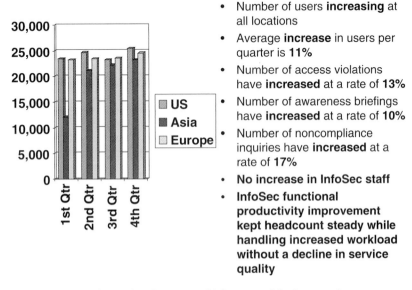

Figure 22-12   An example of a graphic depiction which mapped the increase in systems users at all IWC locations.

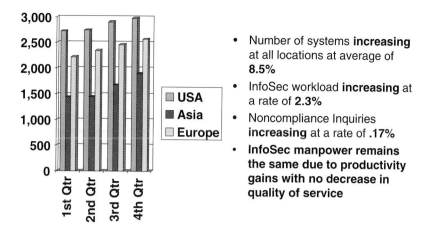

Figure 22-13   An example of a graphic depiction of the metric showing the increase in the number of systems at all IWC locations.

The CISO also developed an overall InfoSec graphic depiction that provides a conceptual look at how InfoSec objectives are supported.

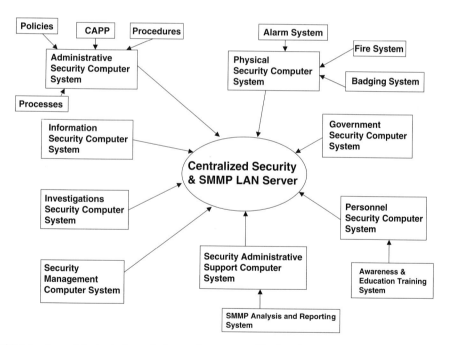

Figure 22-14   A graphic depiction of a (macro) conceptual look at how InfoSec objectives are linked and supported, to include the security metrics management program (SMMP).

INFOSEC CASE STUDY

The CISO was concerned about the increasingly high amount of overtime being charged by InfoSec staff members. The CISO was aware that "burn-out" could occur, which in turn leads to errors in judgment and even health problems for the staff. The CISO discussed the matter with the CSO and sought advice as to how to use a security metrics management process to collect data, analyze that data, and develop an argument for increasing the size of the InfoSec staff.

The CSO not only supported the CISO by providing advice but also by explaining that statement of work (SoW) time and overtime data should be collected, analyzed and graphically depicted in an appropriate way in order to illustrate the increase in the size of the SoW (also referred to as workload). (See Figure 22-15.)

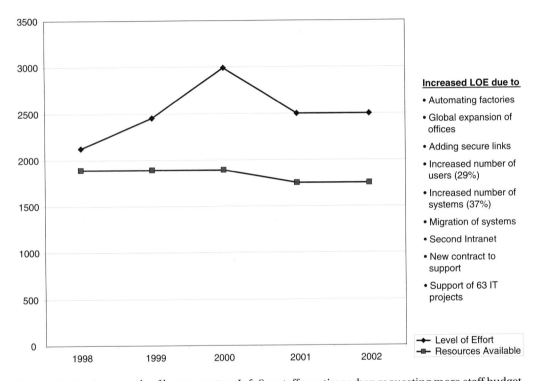

Figure 22-15   An example of how to portray InfoSec staff overtime when requesting more staff budget.

INFOSEC SUMMARY

The InfoSec function has for decades now been one of the functional responsibilities of the IT staff. This is because long ago the security "professionals" abdicated their duties and responsibilities, albeit for what appeared at the time to be seemingly sound technical reasons. It is only now that security professionals recognize the need to bring InfoSec back under the overall security (assets protection) umbrella and are now trying to "get the genie back in the bottle" and under control.

As with all security functions, and InfoSec is no exception, the uses of a security metrics management program can greatly assist in determining the costs, benefits, successes and failures of the InfoSec function.

Chapter 23

Mergers, Acquisitions or Divestitures Security

Mergers and acquisitions, as well as divestitures, are becoming more frequent in the global marketplace. Hardly a business day goes by when one is not announced. Mergers and acquisitions continue to be an important tool to shape the strategic direction of a company. Security has a role to play in this process and, because of that role, security performance should be measured. That process will be discussed in this chapter.[1]

INTRODUCTION

There are hundreds of mergers, acquisitions or divestitures taking place each year. All too often the CSO and security are not part of this process or are brought into the process only during the latter stages of the effort, thus reducing their potential additional value and effectiveness. In order for the merger, acquisition or divestiture (MAD) to be as successful as it can be, it is essential that security be part of the process from the very early stages.

The CSO or the CSO's representative should serve as a team member or at least an "internal consultant" to the MAD team, providing guidance and direction for all security matters. In essence, they are the MAD team's subject matter "expert" for all issues of security and assets protection. In addition to the security consulting role, the CSO also must fulfill the role of a department or functional (e.g., the macro security function) manager responsible for directing and managing all security department-related activities in support of the team and the overall effort.

The role of a security departmental or functional head is similar to the role of any other functional leader on the MAD team. Each is responsible to ensure they manage all activities supporting the MAD-related effort, for their specific discipline and department. For example, the CSO manages all relevant assets protection issues, just as the manager of finance ensures all financial matters are properly handled by his or her organization.

---

[1] This chapter will not repeat what has been said throughout this book when it comes to security metrics management techniques. Suffice it to say that during a MAD project, many of the processes and their measures, discussed earlier in this book, will be used in support of the MAD project. Please refer to those relevant chapters for details. This chapter will deal primarily with the CSO as a project team member in a MAD project. We decided to add this chapter to help the reader involved in a MAD and explain how SMMP can support these by laying out the MAD process.

Support from security for the MAD effort can be divided into two phases:

- Premerger support
- Postmerger support

Furthermore, the contribution security makes to the entire effort can be further segmented into the following three categories:

1) *Protecting the effort itself*: Security measures are applied to the MAD effort to ensure that it is properly protected. That includes the implementation of measures to protect the confidentiality of the effort and its people, information and physical assets.
2) *Providing subject matter expertise*: The security manager or professional serves as a member of the team and provides guidance, direction and consultation on all security-related issues and concerns.
3) *Evaluating the security condition of the target company*: The security manager is charged with assessing the security condition of the target company. Here the CSO conducts a security survey of the target company's security program and overall security condition. That becomes part of the total team's assessment. Any issues identified are given consideration in terms of their effect on closing the deal.

As for the use of the security metrics management process in support of a merger, acquisition or divestiture, it can be useful in all phases of the effort. From the task of integrating the two security organizations of two merging companies into one, to the divesting of a single business unit or significant corporate assets and the impact that will have on the security program, security metrics are used to better understand the effectiveness of the security process in support of MAD. Security metrics are also used to assess the impact of MAD on the security organization itself.

Which metrics are used will depend upon the situation. One can expect that any cost-related metrics along with efficiency metrics will be most useful. This is particularly true when combining two security organizations into one. In this consolidation process, there will be much pressure to reduce costs. Therefore, the CSO must look to find ways to reduce costs. Ideally, the CSO, using metrics management, will be able to analyze the security organization processes, keep the most effective, and change or improve the least effective, thereby creating a better security organization than either one of the two was prior to the merger.

MAD-RELATED SECURITY ORGANIZATION

Most MAD efforts are worked as a project and staffed by a team. That team is usually an integrated (multidisciplines involved) project (or process) team (IPT). In support of the IPT, the CSOs serves as a functional project lead and as a member of the larger project team.

It is structured as such as part of the CSO's organization, and is important enough to report directly to the CSO (see Figure 23-1).

As an integral member of the IWC MAD project team, the CSO also has a place in the project team's structure (see Figures 23-2 and 23-3).

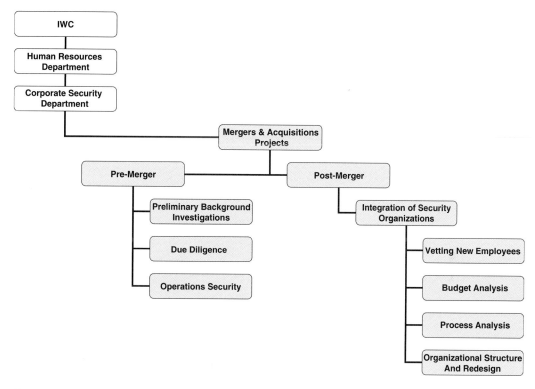

Figure 23-1   The location of the MAD project team as it relates to the CSO's duties and responsibilities.

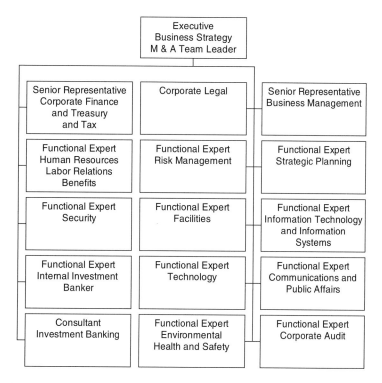

Figure 23-2   The location of the CSO as a member of the MAD project team as it relates to supporting a large transaction.

Figure 23-3   The location of the CSO as a member of a post-MAD project team as it relates to the CSO's duties and responsibilities.

MAD SECURITY DRIVERS, FLOWCHARTS AND CHECKLISTS

What drives the security work for MAD? Obviously, it is governed by the corporation's executive management decisions to divest a portion of the corporation, merge with another, or acquire another business or corporation.

Remember in earlier chapters, flowcharts were used to depict how a process works—the individual steps within that process and sequence in which they occur; as well as the relationship between drivers and processes. Flowcharts and checklists can be useful tools for the CSO in executing performance and management of security processes supporting the MAD.

Since the MAD projects are not under the direct leadership of the CSO, the CSO will serve as a team member providing expertise as required by the team leader. Therefore, the CSO concentrates on developing processes to support the team's objective, one of which is the gathering of information. One important process the CSO must support in the premerger and acquisition phase is the gathering of competitive intelligence. To that end, a checklist (see Figure 24-4) can be very helpful in ensuring that all basic steps in the process are completed.

As part of this effort, the CSO should also establish metrics to track all tasks to include the expenditure of how many hours doing what tasks and their associated costs and materials. This will be useful in that such work should be part of a separate MAD budget and not part of the CSO's security department's budget. Use of the current security department budget should be avoided to ensure that subsequently the CSO does not go over budget. The CSO should determine how others assigned to the MAD team are budgeted for this project and ensure that the same methods are used. If each department

Process Steps	Process Actions
Establishing Needs	• Who needs intelligence? • What information is needed. • Prioritize needs.
Collect Information	• Develop research strategy. • Identify sources. • Collect information. • Review information to ensure you have what is needed.
Analyze Information	• Ensure data is relevant to needs. • Analyze data. • Draw conclusions. • Conduct supplemental data collection if necessary. • Review analysis in context of other known information.
Produce Intelligence	• Package intelligence to meet user expectations and needs. • Protect intelligence—release only to those with a need-to-know.
Distribute to Users	• Deliver intelligence in a timely fashion.
Apply Intelligence	• Integrate intelligence into decision-making process. • Use in context with other relevant intelligence. • Protect the intelligence.
Receive Feedback	• Was the intelligence supplied useful? • Was it delivered in a timely and relevant fashion? • Have use needs changed?

Figure 23-4   A competitive intelligence collection checklist that was developed by the IWC CSO.

is to use its current budget, usually an exception rather than the rule, then so be it, as long as security is treated the same as other departments.

Such data collection will also prove useful for any future MAD projects. These costs should also be tracked to each task's process and each task's process should be flowcharted, as is done with the primary security functions.

MAD—EXAMPLES OF METRICS

As stated earlier, security metrics management techniques in this book support many different security processes and functions. The security effort as part of the MAD IPT draws upon these security processes to support and contribute to the success of a MAD. Moreover, the CSO must use supporting process metrics as a tool to help manage these processes as effectively as possible. Thus, for those affected processes, process metrics management is essential.

Since security metric management for the security processes used in support of MAD were discussed earlier, we will shift the focus of this chapter to the use of other security tools. This section will deal with the appropriate checklists that the IWC CSO will use in support of this project. Supporting a MAD is not an everyday occurrence. Therefore, our intention is to focus in this chapter on what the CSO must do in support of a MAD so that nothing is omitted, overlooked, or forgotten. As part of the checklists, questions will be asked which should drive the CSO to develop measures unique to MAD and useful in assessing security performance.

CHECKLISTS

Premerger and acquisition checklist: During the pre-MAD phase, the high-level objectives for the security manager are to protect the effort and to participate in the due diligence. During this phase, the CSO has many distinct tasks to perform that contribute to the overall success of the effort. Checklists below will be useful to security managers and MAD team leaders as they develop their plans.

Protect the effort: Develop an Operations Security (OPSEC) plan that include guidance and requirements for the following areas:

- Maintain confidentiality of the effort's existence and activities
  - Nondisclosure agreements to be executed by all participants.
  - No public release without team leader approval.
  - Identification of designated project areas.

- Confidentiality of the team's work: Brief team members on:
  - Need for strict compliance with need-to-know.
  - Requirements for protecting information.
  - General procedures, requirements and other obligations.

- Protection of information
  - Define information sensitivity—what must be protected and why.
  - Identify Information Administrator—control and tracking of project documents.
  - Create an information control plan addressing the following areas:
    - Handling of information (paper and electronic).
    - Creation of documents (paper and electronic).
    - Distribution of documents (paper and electronic).
    - Electronic transmission of information and documents.
    - Reproduction of information and documents (paper and electronic).
    - Destruction of documents (paper and electronic).

- Protection of all MAD team members
  - Conduct general threat and vulnerability assessment.
  - Identify all team executives and members.
  - Prepare for international travel.
  - Obtain country risk assessments.
  - Provide team members with travel safety briefings.
  - Develop and brief the cover story for all team members to use.

Due diligence: During the due diligence effort, the security manager has two primary goals:

- The first is continuing to protect the effort, particularly team members as they move from location to location.
- The second is to conduct the security portion of the assessment on the target company.

The results of the due diligence assessment will be used by the CEO and/or board of directors to assist in making decisions relative to proceeding or not proceeding with the merger or acquisition.

- Competitive intelligence assessments: Security must be a member of the competitive intelligence team providing information and investigative support for the following assessments:
  - Market sector.
  - Target companies.
  - Competition intentions.

- Background investigations are to be conducted as needed on the following:
  - Target company executives and board members.
  - Target company affiliates and associates.
  - Target company key supplier executives.

- Evaluation of the target company's security profile
  - Assess current security condition.
  - Collection of data for organizational analysis.
  - Identify potential operational synergies.
  - Identify any major vulnerability.
  - Identify any deal-breaking issues.

Postmerger and acquisition checklist: The major activity of the post-MAD period is combining organizations. The newly acquired company or business unit must be integrated into the acquiring company. Each functional leader must participate. The CSO is responsible for integrating the security department from the acquired business unit into the acquiring company. In the process, there are tasks to accomplish and issues to address:

- Develop plan to combine security organizations
  - Leadership: A single leader needs to be recognized and tasked.
  - Create a single security department.
  - Establish common vision, operating philosophy, goals and objectives.
  - Analyze and define new security statement of work.

- Security operations
  - Implement a common operation—common and consistent application of security services and requirements is essential.
  - Process—analyze all processes—adopt the best, improve the others.
  - Operational synergies—identify areas where savings can be achieved.
  - Best practices—identify practices from both companies and adopt the best, and discard or improve those that are inefficient.
  - Policies and procedures—review all policies and procedures. Ensure they are revised to properly reflect changes made during integration and take advantage of the best both companies have to offer.

- Budget analysis
  - Staffing requirements—aligned with the security statement of work?
  - Reorganization—to ensure security professionals are best matched with security tasks.
  - Cost control—identify ways to improve the efficiency of department processes and procedures.

- Company-wide security issues
  - Identity issues—badges for all new employees.
  - Vetting of new employees—for target company employees never before subjected to a pre-employment or suitability-for-hire background check—consider doing.
  - Work Place Violence prevention—ensure a prevention program is in place, staffed and all intervention team members trained.
  - Customer notifications—as needed.

Divestiture checklist: When a business unit is divested, the CSO has two primary actions to take in support of the activity. One is a protective effort while the other is a management action in separating out those security systems and employees that go with the divested unit. The protective effort could include providing support to the divested business unit should the company decide that is in its best interest.

- Separation of the divested business unit
  - Identification of employees badges—collect company badges from departing employees. Work with acquiring company to establish new identity process.
  - Access controls—ensure departing employees have access only to that information and those areas for which they have a need-to-know.
  - Cost containment—ensure separation occurs as swiftly as possible. Delays translate to added costs and expenditures.
  - Ensure only those assets defined as part of the deal go with the divested company. Anything not part of the deal, stays.

- Security Infrastructure
  - Systems—separate the departing business unit from the security systems being used.
  - Alarm systems—remove from divested buildings and facilities.
  - Access control systems —reconfigure systems to accommodate operational changes.
  - Security information—remove divested employees from the security information systems database. Transfer data to acquiring company (if appropriate).

- Employees—be prepared for employee issues in the following areas
  - Unauthorized removal of assets and information.
  - Potential for workplace violence.
  - Seeking general security guidance about rapidly changing events.
  - Maintaining regular communication with employees advising them of changes, security concerns and events.

Lessons learned checklist: Many companies choose to shape their strategic direction through the use of mergers, acquisitions and divestitures. The likelihood of MAD occurring more than once in any company is increasing. Therefore, it is a prudent action to learn from one transaction in order to better prepare for the next. Below are areas to consider when reviewing lessons learned:

- Use of Competitive Intelligence
  - Did the competitive intelligence produced add value?
  - Did it increase team knowledge of the target company?
  - Did it increase team knowledge of market?
  - Did the intelligence contribute to the team's success?

- Was the effort properly protected?
  - Were there any security failures?
  - Was the effort exposed to anyone without a need-to-know?
  - Were any team members exposed, embarrassed, or harmed?

- Assessment of target
  - Was the target company properly assessed?
  - After the deal was closed, was anything significant about the acquired company learned that could/should have been learned earlier?
  - Did the assessment lead to a realistic valuation?
  - What problems developed?

- Integration success
  - Were the goals and objectives of the team, the CEO and the board of directors met?
  - Did the team perform as expected?
  - Were costs objectives met or exceeded?
  - Did any issues of culture develop—i.e., culture clashes

MAD CASE STUDY

The MAD team has never been involved in such a project before and the team leader has asked the CSO to explain in business terms how the competitive intelligence effort should be handled.

The IWC CSO, an experienced CSO, has always worked to cultivate sources of information that can assist the CSO in protecting the corporate assets. These same sources will prove useful in assisting the CSO support the MAD project team's competitive intelligence collection efforts.

It was decided by the MAD team that one of the primary functions of the CSO as part of the MAD project team would be to lead an effort to gather competitive intelligence on the corporation that has been targeted for acquisition. The CSO developed a simple chart in order to explain to the MAD team the basic philosophy that the CSO uses for such projects (see Figure 23-5).

This is an important function and often accomplished by nonsecurity personnel. However, often the CSO is in the best position to provide this information or at least be part of the project team members responsible for gathering the information. Some corporations have a competitive intelligence organization that specializes in gathering information about its competitors. If so, the CSO should already have opened communication channels with this group and, as part of a MAD, assist them.

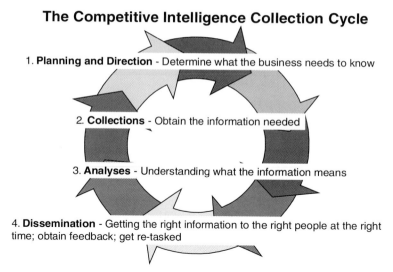

Figure 23-5   One way of looking at competitive intelligence collecting.

MAD SUMMARY

Mergers, acquisitions and divestitures (MAD) are strategic business tools used more frequently in this expanding global marketplace, to enhance the competitive position of the corporation. The CSO must play an important part as an integral member of the MAD team. As such, the CSO has certain responsibilities in the pre-MAD and post-MAD phases. The use of a security metrics management program can greatly assist the CSO in successfully accomplishing the tasks assigned by the MAD team.

Chapter 24

Outsourcing

Outsourcing, like mergers, acquisitions and divestiture (MAD) projects, is a strategy used by management to decrease costs to the enterprise and therefore enhance the corporation's competitive edge in the marketplace. This chapter will address outsourcing and the role security metrics management plays in outsourcing projects.

INTRODUCTION

Outsourcing, by which we mean "contracting for outside services that are a necessary part of doing business but are not core functions or core competencies,"[1] is always an option when a CSO is looking for ways to save money for the corporation and cut costs for the CSO's security department.

There are many advantages and disadvantages to outsourcing a security function. As a CSO, you should look at all security functions (see Figure 24-1) as possibilities for outsourcing, as long as they are not considered "core competencies" by the corporation —and usually they are not.

When considering outsourcing, the CSO should first look at transactional processes (generally the same steps occur within each process transaction) such as pre-employment background investigations and other security processes where there are many capable providers of cost-effective services (such as security guard services). More complex processes such as information systems security are less desirable targets for outsourcing. Outsourcing processes that require a high degree of skill and training means the company no longer has that intellectual capability or asset in-house. This can be a precarious position as there is little to hold or bind the skilled (outsourced) provider to your corporation other than money.

---

[1] Quote taken from the authors' book, *The Manager's Handbook for Corporate Security: Establishing and Managing a Successful Assets Protection Program*, Chapter 10, *Outsourced or Proprietary Security?*, p. 209, published by Butterworth-Heinemann/Elsevier, 2003, and, as stated before, from which much of this book's basic security commentary was derived.

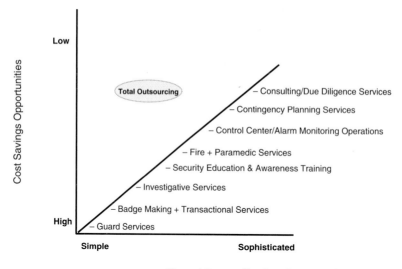

Figure 24-1 Examples of the types of process/services that should be considered for outsourcing.

As a CSO, you more than likely know other corporate CSOs who have been involved in outsourcing some of their security functions. If so, they should be contacted to ascertain what lessons they learned during the process and how the process currently works—are they saving the money they thought they would save and still getting satisfactory service?

It is interesting to note that the estimated savings expected from outsourcing does not always occur. One reason for this is optimistic savings projections for outsourcing. Perhaps the cost-benefit analysis was flawed or over-optimistically skewed. Having a security metrics management program (SMMP) in place, especially a mature program with several years of tracking costs, will help reduce the likelihood of a flawed outsourcing cost-benefit analysis.

As a CSO considering outsourcing a security function, you should seek answers to the following basic outsourcing questions from other CSOs who have outsourced a security function that you are now considering for outsourcing:

- What processes did they outsource?
- What outsource provider did they use?
- What others were considered or not considered, and why?
- Were the expected cost savings achieved?
- If not, did they achieve any cost savings at all?
- Was there degradation in service?
- What other benefits did they derive from outsourcing?
- What pitfalls were encountered?
- Are they a satisfied customer?

The information the CSO obtains from this process will be useful in setting the CSO on a successful path. Learning from the experiences, successes and failures of others can save considerable time and money. Once the CSO has determined candidate security functions for outsourcing, the CSO should also consider the following:

- The processes considered for outsourcing are not core competencies
- There are no proprietary issues to be concerned with
- Company culture or union issues don't exist (or have been reasonably addressed and they will not prevent the CSO from proceeding)
- The CSO has learned from the experiences of other CSOs

OUTSOURCING ORGANIZATION

As with the MAD project, outsourcing is an important project and therefore should be under the direct supervision of the CSO (see Figure 24-2). Don't forget that once a security task is outsourced, the CSO's job is not over. The CSO must provide contractor oversight to ensure that the corporate assets will continue to be protected as if the security function was being performed in-house or, hopefully, even better and at less cost.

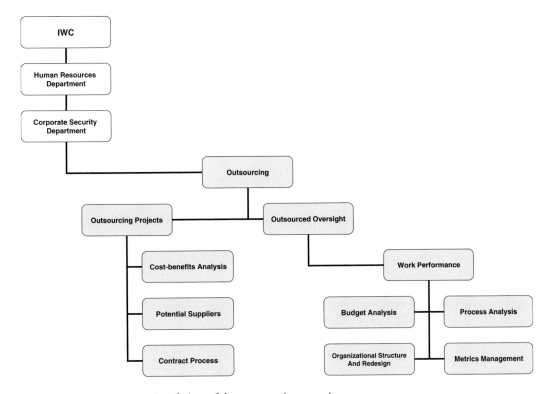

Figure 24-2 An organizational view of the outsourcing security process.

OUTSOURCING DRIVERS AND FLOWCHARTS

The primary driver for outsourcing is of course cost savings. Figure 24-3 depicts the macro decision-making process for outsourcing.

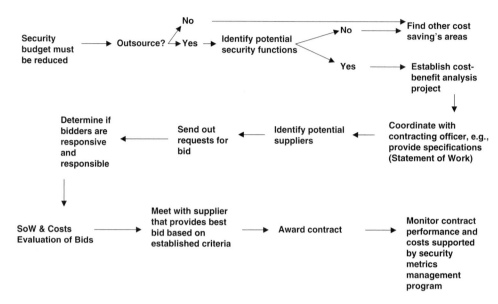

Figure 24-3   An example of a high-level outsourcing cost-benefit decision flowchart.

Once a contract has been awarded to a service provider to perform a security function or deliver a security service, the CSO then transitions into an oversight role to ensure the provider does perform to stated requirements, providing the necessary assets protection service or process at the established cost. The data collection process used while the security function was performed in-house can be used to collect data from the supplier. Thus begins the security metrics management process (costs to be collected and delivered). However, in order to do so, the data to be delivered by the supplier must be a specification of the contract. If not, then you are asking for work to be accomplished that is not part of the contractual agreement. That may add to the cost of the effort. The supplier might so state or possibly just send an additional bill for "services rendered."

As a CSO, you may have obligated the corporation and the additional costs must be paid. So, as the CSO, you should be very clear as to what is in the contract and if you are not clear about it, ask your contracting officer (or procurement official) who is overseeing the contract for you and the corporation. If the data you requested is important and you want it, then a change in contract is the proper way to handle that request. However, be cautious here that you really need the data. You may end up paying more for the outsourced security service than if it were done in-house, at least more than originally expected, if the additional work is not well-defined and is excessive.

OUTSOURCING EXAMPLES OF METRICS

After appropriate research and data collection has been completed, the CSO can then determine if it is time to proceed further with the analysis for finding a capable provider of services. The IWC CSO determined that the IWC procurement office may also be of assistance in identifying potential suppliers. It is necessary to identify a sufficient number of suppliers to hold a true competitive bid process. Usually that means including between three and five (or more but should not be less than three) potential providers. The more potential suppliers included, the better the competition.

The competitive bid process is the best way to ensure the CSO and IWC get the best results. The competitive bid process should provide for a fair assessment of each supplier's capabilities and ability to perform. The process should assess the following:

- Potential suppliers' experience
- Contact references provided
- Response to the security statement of work (SoW)
- Cost and affordability
- Availability for service (time and location limitations if any)
- Responsiveness and flexibility
- Available resources to perform
- Quality and metrics program

The competitive bid process should also allow each potential outsource provider an opportunity to learn more about IWC's security SoW. This can be accomplished through a conference for all bidders and/or a question-and-answer process. The bid process should also include developing a transition plan—for example, one that addresses how the outsource provider will transition from the current proprietary guard force to the contract force. The transition plan can be planned as a major milestone in the outsourcing project plan. As such, it is also to be used as a form of security metrics management.

As part of that outsourcing process, the CSO should use the security metrics management data that has hopefully been collected over the years to help not only in developing a specific SoW but also in knowing the average costs for completing that SoW, which can be used for comparison with the bids received. After all, the bids should always come in lower than doing the work in-house, unless there are some other reasons to outsource the work other than cost savings.

As the CSO proceeds with the cost analysis, the following data (e.g., security guards) should be collected from the proprietary operation for comparison with data provided by potential outsource providers, as applicable and based on the security function outsourced:

1) Budget Category
   - Total department salary by employee
   - Total bonus costs
   - Calculate cost of benefit package for all employees (current and future)
   - Calculate the cost per employee (current and future)
   - Calculate costs by security guard posts to be filled

2) Facilities Category
   - Calculate office space (sq. ft.) occupied by department
   - Calculate cost of that space for the department
   - Cost of department-owned equipment
   - Cost of common use equipment

3) Travel Category
   - Cost of all business travel and associated expenses

4) Training/Development
    • Cost for seminars/courses
    • Cost for internal meetings
    • Cost for other activities

5) Oversight Obligations
    • Cost of time demands placed on line units
    • Development and maintenance of performance measures
    • Cost of reports

6) Other
    • Legal (factor in potential claims of various types)
    • Administrative support

7) Subcontractor Category (if applicable)
    • Total cost of subcontractors to include labor, materials, etc.

A comparison of the data collected from the proprietary operation with data provided by a potential outsource provider should offer an immediate indication as to any cost differences. Placing the data into a spreadsheet listing tasks and costs in time and materials can easily show the variances by line item and in total.

POST-CONTRACT AWARD

Once a contract is outsourced, a security survey/questionnaire may be considered to determine if the IWC internal customers are satisfied with the supplier's services. This is a process for measuring customer satisfaction. Customer satisfaction is an important metric. It does not indicate efficiency, but it certainly does let the CSO know how security's customers feel about the service or products they receive. After all, security is a service and support department and as such must satisfy its customers; therefore, service and support quality is of utmost importance.

The following is a sample survey questionnaire used for outsourcing the IWC access badge process (it can also be used for in-house evaluation).

A)	*How satisfied are you that your employee badge was issued to you promptly?* *1) Very Satisfied 2) Satisfied 3) Unsatisfied 4) Very Unsatisfied*
B)	*The security clerk was able to answer all of your badging related questions.* *1) Very Satisfied 2) Satisfied 3) Unsatisfied 4) Very Unsatisfied*

In a full survey, all responses can be scored, averaged and a baseline established. This baseline should be identified as the level of service provided going into an outsource condition. If the service was poor, the CSO's expectation may be for the outsource provider to deliver better service. If the baseline is high (very satisfied), for the sake of keeping costs low, the CSO may be satisfied with a lower level of service (satisfied), but maybe the customers would not be. Then what would you do?

It is important that services and support satisfaction measurements be identified as a specification of any outsourced contracts.

Once the CSO has made the decision to outsource and has awarded a contract to a selected provider, there are still a few security metrics-related factors that should be mutually agreed to, thus enabling complete success. Doing this will ensure both parties—the customer and the provider—benefit from the newly formed relationship. The areas should be defined, agreed upon, and made part of the contract or process:

- *Identify critical success factors*—Those factors that must be fully achieved, for the effort to be considered a success. For example, if the reason for outsourcing is to reduce cost by 10% or more, then achieving that 10% cost reduction is a critical success factor.
- *Establish goals*—Clearly defined goals are a means of defining expectations.
- *Measure performance to goals*—How well the provider performs to established goals is a measurement of success. Moreover, it is a futile effort if goals are established but performance to them is not measured.
- *Improve*—Performance measurement is a management tool. It establishes where IWC is, as compared to where it expects to be. If performance is below expectations, improvements must be made.
- *Periodic reevaluations*—All relationships require periodic reevaluations. Neither customer nor supplier should assume all is well unless that is validated through some established means. For example, after doing business with a single supplier for several years, the CSO decides to recompete a contract let to that supplier years earlier. Through a competitive bid process, a CSO can validate that the current supplier offers the best deal or select another supplier who does.

OUTSOURCING CASE STUDY

An experienced CSO decided that it might be best for the organization to outsource the security education and awareness training program (SEATP). Several months after outsourcing the SEATP, the CSO was asked to share her experiences on this outsourcing effort. The following is a summary of her experience[2]:

- What made you decide to outsource? *I began to realize that the cost of providing a company-wide SEATP with internal personnel was high and we were not getting all that was needed. I needed a lower-cost program that was cost-effective and still remained interesting and fun for all employees.*
- Did you do a cost-benefit analysis as part of that determination? *I did do a cost-benefit analysis that was sold to the executive staff. Fortunately, as part of my metric management program I had cost trend data for the past 5 years. I was able to use that data and compare it with data provided by experienced service providers. I concluded I could get a better product/service at a lower cost by going outside the company and using an experienced provider. Moreover, with an in-house program, I did not have the flexibility of having the many different skills available for use that a company with a core-competency in SEATP has. I had a security specialist and myself. The service provider I selected has a cadre of experts to draw from.*
- Has it worked out as expected? *Better than expected. We have a more flexible and efficient program provided at lower costs.*

---

[2] This is an actual case study and italics are the quotes of the security manager who outsourced the function.

- What specific services are provided and how are they provided, such as lectures, pamphlets, etc.? *I receive monthly newsletters, weekly news wire clips to send out to the entire organization, a dedicated artist for postings, calendar art as well as newsletter art. I have bi-monthly training, with outside speakers, as well as an entire "Security 101" training day.*
- How did you go about looking for a supplier? *I wanted someone a little "out there" and Winn [Schwartau] was mentioned as a good candidate, along with three other providers. We went through a competitive bidding process, working with the company procurement officer, and we selected Winn. We've been working together ever since.*

OUTSOURCING SUMMARY

In today's business environment there are many providers of a broad range of security services. These providers range from local companies providing few specialized services to international corporations offering security services from the simple to the very complex. A skilled CSO will recognize this and use outsourcing as a tool to help effectively and efficiently manage the security functions.

Never forget that corporate security is part of the business enterprise. Corporate security adds value to a corporation in many ways, but does not usually generate revenue. Therefore, corporate security is a cost center. Keeping costs under control and as low as possible is essential. Outsourcing provides an effective avenue for the CSO to reduce costs or keep them under control.

The security metrics management tool used for data collection, analyses and charting provides the necessary baseline to support a project looking at outsourcing specific security functions.

Section V

The Security Profession and Metrics Management in the Future

...metrics must be more than in-house security tools; they have to be relevant to the people she supports—business executives, plant operators, substation engineers, customer service managers. ...reports must contain information that is important to them, not just to security managers..."also enables us to educate them about this that are important from our perspective, and that give-and-take process we're able to validate the measures that we're using" (Margaret Levine, corporate security manager, Power Georgia)*...Depending on the type of data and compliance requirements, Levine reports her metrics monthly, quarterly or yearly...*[1]

- Chapter 25: Security Metrics Management Technology of the Future and How to Prepare Now to Use It

We will address technology since it is rapidly changing all professions including the profession of security and of assets protection. The discussion will include a proposed direction for the security professionals so that they can prepare now to integrate and apply new technology to more efficiently support future SMMP and systems.

---

[1] Quoted from CSOONLINE.COM, "Where the Metrics are" article, February 2005 issue.

Chapter 25

Security Metrics Management Technology of the Future and How to Prepare Now to Use It

Technology is rapidly changing all professions and the profession of security, protecting assets, is no different. This chapter will provide guidance for security professionals so that they can prepare now to integrate and apply new technology to more efficiently support future security metrics management systems.

INTRODUCTION

No matter how old you are, in your lifetime you have seen many changes brought on by technology—primarily technology based on the microprocessor. Many of us saw the first computers, which occupied massive amounts of space and where the room temperatures were cold enough to hang meat in them. That was necessary in order to prevent the intense heat given off by the vacuum tubes from "frying" the computers.

During this period of rapid improvement of information systems, security professionals, except for possibly the current generation, have been slow to adopt computers as tools to support their assets protection program and related security functions. However, that is changing.

> *Interactive TV poised for rollout…Dozen markets will see form of IPTV later this year… NEW YORK (AP) — Internet Protocol, the language of most online communications, was supposed to have revolutionized the way we watch television by now, enabling a wide range of multimedia bells and whistles: from multiple camera angles to on-screen Web searches while viewing Gilligan's Island to see which actors are still living.*[1]

Because the security function is like most any other business function in that it needs to be as efficient and effective as possible, the use of computers—information systems—in support of the corporate asset protection program is growing. Information systems[2] are more and more being used to facilitate work flow. In many cases, the automation

---

[1] http://www.cnn.com/2005/TECH/02/14/interactive.tv.ap/index.html
[2] By information systems, we mean all microprocessor-based systems to include PDAs, cell phones, integrated, multifunctional, microprocessor-based systems such as today's and tomorrow's cellular telephones, wireless computer systems, and the like.

of work flow has reduced the number of persons previously involved in the work-flow process.

The use of information systems in the work-flow process actually facilitates data collection and data analysis. It is reasonable to expect that information systems will play a major role in the development and evolution of security metrics and a security metrics management program (SMMP).

NEW TECHNOLOGY

> *2005 "year of mobile broadband"…STOCKHOLM, Sweden (AP) — LM Ericsson said Tuesday that 2005 is set to be the year of mobile broadband, painting a portrait of fast downloads for cell phone users who want information quickly.*[3]

New technology is proceeding at a fast pace and into new frontiers. Developments such as "nanotechnology" offer great potential for computing capabilities to include bio-computing. Nanotechnology really gives new meaning to the term "microtechnology." It is so small that it will not be visible to the naked eye. Such technology is being considered for implanting in the body to fix blocked arteries, repair brain damage and generally repair the body—to paraphrase Star Trek—"to go where no computer has gone before!"

Today, there are experiments taking place in laboratories, research centers and hospitals around the world attempting to help paralyzed people walk with the aid of computers and even one day to provide blind people the ability to see with the use of advanced technology. Just a few years ago, these and many more such projects were only thought to be in the realm of science fiction.

In England, one scientist went so far as to attach a computer to his body to conduct interface experiments.

> … *"Is the human body a fit place for a microchip? The debate is no longer hypothetical. The same computing power that once required an entire building to harness now can be inserted in your left arm…*
>
> *Professor Kevin Warwick, director of cybernetics at the University of Reading in the U.K., is that somebody else…Warwick became the first human to host a microchip. During a 20-minute medical procedure described as "a routine silicon-chip implant" by Dr. George Boulos, who led the operation, doctors inserted into Warwick's arm a glass capsule not much bigger than a pearl. The capsule holds several microprocessors. The British Broadcasting Corp. was on hand to document the historic event—and to trouble the professor's already frayed nerves. "In theory, I was able to see what was going on," Warwick says in a phone interview several days after the operation (which he described as slightly more pleasant than a trip to the dentist), "but I was looking in the opposite direction most of the time."…"*[4]

Regardless of how one feels about technology, it cannot—will not—be stopped. Where it will all end, no one knows. Think about what has occurred during the last 50 years of technology development and the rapid changes we now experience. It seems

---

[3] http://www.cnn.com/2005/TECH/02/16/3gsm.ericsson.ap/index.html
[4] IDG, January 14, 1999, Web posted at: 3:21 p.m. EST (2021 GMT) on CNN.com article by Sam Witt.

that progress and development have occurred exponentially. Now, project out 50 years and one can only imagine the new technological developments. It seems reasonable to believe we will all carry or even have embedded in the human body computers that we interact with as naturally as we do our apparel today. Keyboards will almost be a thing of the past as the true environment of the future will be more like Star Trek than ever thought of before.

For the security professional and their assets protection programs, now is the time to look into the future and prepare to adopt new technology to not only support the assets protection program but also their SMMP.

APPLYING HIGH TECHNOLOGY TO THE SECURITY METRICS MANAGEMENT PROGRAM

Measuring performance and developing a security metrics management program is of course very different from technology and computers embedded within the human body. However, using new developments in information technology to assist the CSO in better knowing and managing a CAPP is not.

In today's assets protection and security organization environments, one already has access to hardware and software for collecting, analyzing and reporting data and information as part of an SMMP.

A few words of caution: data for an SMMP can today be collected manually or automatically, as we previously discussed. What system one wants to use in the future should depend on several factors:

- If the amount of data being collected is relatively small, then maybe an automated system is not needed. If only small amounts of simple data are to be collected, then a manual system will probably suffice as it will be efficient and effective—fast and cheap.
- If the amount of data to be collected is large and more complex, then an automated system might be faster and more economical.
- Somewhere in between, you might want to consider a manual system and a project to go from manual collection, analysis and reporting of data to an automated process as technology develops.

> *Establish a detailed plan for an ideal and totally automated data collection and charting system for your SMMP. As technology develops to meet your requirements, integrate it into your SMMP.*

However, in the future, we suspect automation will be the primary if not the only process for data collection and most of data analysis. Regardless of how you choose to build your SMMP, technology will always be an option that must be considered.

Today, there are many simple application programs that can be used, as well as some complicated and very sophisticated ones. For large mainframe systems, data is collected by the information technology (IT) organization relative to their needs. If you have such systems and they play a part, other than physical controls, in your CAPP, you should work with the IT staff and determine what data they collect and some specific applications that can be written to meet your data collection needs. The same holds true for wide area networks (WANs) and local area networks (LANs). Some of these may already have applications available that are applicable to your data collection needs, as do the larger, sometimes called "legacy" systems.

You should coordinate with the IT organization to stay abreast of technological developments and IT systems upgrades. That way, you can plan now for the future and, when that future arrives, you will be ready to adopt and adapt the new technology to both your assets protection needs and your SMMP.

Since LANs have a file server to monitor, manage and maintain the LANs, that may be the point of data collection that you could use as your SMMP matures over time, instead of trying to collect data off each individual computer on a LAN. Systems used for controlling physical access to buildings, areas and offices should also have data collection capabilities, as should fire control systems' computers.

Ideally, these systems can be eventually linked together to download relevant SMMP data to a computer in the office of the security department. With the help of future artificial intelligence and neural networks that continue to mature, your SMMP could include a process to dump data into databases and automated tools could be used for analyzing and reporting the data collected. This would include the "intelligent" SMMP which can learn over time. For example, the data collected may include all physical and logical access violations indicating patterns of abuse and attempts to steal assets, such as information which the individual is not authorized to have.

> *Do you currently have a system in place to view and analyze, in a holistic manner, security infractions by individuals which may indicate a pattern of attempts at stealing sensitive corporate information or equipment? If not, why not?*

The system could continually analyze these security infractions and establish a reporting criterion by department, person, area, and so forth. That information could be automatically fed into reports and sent to the departments where the violations have occurred, based on a set of reporting parameters. The system could automatically input the data into charts by department and periodically send the reports to all department heads for their information and/or action with automated reply suspense dates. In addition, automatic analyses could provide recommendations to improve access control processes to mitigate future infractions.

> *Think of the detailed processes of an SMMP and think of how future technology can replace the human in the data collection, analyses, charting, reporting, and risk mitigation processes to the point where it is entirely automated.*

In addition, some of today's security departments have their own security LAN, which can be used to collect data from the various systems and used as a tool to support the various security functions identified in this book. You may want to look at eventually integrating the security links into every system in order to monitor its secure use in a fully automated fashion, like the tentacles of an octopus.

When developing SMMP automated support tools, a holistic approach should be taken. This approach, often also called a systems approach, should provide for automated collection mechanisms into individual databases applicable to each of the primary security functions' computers, and also a centralized computer to collect data from all the individual security functional computers.

For now, a manual collection system may be the best solution requiring that the data collected manually be entered into databases, spreadsheets and the like for easier and automated compilation, analysis and reporting.

APPLICATION SOFTWARE TOOLS FOR TODAY

Application software tools are readily available for use to support an SMMP. These tools include word processing, spreadsheet and graphics design software. Many of these tools are simple and integrated so that once the information is entered, it can be applied to various reports and briefing charts.

> *The use of generic software is more cost-effective than developing your own application software.*

For briefing purposes, software that takes information from a database or spreadsheet and automatically makes charts and reports would be very useful. Using a word processing program, these spreadsheets, charts and other graphics can easily be added to make reports on the status of the CAPP and the security department. This may be considered an interim, "semi-automated" process.

EVALUATING CURRENT AND FUTURE DATA COLLECTION NEEDS

Before we continue further with practical methods for data collection, measurement and analysis today, a few thoughts about better types of metrics (measurements) as we head into the future are called for. Determine where you are today in your security metrics measurement processes and compare it to the following comments.

Current common measures for the CAPP and security processes focus on "how much" and "how fast" at the process and program level. For example, many security organizations measure the cycle time for conducting a background investigation on a prospective employee. How long that process takes is important as it may affect how quickly a corporation can hire a new employee and get them working. Another frequently used measure is the number of security violations or security infractions that occur within a period of time. These incidents are violations of security policy that can adversely affect the CAPP and the security of the corporation.

The types of measures that are less frequently used are those indicating efficiency and effectiveness. Of these, some of the more common are comparisons of trends and performance to goals. With the comparison to trend, a data point (e.g., security costs) is compared over a period of time (years) to determine if costs are increasing, decreasing or remaining constant. In measuring performance to goals, the actual performance of a process or objective is measured against the established goal (e.g., conduct security awareness training for all employees).

Comparing performance to objective can be a simple and effective measure in terms of what was planned to be achieved. This type of measure allows the CSO to know if goals were or were not achieved. These and other measurement philosophies and methodologies explained in this book should be installed and given a chance to mature prior to seeking a fully-automated SMMP. If not, the adoption and adaptation of new technology may not provide the desired results at the desired cost savings.

What has been missing from the security community is a more sophisticated metric, or set of metrics—keep in mind, simple and few are best—that provide an immediate and meaningful measure of effectiveness and/or efficiency. That is to say, a meaningful measure that is understandable to all and that allows any change to be instantly recognized and reacted to. For example, Wall Street and the investment community have many metrics that are used to help investors understand the direction and health of the market and economy. Using the Dow Jones index—a representative mix of stocks from the New York Stock Exchange—an investor can determine at any point in time what is occurring with stocks (on average) listed on the New York Stock Exchange.

Individual investors recognize that a 200-point increase in the Dow Jones index over the course of the day is a positive trend. Investors also recognize the opposite in that a 200-point decrease in the Dow Jones index over the course of the day is generally a negative trend. The Dow Jones index, as a metric, simply and effectively communicates an instant message to investors, at any moment in time, regarding the direction of stocks listed on the New York Stock Exchange. This is a very powerful metric as it allows the individual or institutional investor to instantly make an informed decision and take action or not take action.

Within the security community, security professionals ought to strive for the development of similar metrics. Metrics—particularly macro metrics—that can be simply and instantly expressed and that meaningfully characterize the direction, condition, or health of the entire CAPP are uncommon or nonexistent. With continued technological advances in information systems capabilities and the application of scientific measures such as Six Sigma, the next step in developing meaningful metrics for measuring security performance must take us in the direction of others, such as the investment community, toward the development of more simple, meaningful and common measures.

We should eventually get to a point where individual security metrics for each security function roll-up to provide the specific security function's successes, failures, costs, and benefits. These would then roll-up into a total CAPP status of assets protection, costs, benefits, successes and failures.

In the meantime, the CSO should continue to review, analyze and improve on the SMMP and evaluate the SMMP periodically for relevance and utility of each measure:

- Are they meaningful?
- Do they provide an understanding or insight into the security process or function?
- Do they contribute to the understanding of the effectiveness, efficiency, success or failure of security processes and the security program, e.g., CAPP?
- And, perhaps most importantly, do they help the CSO make needed changes and decisions?

These are the questions each CSO and security professional should ask and answer to ensure that the SMMP is successfully supporting the CSO as it was intended to do.

CURRENT AND FUTURE—"TOOLS"—HARDWARE AND SOFTWARE TO SUPPORT AN SMMP

One of the ways that a security professional can now begin to collect information is through a dictation system. The software available for dictation several years ago was not very accurate. That has changed over the years. One software dictation vendor claims a 99% accuracy in taking verbal dictation to text in word processing formats. In addition, today's digital microrecorders are also reliable and can be used to convert verbal dictation to text.

The dictation type of software will continue to improve and can be used to collect data concerning applicable security functions. In addition, combining such a system with wireless technology of the future will truly make for "Star Trek" computer use. As a security professional, one should begin looking at such systems through an assets risk management perspective, as well as how to use such a system to collect security metrics data.

Looking at today's hardware and software trends, one can see their power increasing and their price and size decreasing. Therefore, as a security professional or one involved in management and assets protection, now is the time to start planning on upgrading to a more sophisticated and automated SMMP over time:

1. Be sure that the architecture, procedures and processes related to your SMMP are current and meeting your needs, to include effective, efficient and accurate data collected. If not, then make them so.
2. Identify all the manual data collection points and establish at least an outline of a project plan to automate and integrate them where it is cost-beneficial to do so. When your criteria for automation is reached, establish and implement a project plan to automate an integrated data collection process.
3. Identify the security department's hardware that is now being used—make, model, capacity, capabilities, location, and purpose. For example, their:
   - Speed (e.g., 3.2 GHz)
   - Number of hard drives and their size
   - Memory size
   - Whether or not they are networked and to what and where
   - Whether or not they have a CD, DVD, read/write capabilities
   - Etc.

4. Identify the security department's software on each piece of hardware and their capabilities to include:
   - Word processing
   - Spreadsheets
   - Graphics development
   - Database
   - Report writing
   - Forensics
   - Telecommunications
   - Web development
   - Etc.

Once you have identified and documented the architecture, policies, procedures and processes used for your SMMP, it is now time to plan to upgrade and integrate your hardware and software where it is cost-beneficial to do so.

While you are doing this, be sure to continually look at trends, hardware and software vendor announcements, technology trends studies, and other sources of information so that you will know when a particular technology will be available that will meet your needs.

You should identify the specific criteria needed for each piece of hardware and software to replace what you now have in place. In addition, you should also have a documented overall strategy for integrating new technology concepts into the overall SMMP support toolbox—such as the application of nanotechnology, the application of artificial intelligence, the application of sensor or scanning technologies, the application of neural networks and the like.

Using the badge-making process, for example, perhaps a sensor at the entrance and exit can be used to identify the customer entering for service to include their name, organization, date, and time of entrance and time of exiting the badge-making office. This would eliminate the need for a manual sign-in and sign-out sheet to be filled out and then manually typed into a database for later analysis and reporting.

In addition, that system could be networked with or be the same system used by the badge maker to make the badges, which includes the type of badge, reason for the badge, etc. That way, the database would provide all the required information that can be analyzed and reported using a standard, approved format. Furthermore, it should be integrated into a security LAN and automatically compiled with other data as applicable, such as the total number and cost of security hours for the month, quarterly or annually.

An integrated SMMP can be built over time. (See Figure 26-1 and 26-2 as examples.)

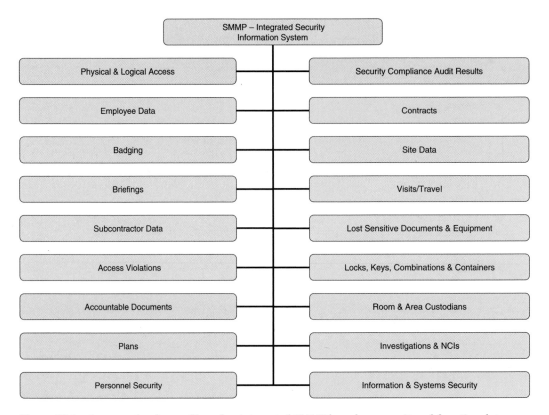

Figure 26-1   An example of an outline of an integrated SMMP based on security subfunction data.

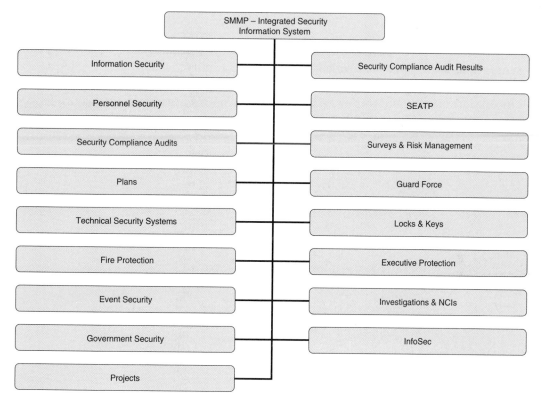

Figure 26-2 Another example showing the architecture of an integrated SMMP using the security departments primary security functions and subfunctions.

Your decision to upgrade should be carefully considered and requested only when it can be clearly shown, using the most conservative estimates, that it is worth the expenditure of your budget to upgrade.

In addition, you should also begin monitoring robotic activities to replace security specialists and also for data collection. That may seem very far-fetched now, but it won't be in another decade or so.

Also, from an assets protection or surveillance viewpoint, think about this:

> "...*High-tech cloaking machines could one day render very small objects nearly invisible and perhaps improve military stealth technology, scientists said...The idea is straight out of science fiction—cloaking technology made Romulan spaceships disappear in Star Trek. A humble version of the device could become a reality, according to Nader Engheta and Andrea Alu of the University of Pennsylvania[5]...*" (May be used to hide assets for additional protection when they are not in use.)

Today's advanced technology-driven world, when projected into the future, leads one to believe that nothing is impossible. Keep an open mind when it comes to applying today's science fiction to tomorrow's assets protection and SMMP issues. Start now so that the high technology-based future doesn't continue to speed by many of you in the security profession.

---

[5] http://www.livescience.com/technology/050228_invisible_shield.html; New Theory: How to Make Objects Invisible By Robert Roy Britt; LiveScience Senior Writer posted: 28 February 2005; 01:00 pm ET

SUMMARY

Today's security professionals and assets protection management must be constantly looking at tools to not only provide for more effective and efficient assets protection and security operations. They should also be looking at the future of technology and applying it to support current and future SMMP operations and processes when it is prudent to do so.

Guthrie Research Group, Inc.

Security

Benchmarking Group

SURVEY

Prepared by : Dr. Lou Guthrie, President, Guthrie Research Group, Inc.
16509 Woolwine Road, Charlotte, NC 28278
704-583-2634 Fax: 704-583-2643 Email: guthrielou@aol.com

All Rights Reserved

SECURITY BENCHMARKING GROUP - Data Year 2004

Guthrie Research Group, Inc.

16509 Woolwine Road, Charlotte, NC 28278

704-583-2634   Fax: 704-583-2634   Internet: guthrielou@aol.com

General Directions

The study includes both Corporate Security functions and Site Security functions. The Corporate functions are those that are not site specific but are done for numerous company locations. They do not pertain to the security at a specific site.

Corporate Security would include functions such as Executive Protection, Employee or Vendor Background Checks, Corporate Asset Protection, Security Policy and Procedure Formulation for the entire Corporation, Information Security/Document Destruction, Corporate-wide IT Security, Business Continuity Planning, Off-site Meeting Security, Travel Security, and Security Education & Training. Any functions that are done for more than one location would be considered Corporate Security.

If you have a question about including or excluding a specific function not mentioned, please call.

Please complete the input schedules using ANNUAL figures. Your most current year-end numbers should be used for costs as much as possible and year-average or mid-year numbers for personnel levels should be used. If you are using other than US dollars and Square Feet please indicate currency and use the same throughout the survey.

If the answer to a question is zero, please put a 0 on the answer line. Do not use dashes, which could mean anything.

For answers where a description is required your full answer may not show in the cell, however the information is in the spreadsheet and will get included in the report.

Be sure to use matching cost and square footage data. Also, please do not duplicate costs unless specifically instructed to in the question. If a cost is included in one part of the questionnaire do not include it on another schedule. Space has been added to the schedules for footnotes that you would like to appear with the data. Please feel free to use footnotes to explain any figures, or relate unusual circumstances. **USE ONE COLUMN PER SITE.**

Please read the directions and definitions in each schedule carefully before you answer the questions. **If different people respond to the various schedules please make sure copies of these directions are included with the schedules.** Please have the person completing each schedule fill in his/her name and telephone/fax numbers at the top of each schedule. The data input schedules are provided on disks using the Microsoft Excel XP program. Do not add lines or columns to the data input disks. If you need assistance using the disks please call.

If you have more than one site and want to print the survey with multiple columns you will need to revise the print settings.

	All Answers Must Be In This Columns

SECURITY BENCHMARKING GROUP - Data Year 2004

Guthrie Research Group, Inc.
16509 Woolwine Road, Charlotte, NC 28278
Voice: 704-583-2634 Fax: 704-583-2643
Email: guthrielou@aol.com

Contact:	
Company:	
Voice:	
Email:	

Data Input Module Security 1: CORPORATE SECURITY

Peer Group: Security

This page covers only Corporate Security. Corporate security includes functions that are not site specific.

If you are including site information only for the study please leave this Corporate page blank.

SITE CODE:	
Currency:	
Meters	

Corporate Locations

1 Data is for month and year ending: Most current year-end preferred.	Month/Year	
2 # of Locations covered by Corporate Security	#	
3 Locations are Regional, US-wide, or International	R, US, I	
4 Approximate Number of Employees covered by Corporate Security	#	
5 Approximate Number of Executives covered by Corporate Security	#	
6 Approximate Gross Square Footage covered by Corporate Security	1,000 sq. ft.	

Corporate Products/Security Risks

Please rank each of the following at the site. High risk=5 down to no risk=1

7 Products	5 to 1	
Products that are easy to steal, highly desirable, easy to re-sell. Examples drugs, electronics, radioactive materials, etc.		
8 Industrial Espionage, Intellectual Property	5 to 1	
Highly competitive industry where patents and inventions play a large role in the future of the business.		
9 High-risk locations	5 to 1	
Site is located in high crime area.		
10 Animal testing	5 to 1	
Site has animal laboratories.		
11 Other, please describe.	description	
Any other situations that increase the security risks for the site.		

Functions

Place an X in the box if your In-house Corporate Security does the following or provides support to sites in the following areas. If this function is performed by a vendor put a V in the box. You may use a B if the function is done by both. If function is done at site level put an S.

12		
a	Executive Protection,	X, V, B, S
b	Employee Background Checks	X, V, B, S
c	Corporate Asset Protection,	X, V, B, S
d	Security Policy and Procedure Formulation for the entire Corporation	X, V, B, S
e	Information Security/Document Destruction	X, V, B, S
f	Corporate-wide IT Security	X, V, B, S
g	Business Continuity Planning	X, V, B, S
h	Off-site Meeting Security	X, V, B, S
i	Travel Security (issue travel advisories, visa assistance, etc.)	X, V, B, S
j	Security Education & Training (conducts or administers training programs)	X, V, B, S
k	Vendor Background Checks	X, V, B, S
l	Site Security Audits	X, V, B, S
m	Corporate Level Investigations	X, V, B, S
n	Intellectural Property Security	X, V, B, S
o	Disaster Planning (Corporate Level or consolidates plans)	X, V, B, S
	Government Security (classified programs; classified document control; classified	X, V, B, S
p	visitor control)	
q	Other	description
r	Other	description

Corporate Security Costs

13 Annual costs for salary labor including benefits — In $1,000
Include labor costs for VPs, directors, managers dedicated to corporate security function. Do not include site specific personnel.

14 Annual costs for hourly labor including benefits — In $1,000
Include labor costs for administrative assistants, clerks, receptionists, and any other hourly employees working in corporate security. Do not include site level guards or other staff members.

15 Annual cost for company purchased materials & supplies — In $1,000
Include costs for department functioning (paper supplies, training, travel, vehicles, computers, phones, etc.) and allocated costs such as space costs, IT costs, etc. Do not include site level department costs.

16 Annual contract costs, including fees — In $1,000
Include costs for service contracts, consultant contracts, and all other contracts relevant to corporte security functions.

17 TOTAL ANNUAL CORPORATE SECURITY COSTS — In $1,000 — $0

Headquarters and Offices Benchmarking Group

Corporate Security Staffing: In-house and Contract

18 Security VPs, directors, managers (**company** employees) whose main focus is corporate level security   Headcount

Should correspond to costs in Q. 13 above.

19 Administrative assistants, clerks, receptionists and other **company** hourly employees whose main focus is corporate level security   Headcount

Should correspond to costs in Q. 14 above.

20 Security VPs, directors, managers (**vendor** employees) whose main focus is corporate level security   Headcount

Costs should be included in Q. 16 above.

21 Administrative assistants, clerks, receptionists and other **vendor** hourly employees whose main focus is corporate level security   Headcount

Costs should be included in Q. 16 above.

Business Continuity Planning

22 Is Business Continuity Planning done by security?   YES or NO

23   If not, who (department) is in charge of this function?   department

24   How many sites are included in your Business Continuity Plan?   #

25 When was your plan last updated?   year

26   Estimated # of man hours spent in updating plan   man hours

Information Technology Security (Internet, Intranet, etc.)

27 Is IT security done by security department?   YES or NO

28   If not, who (department) is in charge of this function?   department

29 How many of the IT incidents did Security respond to during the data year?

a   Hackers/system intruders   #

b   Virus infestations   #

30 **List one corporate security "best practice" that is done by your company.**

31 Footnotes for Corporate Security: Type here

END OF SCHEDULE

SECURITY BENCHMARKING GROUP - Data Year 2004

Guthrie Research Group, Inc.
16509 Woolwine Road, Charlotte, NC 28278
Voice: 704-583-2634   Fax: 704-583-2643
Email: guthrielou@aol.com

	All Answers Must Be In This Columns
Contact:	
Company:	
Voice:	
Email:	

Data Input Module Security 2:   SITE BACKGROUND DATA

Peer Group: Security   SITE CODE: [   ]

Site Information

1 Data is for month and year ending: Most current year-end preferred.   Month/Year [   ]

2 Location is downtown (D), suburban (S), or isolated (I)   D, S, or I [   ]
Downtown: in one of the prime business districts of a major city. Suburban: in a suburb or a small satellite town. Isolated: outside normal business areas; no companies close by; site that is surrounded by undeveloped land or residential areas.

3 Site is campus (C) or stand alone building (S)   C or S [   ]
Campus site includes multiple buildings with open space or acreage. A stand alone building is a single building with little or no lawn/green space surrounding it.

4 Number of buildings   # [   ]
Total number of buildings included in the site data.

5 Buildings age

Percent of space over 19 years old   % [   ]

Percent of space 8 to 19 years old   % [   ]

Percent of space less than 8 years old   % [   ]
Must add up to 100%.

6 Has the building had extensive renovations to the building security systems?   YES or NO [   ]
New access control systems, new sprinkler systems, new monitoring systems, etc.

7 Please describe your most important current renovations.   Describe [   ]

8 Percent of total area owned   % [   ]

9 % of full 8760 hour year office buildings are normally operated   % [   ]
Include the normal working hours for building participants. To be 100% you would need to have the building fully functioning (air, heat, all lights) 24 hours a day, 7 days a week, every week of the year.

Business at Site

10 Company's type of business at site (indicate percentages)

a	Retail/Wholesale	%
a	Financial	%
a	Institutional	%
a	Industrial/Manufacturing	%
b	Healthcare	%
e	Service Industries	%
f	Research & Development	%
g	Warehouse Facility	%
h	Government	%
i	Other	%
j		%

Population

11 Permanent site population (all shifts, include employees and contract workers)   Headcount

The total headcount on all shifts. Include all site employees and contract workers who make the site their "home" base.   Part-time personnel only on-site one or two days a week or ½ days should be prorated.

12 Permanent **day shift** population (all)   Headcount

13 Number of work shifts at site?   #

Day shift only = 1; day and evening shifts, no week-ends =2; 24 hour operation, no week-ends = 3; 24 hour operation including week-ends and holidays = 4

14 Site visitors   #

Number of visitors processed through security for the data year.

Space Information

15 Total Gross Square Footage   1,000 sq. ft.

Gross sq. ft. is the total of all floor areas of a building. It is measured from the outside walls and includes the boiler, mechanical, electrical, basements, and other building system areas, but does not include parking garages

(These are covered under paved areas.). Gross sq. ft. shall be derived by including common areas. BOMA definition used.

Square footage of types of space in building(s):

Some categories of space may not be present at your site and should be marked with a zero.

The sum of the sq. ft. for the following types of space (next page) should equal the **gross** square feet of the site. Each type of space category should be net usable area including internal aisles.

If an area is not covered by one of the following categories, choose the descriptions that most closely describes the type of operating cost experienced for the area. Account for all space.

16 Vacant Space
Covers full buildings or portions thereof, not occupied or serviced; this space may receive minimal electrical or air supply if needed for maintenance requirements. Also includes mothballed space. Only unassigned space should be included.

_____ 1,000 sq. ft.

17 Storage/Warehouse Space
Used for storage or storage related activities. Indoor space with low utility requirements and very low occupancy. Examples: stores, shipping, receiving, enclosed docks, storage closets, chemical storage, and materials stores.

_____ 1,000 sq. ft.

18 Common and Circulation Space
Areas used by all building occupants. Examples: lobbies, stairs, elevators, main aisles, mail rooms, restrooms, security centers, major copy rooms, auditoriums, libraries, training areas, nurses or first aid stations, and other areas that are used by the majority of the site population.

_____ 1,000 sq. ft.

19 Amenity Space
Includes cafeteria and kitchen areas, vending areas, day care centers, fitness centers, employee lounges, locker rooms, company stores, and other areas designed to serve employees in non-work related matters.

_____ 1,000 sq. ft.

20 Total Office and Office Support Space
Includes all offices, including both open landscape and private offices. Includes conference rooms, file areas, department copy and printing areas, PC computer areas, secondary aisles, area lobbies and reception areas, and areas designed to support a selected group of offices.

_____ 1,000 sq. ft.

21 Production, Assembly, Testing and Factory Space
Areas for product manufacturing, assembly, quality control, and testing. High density of work stations and related production equipment. Medium utility requirements, additional air conditioning capacity to meet higher heat load requirements, and high lighting requirements. Examples: assembly, test, inspection and circuit card assembly, and maintenance shop areas.

_____ 1,000 sq. ft.

22 Laboratory or R&D Space
Areas with work stations and/or multiple pieces of equipment for R&D, or repair. Higher power and utility requirements than offices. Typically operate 24 hours/day.
Examples: chemical labs, wet labs, SEM labs, systems training rooms, electronic labs, software labs, and call centers.

_____ 1,000 sq. ft.

23 Computer Rooms & Controlled Areas
Areas with higher air flow, humidity, and temperature control requirements. High utilities cost. Could have raised flooring. Examples: assembly of close tolerance parts, computer rooms, print & develop rooms, and metrology lab.

_____ 1,000 sq. ft.

24 Clean Room
Area used as clean room with multiple pieces of equipment. Very high utilities including process gases and RODI water. Examples: IC fabrication, microcircuit fabrication, R&D, and pharmaceutical labs.

_____ 1,000 sq. ft.

25 Mechanical, Electrical, Central Plant Areas
Physical or central utility plant areas, mechanical rooms, electrical rooms and janitorial closets.

_____ 1,000 sq. ft.

26 Gross Sq. Ft. of Types of Space Summed

#VALUE!   1,000 sq. ft.

Outdoor Spaces

27 Total acreage of site _____ Acres

Include the footprint of the building, all acres -- landscaped or wild, all parking, roads, etc.

Net Book Value

28 Net Book Value of the Site $ _____

29 Footnotes for Background: Type here

SECURITY BENCHMARKING GROUP - Data Year 2004

Guthrie Research Group, Inc.
16509 Woolwine Road, Charlotte, NC 28278
Voice: 704-583-2634   Fax: 704-583-2643
Email: guthrielou@aol.com

	All Answers Must Be In This Columns
Contact:	
Company:	
Voice:	
Email:	

Data Input Module Security 3:   FUNCTIONS & PHYSICAL SECURITY

SITE CODE:

Peer Group: Security

Functions

Place an X in the box if your Site Security performs or manages the following. If this function is performed by a vendor put a V in the box. You may use a B if the function is done by both. If the function is performed mainly by Corporate Security, put a C. It the function is not done or not applicable to the site use a O.

	Functions	
1	X	
b	Aircraft Security/Airborn Response	X, V, B, C, O
c	Alarm Monitoring and Response	X, V, B, C, O
d	Automobile unlocks/jump starts	X, V, B, C, O
e	CCTV Monitoring	X, V, B, C, O
e	Contractor on-Off Boarding	X, V, B, C, O
f	Control Access Systems Reports	X, V, B, C, O
g	Control Center	X, V, B, C, O
h	Emergency Communications	X, V, B, C, O
i	Emergency Planning	X, V, B, C, O
j	Emergency Response (note below which functions apply)	X, V, B, C, O
k	Fire Department on Site	X, V, B, C, O
l	First Aid by On-site Firemen	X, V, B, C, O
m	Medical Responders, On-site EMTs	X, V, B, C, O
n	HAZMAT Response	X, V, B, C, O
o	Municipal HAZMAT support (offer off-site assistance)	X, V, B, C, O
c	Disaster Preparedness	X, V, B, C, O
q	Emergency Telephone Monitoring	X, V, B, C, O
r	Employee Background Checks	X, V, B, C, O
s	Energy System Monitoring	X, V, B, C, O
t	First Aid Response by Security Officers	X, V, B, C, O
	Government Security (classified programs; personnel clearances; classified document control; classified visitor control; federal govt. liaison on such programs)	
u	X	X, V, B, C, O
v	ID Badge Making/Issuing	X, V, B, C, O
w	Incident Evaluation/Response	X, V, B, C, O
x	Inclement Weather Procedures	X, V, B, C, O

		X, V, B, C, O
y	Information Security/Document Destruction	X, V, B, C, O
z	Investigations	X, V, B, C, O
aa	Key Production	X, V, B, C, O
aa	Key Control	X, V, B, C, O
ab	Law Enforcement Liaison	X, V, B, C, O
ac	Lost and Found	X, V, B, C, O
ad	Mail Inspections	X, V, B, C, O
ad	New Hire Orientation	X, V, B, C, O
ad	Parking Management	X, V, B, C, O
ae	Patrols	X, V, B, C, O
aa	Product Security	X, V, B, C, O
ab	Security Education, Awareness & Training	X, V, B, C, O
ac	Security Reviews/Presentations/Audits	X, V, B, C, O
ac	Security Trend Analysis and Reporting	X, V, B, C, O
ad	Shipment Inspections	X, V, B, C, O
ad	Special Event Security (Off-site, VIP's, etc.)	X, V, B, C, O
ae	Switchboard	X, V, B, C, O
ae	Traffic Control	X, V, B, C, O
ae	Traffic Enforcement	X, V, B, C, O
aa	Travel Security & Advice	X, V, B, C, O
ab	Unlock Doors (buildings)	X, V, B, C, O
ac	Vendor Background Checks	X, V, B, C, O
ac	Visitor Management	X, V, B, C, O
ad	Other (please list below)	X, V, B, C, O
ae	Other	description
aa	Other	description

Access Control

Access Control includes guards and systems (both operations & maintenance) to control entrances, loading docks, garages, badge readers, and other electronic access control devices.

2 Is the perimeter of the site fenced or open? `F, O`

3 What type of fencing is used? `description`

4 Access control is at the site perimeter (P), at each building (B), or at groups of buildings (G)? `P, B, G`

This question and the questions below, refer to the initial controlled points of entry, not to controlled areas within a building. Site perimeter may be inside the parking lot but external to the buildings. Groups of buildings may be connected by a fence, wall of by buildings abutting each other while having one or a few controlled points of access. More than on one answer is allowed, for example you may put PB for perimeter and building access control.

5 If access control is at perimeter what method is used to monitor all incoming traffic? `GB, G, BR, O`

Guard booth (GB), Posted Guards (G), Badge Readers (BR), or other. Combinations are allowed.

6 Total number of controlled access points used for entry on **day shift** `#`

7 ___ of these, number controlled by guards **only** `#`

8 ___ of these, number controlled by electronic devices (CCTV, badge readers, etc.) **only** `#`

9 ___ of these, number controlled by **both** guards and electronic devices together `#`

10 Total number of controlled access points, **2nd or 3rd shifts and weekends** `#`

11 ___ of these, number controlled by guards **only** `#`

12 ___ of these, number controlled by electronic devices (CCTV, badge readers, etc.) **only** `#`

13 ___ of these, number controlled by **both** guards and electronics devices together `#`

14 What type of badge readers does you site use?

NEED HELP HERE IDENTIFYING COMMON TYPES (Badge swipe, walk through, badges flashed at electronic eye, etc.

15 Are some areas of the site protected by higher levels of security? `Yes or No`

16 Are any palm, eye or voice readers use? `Yes or No`

17 Are additional guarded check points used? `Yes or No`

Visitor Centers

18 Does your site have a separate visitors center? `Yes or No`

A separate building or entrance used solely by visitors where they are checked in and given a badge.

19 Which of the following are required of visitors?

a	Proof of citizenship	X
b	Picture ID	X
c	Business Card	X
d	Advance appointment	X
e	Escort by employee	X
f	Search of briefcase, bags	X
g	Visitor Badge	X
h	Reading/Signing of Company Security Statement	X
i	Surrender of cameras, video equipment	X
j	Process through metal detectors	X
k	Other, (safety briefings, non-disclosure statements, etc.)	X
	Please list:	list
		list

CCTV

20 Does your site have a CCTV system for security purposes?	Yes or No
21 How many cameras are used?	#
22 How many monitors are used?	#
23 During the day, how many security officers are used on CCTV monitoring duty?	#
24 Does the CCTV system cover both interior and exterior views?	Yes or No
25 Can multiple sites be monitored remotely by your CCTV system?	Yes or No
26 Does the CCTV system record and store the images for future investigations?	Yes or No
27 Does your site use intelligent video surveillance software?	Yes or No
Runs objects in a camera's view against threat-specific pre-programmed rules and alerts security personnel by phone, pager, on alert on console when rules are broken.	
28 If intelligent software is used, how effective and beneficial would you evaluate it to be?	Yes or No
5=Very effective and beneficial; 4=somewhat effective and beneficial; 3=neutral; 2=not very effective or beneficial; 1=not effective and of no value to site	

Security Vehicles

29 How many automobiles/trucks are in your security fleet?	#
30 Indicate the # of these other transportation methods that are used on the site?	
Motorcycles	#
Golf Carts	#
Bicycles	#
Other, write in number and item. For example 5 ATVs (All Terrain Vehicles).	#

Best Practices

31 List one site security "best practice" that is done by your company.	Type here
32 Footnotes for Physical Security:	

SECURITY BENCHMARKING GROUP - Data Year 2004

Guthrie Research Group, Inc.
16509 Woolwine Road, Charlotte, NC 28278
Voice: 704-583-2634   Fax: 704-583-2643
Email: guthrielou@aol.com

Contact:	
Company:	
Voice:	
Email:	

All Answers Must Be In This Columns

Data Input Module Security 4:   Site COSTS

This section of the survey includes all costs for security personnel (in-house and contract), service contracts and costs for security supplies and equipment and the repairs for security equipment. Supplies include items such as uniforms and equipment guards carry, access cards, security vehicles, computer equipment used in security,

SITE CODE:

Security Expenditures

1 Annual costs for salary labor including benefits — In $1,000

Include labor costs for VPs, directors, managers dedicated to site security function. Do not include staff with corporate-wide job functions.

2 Annual costs for hourly labor including benefits — In $1,000

Include labor costs for security guards, administrative assistants, clerks, receptionists, and any other hourly employees working in site security.

3 Annual cost for company purchased materials, equipment & supplies — In $1,000

Include costs for department functioning (paper supplies, training, travel, vehicles, computers, phones, etc.) and allocated costs such as space costs, IT costs, etc. Include uniform costs and guard equipment, access control equipment & maintenance, key/locksmith services, and any other costs to provide security at the site. Include repair costs here if they are not contracted.

4   Purchase of New Equipment — $

5   Repair of Existing Equipment — $

6   Replacement of Existing Equipment — $

7   Purchase of Vehicles — $

8   Repair, Maintenance, Operation of Security Vehicles — $

9   Other materials, equipment, supplies, training, & allocated costs — $

Questions 5-10 should add up to 4.

10 Annual contract costs, including fees — In $1,000

Include costs for service contracts, consultant contracts, and all other contracts relevant to site security functions.

11 TOTAL ANNUAL SITE SECURITY COSTS (Sum of 2, 3, 4, & 11) — In $1,000   #VALUE!

Capital Security Expenditures

Capital expenditures are usually project related and specific to the data year (not annual, or on-going costs). They would include upgrades to CCTV systems, new alarm systems, new access control devices, and other additions or changes that would add value to the site.

12 Total annual costs for all capital security projects — In $1,000

Headquarters and Offices Benchmarking Group

Breakdown of Security Expenditures into the following functions:

Break down the total site security expenditures into the following categories. Estimates are acceptable.

13 Department Administration, Overhead, and Management

May include some labor costs, some equipment costs and some contract costs. Include front office management, contract administration, phones, computers, training costs, etc.

$ ☐

14 Access Control

How much does your access control cost? Access Control costs includes guards labor, and systems (both operations & maintenance) to control entrances, loading docks, garages, badge readers, and other electronic access control devices. Do not include CCTV monitoring or alarm monitoring.

$ ☐

15 Visitors Centers or Reception

How much does it cost to operate your visitors' center or visitors reception? All costs for a separate building or entrance used solely by visitors where they are checked in and badged. Include the cost of operating the building , if a separate building is used for visitors. Include the labor costs for guards or receptionists and escorts for this function and the cost (maintenance & annual purchase) of any special equipment that is used (metal detectors, etc.).

$ ☐

16 Provision of Physical Security Services

Expenses related to patrols and other guard costs (except access control & visitors), incidents and investigations, security systems (monitoring & repairs), CCTV and control rooms. Include things like mail & shipment inspections, traffic control/enforcement, and other functions related to the physical security of the building and occupants. Exclude access control & visitor center costs.

$ ☐

The following questions break out the costs for some specific functions of physical security services at the site.

17 Security System Operations & Maintenance

Included in 16, break out the costs for just your security system such as alarms, CCTV. This excludes any labor costs.

$ ☐

18 Incident Investigations (exclude pre-employment screening)

How much does investigating incidents cost annually? Included in 16, breakout investigation costs including the labor for investigations and any incidental costs the investigations might entail. Computer searches, photography services, background checks, etc. should be included.

$ ☐

19 Pre-employment Screening

How much does pre-employment screening cost annually? (also included in 16) Include the labor for this and any incidental costs the investigations might entail. Computer searches, photography services, background checks, etc. should be included. Badges/ID costs are not included here. Include contractors if they are screened.

$ ☐

20 Badging Costs

How much do you spend on badges/IDs annually? (Also included in 16.) Include the labor for this and any incidental costs such as supplies, database maintenance, etc.

$ ☐

21 How many badges did your site issue in the data year?

Include new employees and remakes for lost IDs, name changes, etc.

☐

22 Provision of Emergency Response Security Services

All costs for emergency communications, emergency planning, emergency response, fire departments, first aid, medical responders, HAZMAT, disaster preparedness and other safety functions. Maintenance of sprinkler systems and other fire control systems should be included here. Alarms, CCTV, control rooms, alarm monitoring are included in 16 above unless there are separate systems for safety, such as panic buttons, chemical spill monitors, etc.

$ ☐

23 Cost of Special Services

Special security for meetings, events, driver services, executive protection (if provided at site level),

$ ☐

24 Expenditures for other functions that don't fit into any of the above categories.

$ ☐

25 Please list functions:

list ☐

Headquarters and Offices Benchmarking Group

SECURITY BENCHMARKING GROUP - Data Year 2004

Guthrie Research Group, Inc.
16509 Woolwine Road, Charlotte, NC 28278
Voice: 704-583-2634   Fax: 704-583-2643
Email: guthrielou@aol.com

		All Answers Must Be In This Columns
	Contact:	
	Company:	
	Voice:	
	Email:	

Data Input Module Security 5: RESOURCING

Include information only on officers (either proprietary or contract) that work at the site.

This section covers all security personnel used at the site. Include management, guards, security receptionists, etc.

		SITE CODE:

Operating Model

1	Security at site is Proprietary (in-house) (P), Contracted (C), or Both (B)	P, C, B
2	% of site security that is contracted?	%
3	Are security officers managed in-house (Proprietary) or by the Contractor, or Both?	P, C, B
4	What type of contract security firm do you use?	
	National (N), Regional (R}, Local (L), Temporary Agency (T), or Police Agency (P)	N, R, L, T, P

Employee Security Officers

5	Employee security officers are primarily union (U) or non-union (NU)	U or NU
6	Average headcount of the following security department employees:	
a	VPs, Directors, Managers of Security	Headcount
b	Security Contract Administrator	Headcount
c	Security Supervisors	Headcount
d	Administrative Assistants, Clerical	Headcount
e	Reception Duty Officers/Escort Duty Officers	Headcount
f	Post Duty Officers	Headcount
g	Vehicular Patrol Officers	Headcount
h	Foot Patrol Officers	Headcount
i	CCTV/Alarm Monitoring Officers/Safety Inspections	Headcount
j	Investigating Officers (including background checks)	Headcount
k	IT Security Specialists/Intellectual Property	Headcount
l	Other Specialists	Headcount
m	Key control officers	Headcount
n	Other	Headcount
	Please list	list

7 Average wage rate (w/o benefits) for employee security officers

a	Post Duty, Reception Duty, Vehicular or Foot Patrol Officers	$ per hour
b	CCTV/Alarm Monitoring Officers/Dispatch Operations	$ per hour
c	Investigating Officers (including background checks)	$ per hour
d	IT Security Specialists/Intellectual Property/Other Specialists	$ per hour
e	Physical Security Specialists	$ per hour
f	Other Specialists	$ per hour
g	Shift Supervisors	$ per hour

8	Average benefit rate as a percent (fully loaded) for employee security officers	%
9	Percentage of overtime for employee security officers (use average overtime for year)	%

Contract Security Officers

10	Contract security officers are primarily union (U) or non-union (NU)	U or NU

11 Average headcount of the following security contract workers:

a	VPs, Directors, Managers of Security	Headcount
b	Security Contract Administrator	Headcount
c	Security Supervisors	Headcount
d	Administrative Assistants, Clerical	Headcount
e	Reception Duty Officers/Escort Duty Officers	Headcount
f	Post Duty Officers	Headcount
g	Vehicular Patrol Officers	Headcount
h	Foot Patrol Officers	Headcount
i	CCTV/Alarm Monitoring Officers/Safety Inspections	Headcount
j	Investigating Officers (including background checks)	Headcount
k	IT Security Specialists/Intellectual Property	Headcount
l	Other Specialists	Headcount
m	Key control officers	Headcount
n	Other	Headcount
	Please list	list

12 Average wage rate (w/o benefits) for contract security officers

a	Post Duty, Reception Duty, Vehicular or Foot Patrol Officers	$ per hour
b	CCTV/Alarm Monitoring Officers/Dispatch Operations	$ per hour
c	Investigating Officers (including background checks)	$ per hour
d	IT Security Specialists/Intellectual Property/Other Specialists	$ per hour
e	Physical Security Specialists	$ per hour
f	Other Specialists	$ per hour
g	Shift Supervisors	$ per hour

13 Average benefit rate as a percent (fully loaded) for contract security officers   %

14 Percentage of overtime for contract security officers (use average overtime for year)   %

Training for Security Officers

15 Average # of technical security training hours per **proprietary** security officer   # of hours

Technical training hours include training for crowd control, firearms, self defense, threat assessment, etc.

16 Average # of Life Safety training hours per **proprietary** security officer   # of hours

Life Safety training would include EMT training, HAZMAT, CPR, etc.)

17 Average # of non-technical training hours per **proprietary** security officer   # of hours

Team building, HR skills and other similar training classes.

18 Average # of technical security training hours per **contract** security officer   # of hours

Technical training hours include training for crowd control, firearms, self defense, threat assessment, etc.

19 Average # of Life Safety training hours per **contract** security officer   # of hours

Life Safety training would include EMT training, HAZMAT, CPR, etc.)

20 Average # of non-technical training hours per **contract** security officer   # of hours

Team building, HR skills and other similar training classes.

Turnover Rates

Turnover is determined by dividing the number of officers who left the company in a year by the total number of officers scheduled for the year.

21 Average turnover of proprietary security officers at the site for the data year   turnover rate

22 Average turnover of contract security officers at the site for the data year   turnover rate

Hiring Requirements for Security Officers

23 Minimum level of education your site requires for **proprietary** prospective officers   N,HS, JC, C

None (N), High School Diploma or Equivalent (HS), Junior College (JC), 4 year College {C}

24 Minimum level of education your site requires for **contract** prospective officers   N,HS, JC, C

None (N), High School Diploma or Equivalent (HS), Junior College (JC), 4 year College {C}

25 Minimum level of security experience required for prospective officers   # of years

Use 0 if no security experience is required.

Check the following types of screening used at your site in the selection of prospective

26 security officers. Indicate who provides this service, proprietary or contractor. Use a O if the
service is not done. More than one code may be used.

a	Integrity Testing	P,C,O
b	Drug Screening	P,C,O
c	Psychological Evaluation	P,C,O
d	Physical Fitness Test	P,C,O
e	Proof of Citizenship	P,C,O
f	Reference Check	P,C,O
g	Credit Check	P,C,O
h	Criminal Records Check	P,C,O
i	Fingerprint Check	P,C,O
j	Other	P,C,O
	Please list	list

27 Are your security officers required to wear a uniform   YES or NO

Equipment Used by Security Officers

28 What types of equipment do your security officers use? Who provides the equipment --
Proprietary or Contractor. Use a O if the item is not used. More than one code may be used.

a	Computer	P,C,O
b	Tour System	P,C,O
c	Flashlight	P,C,O
d	First Aid Equipment	P,C,O
e	2-way Radio/Pages	P,C,O
f	Cell Phones	P,C,O
g	PDAs	P,C,O
h	Firearms	P,C,O
i	Tasors	P,C,O
j	Handcuffs/Restraints	P,C,O
k	Chemical Agents	P,C,O
l	HazMat, Safety, or Fire Equipment	P,C,O
m	Wheel Clamps	P,C,O
n	Vehicles	P,C,O
o	Other	P,C,O
	Please list	list

29 Footnotes for Officers   Type here

END OF SCHEDULE

SECURITY BENCHMARKING GROUP - Data Year 2004

Guthrie Research Group, Inc.
16509 Woolwine Road, Charlotte, NC 28278
Voice: 704-583-2634   Fax: 704-583-2643
Email: guthrielou@aol.com

Contact:
Company:
Voice:
Email:

All Answers Must Be In
This Columns

Data Input Module Security 6:   SECURITY INCIDENTS

Include information only on incidents that happened at the site.

SITE CODE:

Personnel Security (On-boardng/Off Boarding)

1	Number of new employees processed by site during the data year	#
2	Number of employees exiting company site during the data year	#
3	Number of contract personnel processed (on-boarded) by site during the data year	#
4	Number of contract personnel exiting (off-boarded) site during the data year	#
5	Does security department:	
a	Conduct security or safety training for new hires	Yes or No
b	Conduct exit interviews	Yes or No
c	Collect badges, keys, documents, etc. from exiting employees	Yes or No
d	Inspect exiting employees offices, observe while packing personal belongings, etc.	Yes or No
e	Other, please describe	description

Security Incidents

6 How many of the incidents did Security respond to during the data year?

a	Thefts	#
b	Burglary/Intrusions	#
c	Trespassing	#
d	Eviction of Personnel	#
e	Assault	#
f	Sexual Assault/Rape	#
g	Robbery	#
h	Fires	#
i	Chemical Spills/HazMat incidents	#
j	Vehicle Accidents	#

k	Personnel Accidents	#
l	Disorderly Conduct	#
m	Medical Emergencies	#
n	Bombings/Bomb Threats	#
o	Power Failures	#
p	Demonstrations	#
q	Colleague Assistance Incidents (unlocking doors, vehicle assistance, etc.)	#
r	Suspicious Packages/Bomb threats	#
s	Other	#
	Please list	list

Has your company been a party to any legal action as a result of the action of any of your

7   security officers in the data year?   Yes or No

Site Security Risks

Please rank each of the following at the site. High risk=5 down to no risk=1

8   Products   5 to 1
Products that are easy to steal, highly desirable, easy to re-sell. Examples drugs, electronics, radioactive materials, etc.

9   Industrial Espionage, Intellectual Property   5 to 1
Highly competitive industry where patents and inventions play a large role in the future of the business.

10   High-risk locations   5 to 1
Site is located in high crime area.

11   Animal testing   5 to 1
Site has animal laboratories.

12   Other, please describe.   description
Any other situations that increase the security risks for the site.   5 to 1

13   Footnotes for Incidents: Type here

About the Authors

Dr. Gerald L. Kovacich has over 40 years of counterintelligence/counterespionage, business security, criminal and civil investigations, anti-fraud, information warfare, and information systems security experience in the US government as a special agent and in the international business sector. He has also worked for numerous technology-based, international corporations as an information systems security manager, information warfare technologist, investigations and security audit manager, and anti-fraud program manager; as well as an international lecturer and consultant on these topics. Dr. Kovacich is currently living on an island in Washington State where he continues to write and conduct research relative to these topics. More information about Dr. Kovacich, as well as numerous security-related articles and books, can be found on his web site: http://www.ShockwaveWriters.Com.

Edward P. Halibozek has over 26 years of security experience. He is currently the Corporate Director of Security for a Fortune 100 company. He is a member of the Board of Directors for the Chief Special Agents Association in Los Angeles, California. Furthermore, Ed served four years (1997–2000) as an industry member to the National Industrial Security Program Policy Advisory Committee (NISPPAC). Ed holds a bachelor of science degree and master of science degree in criminal justice from California State University, Long Beach. He also earned an MBA from Pepperdine University, Malibu, California.

Index